"This book is a sumptuous feast for preachers which, if savored and digested, will prepare a banquet of life for those who listen to it. It is a delight to read from beginning to end. Formed by a deep love of the Bible and for the God who gave it, O'Donnell and Ryken have given us a wonderful gift. Whether you are a novice preacher who wishes to have your mistakes corrected gently but wisely, a tired preacher who has lost the romance of the art form, a burdened preacher who is taking shortcuts because of the demands of ministry, or an experienced preacher for whom well-worn homiletical paths have become second nature, there is something here to edify you richly. This book will make you smile and provide fresh enchantment with the text of holy Scripture. Read and enjoy!"

David Gibson, Minister, Trinity Church, Aberdeen, Scotland; author, *Living Life Backward* and *Radically Whole*

"With masterful and inspirational challenges to preachers, O'Donnell combines his and Ryken's years of biblical preaching insights into a descriptive and useful manual for biblical exposition. This work, with its relevant examples, encourages preachers to read the Bible through the lens of various literary genres of Scripture while faithfully preaching the word of God with authorial intent and transformative purpose."

Robert Smith Jr., Charles T. Carter Baptist Chair of Divinity, Beeson Divinity School, Samford University

"As Virgil once stood before Dante, this volume now stands before you as a wise tour guide of the contours and depths and great beauty of the Bible's literary genres. Preachers will benefit from numerous insights packed into each chapter (as will their congregations), and all readers will have their appreciation of the Scriptures enriched by the obvious affection that O'Donnell and Ryken have for God's word. Let this book encourage you in your word work."

Robert S. Kinney, Director of Ministries, Charles Simeon Trust; Priest, Christ Church, Vienna, Austria

"Preaching faithfully and well is the challenge of a lifetime. We need all the help we can get. There is much wisdom here, the fruit of long experience and careful study, all compiled with warmth and clarity. This book will be a helpful resource for preachers and for those who seek to train preachers."

Christopher Ash, Writer in Residence, Tyndale House; author, *The Priority of Preaching*

"Leland Ryken has been perhaps the clearest and most helpful voice in understanding the literature of the Bible for our generation, and here Douglas O'Donnell ably brings Ryken's insight and voice specifically to the preaching task. The strength of this book lies especially in its affirmation of the importance of paying attention to the function and beauty of literary form, but also in its setting forth of particular strategies for reading and for preaching, helpfully illustrated through particular examples. Clearly, literary form matters to God; and as preachers, it should matter to us, in both our preparation and our delivery. *The Beauty and Power of Biblical Exposition* will serve you well on both fronts. It is a compelling testimony to the power and profitability of God's beautiful word."

Mike Bullmore, Senior Pastor, CrossWay Community Church, Bristol, Wisconsin

"One of the great needs of our day is for pulpits to be manned by preachers who are committed to proclaiming the truth of Scripture and equipped to sound the beauty of the gospel. This work has drawn its bow toward a worthy and unmoving target. These two men have each been shaping voices in my life as a preacher and a hymnwriter, and I am expectant to see how the Lord will use this contribution to mold the next generation of expositors."

Matt Boswell, Lead Pastor, The Trails Church, Celina, Texas; hymnwriter

The Beauty and Power of Biblical Exposition

The Beauty and Power of Biblical Exposition

Preaching the Literary Artistry and Genres of the Bible

Douglas Sean O'Donnell
and Leland Ryken

CROSSWAY®

WHEATON, ILLINOIS

Library of Congress Cataloging-in-Publication Data

Names: O'Donnell, Douglas Sean, 1972– author. | Ryken, Leland, author.
Title: The beauty and power of biblical exposition : preaching the literary artistry and genres of the Bible / Douglas Sean O'Donnell and Leland Ryken.
Description: Wheaton, Illinois : Crossway, 2022. | Includes bibliographical references and index.
Identifiers: LCCN 2021044841 (print) | LCCN 2021044842 (ebook) | ISBN 9781433570445 (trade paperback) | ISBN 9781433570452 (pdf) | ISBN 9781433570469 (mobipocket) | ISBN 9781433570476 (epub)
Subjects: LCSH: Preaching.
Classification: LCC BV4211.3 .O33 2022 (print) | LCC BV4211.3 (ebook) | DDC 251—dc23
LC record available at https://lccn.loc.gov/2021044841
LC ebook record available at https://lccn.loc.gov/2021044842

To R. Kent Hughes

Contents

Tables and Diagrams

TABLES

DIAGRAMS

Introduction

NEARLY THIRTY YEARS AGO I took Dr. Leland Ryken's *Literature of the Bible* course. It was the first time I was introduced to Lee's wit, wisdom, and unfair grading policies. He gave me a B. It was also the first time I was introduced to literary genres and the way in which the teacher of God's Word, if he desires to be a good and faithful (as well as insightful and interesting!) instructor, needs to understand how each genre works.

What I remember most about that class, besides the cute petite brunette who would become my wife, was Lee's retelling of the story of the left-handed judge Ehud from the tribe of Benjamin, who assassinated the arrogant and obese Moabite King Eglon (Judg. 3:12–30). In their private meeting, Ehud grabbed his concealed double-edged sword from his right thigh and thrust it into the unsuspecting Eglon with his left hand. The sovereign's stomach swallowed the sword, and he died as Ehud escaped. As Dr. Ryken retold the story, pointing out the important details, and how the genre of narrative worked and is to work on our intellects and emotions, I was captivated. "That will preach," I thought to myself.

From that day until today, I have continued—in the form of his books and friendship—to sit under Dr. Ryken's tutelage. I have learned a lot! I deserve an A, or some honorary acknowledgment from him that he approves of my development! Well, I suppose his offer to coauthor this tome is just that; or, at least I'll take it as that, and I will notify the Wheaton College registrar posthaste to change my GPA!

When Lee approached me and asked if I would team up with him on writing a book on preaching the literary genres of the Bible, I was honored. When he told me that he would like me, as the preacher, to be "the voice" of the book,[1] I was doubly honored. The deal was that he would write on the topic of each chapter, then I would have total freedom to use what I wanted, restate it in my own words, and add a preacher's perspective. He said that he didn't need to see anything I wrote. Trust. Freedom. Wings to write!

As I began to soar—sifting through his words with delight and as the air beneath my flight—an idea came to mind to honor him as he had honored me. Yes, what you have in hand is my personal festschrift to him. I have taken both the new material he has written for this particular project and some of the most applicable tidbits from some of his seventy-plus monographs, articles, and essays, to give voice to *our* thoughts on how to preach the genres of narrative, parable, epistle, poetry, proverbs, and visionary writing. The purpose of our shared endeavor is simple. We want to help you "bring the thunder," as preachers often say to and pray for each other. In the process of determining this book's title, at one point I suggested "Reversed Thunder" while reading Ryken's perceptive commentary on George Herbert's poem "Prayer."[2] One

---

1   As a personal aside, Lee knows that English literature is his expertise. He is not a preacher. I believe he stepped back from having two voices to this book—half a chapter by him and half by me—because he has such a high respect for the pastor's calling and he thought my voice, as a preacher, would be more directly relevant to our readers.

2   Leland Ryken, *The Soul in Paraphrase: A Treasury of Classical Devotional Poems* (Wheaton, IL: Crossway, 2018), 88–89.

of Herbert's images to describe prayer is reversed thunder, in the sense that, through prayer we fire up petitions to heaven like a thunderbolt.[3] I'm borrowing that compelling metaphor, but using it in a different way. The idea is this: what is going on behind the powerful thunderbolt of the Sunday morning thunder? What happens, in other words, if we reverse the timeframe from Sunday's strike from Scripture to the pastor's calm study of Scripture in the days before? What is behind the heat and light? My point is plain, or I hope is plain. I will make it plain now: Understanding what happens in the pastor's study, as he seeks to understand, and then explain, illustrate, and apply God's Word, can help everyone who regularly teaches God's Word tap into the surge behind the storm.

SEVEN SHARED CONVICTIONS

Before we peer into that power source, it is important to say something of the shared convictions behind this collaborative endeavor, or "our book," as we would so often title our many emails to each other. We have at least seven. First, a literary approach to the Bible is essential to good preaching because the Bible is literature. To rightly divide the word of truth requires an understanding of how the Bible is put together. Faithful biblical exposition necessitates careful literary analysis. As Martin Luther once stated, "I am persuaded that without knowledge of literature pure theology cannot at all endure." The context of that quote is that Luther is expressing his "desire that there shall be as many poets and rhetoricians as possible" in the pulpit because he sees that "by these studies, as by no other means, people are wonderfully fitted for the grasping of

---

3   For further explication on the poem, see Leland Ryken, *The Devotional Poetry of Donne, Herbert, and Milton*, Christian Guides to the Classics (Wheaton, IL: Crossway, 2014), 54–55.

sacred truth and for handling it skillfully and happily."[4] Likewise, we are convinced that, on the negative side, a handling of the Bible that ignores its literary nature is a sin of omission;[5] and, on the positive side, a handling of the Bible that recognizes that the Bible is a literary anthology in which the individual parts belong to various literary genres and embraces "even a modicum of self-conscious literary analysis" will greatly enhance the proclamation of God's Word.[6]

Second, a literary approach to the Bible helps avoid reductionistic preaching. Some pastors think that expository preaching is just the homiletical equivalent of expository writing, the sole aim of which is to convey facts and information. The point of preaching Psalm 23, it might be said, is to reduce all the images to ideas. But why would we take the poetry out of the poem? Psalm 23 is not a collection of ideas; it is a beautiful short poem that God inspired David to write so that we might understand the picture it paints, the emotions it expresses, and the timeless truths it propounds. Here's another example, from a biblical story Ryken often uses to defend and illustrate the point, and for good reason. In his own words,

> The sixth command tells us, "You shall not murder." The story of Cain (Gen. 4:1–16) embodies that same truth by means

---

4   Martin Luther, "Letter to Eoban Hess, 29 March 1523," in *Luthers Briefwechsel*, in *D. Martin Luthers Werke*, 120 vols. (Weimar, Germany: Böhlhaus, 1883–2009), 3:50.

5   "There is a . . . sense in which the Bible, since it is after all literature, cannot properly be read except as literature; and the different parts of it as the different sorts of literature they are" (C. S. Lewis, *Reflections on the Psalms* [New York: Macmillan, 1958], 3).

6   Leland Ryken, "The Bible as Literature and Expository Preaching," in *Preach the Word: Essays on Preaching: In Honor of R. Kent Hughes*, ed. Leland Ryken and Todd Wilson (Wheaton, IL: Crossway, 2007), 39.

of characters and events. The story of Cain does not use the abstract word *murder*, nor does it contain a command not to murder. It *shows* that we should not commit murder. The author of any story wants us to vicariously relive an experience in our imagination, and by that means encounter truth. That is how literature works. If the author of Genesis 4 had primarily wanted us to grasp an idea with our minds, he would have given us an idea. The fact that he gave us something else obligates us to take account of this "something else." The biblical authors need to be allowed to set the agenda for how we are expected to assimilate what they wrote. What happens when we ignore the narrative form of the story of Cain? The most customary result is that the text is reduced to an idea. Reductionism in this form is the only thing left to do with the text if we ignore the story with its characters, settings, and events. If we ignore the narrative form, we are not dealing with the text in terms of its intended mode of operation, which is to get us to share an experience. Kenneth Bailey has correctly written that a story (and by extension any literary text) is "not a delivery system for an idea that can be discarded once the idea (the shell) is fired. Rather [it] is a house in which the reader or listener is invited to take up residence . . . and look out on the world from the point of view of the story."[7]

---

7   Leland Ryken, "Why We Need to Read and Interpret the Bible as Literature," unpublished, quoting Kenneth Bailey, *The Cross and the Prodigal* (Downers Grove, IL: InterVarsity Press, 2005), 87. A number of ideas and expressions in this introduction come from Ryken's unpublished article. Elsewhere, Ryken writes of Genesis 4, "A person listening to an expository sermon on the story of Cain should be aware from start to finish that the text being explicated is a narrative, not a theological treatise. The text exists to be relived in its fullness, not dipped into as a source of proof texts for moral and theological generalizations" (Ryken, "Bible as Literature and Expository Preaching," 43).

Third, and closely related to the second, a literary approach to the Bible acknowledges that, throughout the Bible, meaning is communicated through various literary forms.[8] There is more to the story of Cain's murder of Abel than the application "don't kill your brother." Likewise, the nature of the Canaanite woman's "great faith" in Matthew 15:21–28 is understood only through her dialogue with and response to Jesus.[9] Faith is defined only once in the Bible (Heb. 11:1), but it is illustrated in narrative form hundreds of times. Think of the stories of Abraham, Job, and Habakkuk. Think also of the poems of the Sons of Korah. In Psalm 46:1–3, the sons sing of resilient faith:

> God is our refuge and strength,
>> a very present help in trouble.
> Therefore we will not fear though the earth gives way,
>> though the mountains be moved into the heart of the sea,
> though its waters roar and foam,
>> though the mountains tremble at its swelling.

It would be ridiculous to ignore or disregard this poem's literary form and features, for the truths of the text come through the form and features. It is only as we imagine God like a mighty unshakable and secure fortress (the image used in the final line of the poem, "the God of Jacob is our fortress," v. 11) when a sudden powerful

---

8 "There is no content without the form in which it is expressed" (Leland Ryken, *Literary Introductions to the Books of the Bible* [Wheaton, IL: Crossway, 2015], 10).

9 As Flannery O'Connor notes of narrative, "the whole story is the meaning, because it is an experience, not an abstraction" (*Mystery and Manners: Occasional Prose* [New York: Farrar, Straus, & Giroux, 1969], 73). For an example on how doctrine is taught in narrative form, see Douglas Sean O'Donnell, *"O Woman, Great Is Your Faith!": Faith in the Gospel of Matthew* (Eugene, OR: Pickwick, 2021).

earthquake causes the side of a mountain to crash into the sea, that we grasp the point of the poem. The images embody the idea. The poets could have simply said, "God is our security in times of calamity," but instead they provide pictures that make the very point more memorable and tangible. The medium is not the message, but the message cannot be fully obtained without the medium. We cannot discard the form once we have deduced the idea. To merely preach an abstract idea is to fail to do justice to the authors' intent (the Sons of Korah wrote a God-inspired poem!)[10] and to pull the plug on the power of word pictures in preaching the Word.

Fourth, a literary approach to the Bible helps the preacher help his congregation to relive the text as fully as possible, so as to live out the message of the text. Years ago, Professor Richard Pratt wrote a book on interpreting Old Testament narratives called *He Gave Us Stories*. Yes, God gave us stories! He also gave us poems, parables, proverbs, laws, lists, letters, doxologies, debates, dialogues, lamentations, hymns, apocalyptic visions, chronicles, encomiums, treaties, and more. He gave us these various genres for various reasons, one of which is to re-experience in community the ideas, expressions, emotions, and applications of each unique text. For example, we cannot relive a story without encountering and analyzing the settings, characters, and plots; and, we cannot relive a poem without assimilating the structure and symbols of the poem. The Bible is

---

10 Here is where the doctrine of inspiration comes into view. Did God inspire the forms of the Bible, or only the content? Both! God led some biblical authors to write stories, others to write poems, others to write satire and proverbs and epistles. The Holy Spirit superintended the process of composition undertaken by biblical authors and also the resulting products of that composition (see 2 Pet. 1:21). Thus, whenever a biblical author expressed the content of a passage in a literary form, we can safely conclude that he *intended* that the preacher interpret the passage using ordinary literary methods of analysis. Put differently, whenever a biblical author embodies his message in a literary genre and by means of literary techniques, he *intends* that pastors engage in literary analysis.

not predominantly an ideational book—a book of randomly disassociated lists of theological propositions. Christians sometimes treat the Bible that way. What a shame. Christian preachers sometimes preach the Bible that way. A double portion of shame!

When a preacher and his congregation fail to relive a text, they fail to enter into the human experience so carefully and vividly expressed in Scripture. The Bible embodies human experience—the tears of death, the sadness of sickness, the sting of betrayal, the flush of sexual arousal. It is a book of human experience, not merely or mainly a book of religious and moral ideas. The nightly news might tell us what *happened*, whereas the Bible tells us what *happens*—what is true for all people in all places and times. Thus, "to gain relevance, all a preacher needs to do is explicate the human experience embedded in the literary parts of the Bible."[11] Indeed, he needs to "resist the impulse immediately to reduce every biblical passage to a set of theological ideas,"[12] and use the human experience expressed in Scripture to bridge the gap from the ancient world of the text to today. As Ryken exhorts, "We need to hear the voice of human experience from the pulpit." For to hear that voice is to deeply connect God's breathed out word with God's gasping people—to teach, reprove, correct, and train them in righteousness, to equip them for every good work (see 2 Tim. 3:16–17). "The test of whether an expository preacher has dealt adequately with a text," Ryken continues, "is simple: if listeners have been led to see their own experiences in the text and exposition, the expositor has interacted with the subject matter in keeping with its literary nature."[13]

---

11 Ryken, "Bible as Literature and Expository Preaching," 42.
12 Leland Ryken, "Reading the Bible as Literature," in *The ESV Study Bible* (Wheaton, IL: Crossway, 2008), 2570.
13 Ryken, "Bible as Literature and Expository Preaching," 42, 44.

Fifth, a literary approach to the Bible offers an awareness and appreciation of the artistry of God's inspired Word. While the Bible is written in plain and common ancient languages, and much of the Bible uses plain talk to talk about profound realities, the beauty of expression and artistry of arrangement is everywhere. Just as we are called to worship the Lord "in the beauty of holiness" (Ps. 96:9 KJV), preachers should preach, and all Christians should delight in, the beauty of the holiness of God's Holy Word. Beauty mattered to God when he created the world, and it mattered to him as he moved the authors of the Bible to compose. "The writer of Ecclesiastes states his philosophy of composition, portraying himself as a self-conscious stylist and wordsmith who arranged his material 'with great care' and who 'sought to find words of delight' (Eccles. 12:9–10). Surely other biblical writers did the same."[14] Every Bible preacher has the responsibility to do something with that beauty. To underscore, explain, illustrate, and apply the imagery, metaphors, similes, hyperboles, apostrophe, personification, paradox, and pun, and lots of other literary devices is a sacred duty and delight![15] If artistry is found on every page of the Bible, Bible preachers need to expound the Bible with that in mind.

Sixth, a literary approach to the Bible opens the entire canon of Scripture to exploration and exposition. Ryken recounts the time when a longtime minister confided that before he mastered literary analysis of the Bible, he would often read a psalm to patients in a hospital but would never consider preaching from a psalm because he "didn't know what to do with it." Mastering all the literary

---

14 Ryken, "Reading the Bible as Literature," 2570.

15 See Leland Ryken, *A Complete Handbook of Literary Forms in the Bible* (Wheaton, IL: Crossway, 2014); and "Glossary of Literary Terms and Genres," in *The Literary Study Bible, English Standard Version* (Wheaton, IL: Crossway, 2019), 1975–1988.

genres and understanding how various literary devices work gives the expositor the confidence and skill to cover all of the Bible. When he comes to the opening scene of the Song of Solomon, the Olivet Discourse, a parable of judgment, a paradoxical proverb, or John's visions on Patmos, he doesn't ask, "What do I do with this?" and "Oh, heavens, how on earth do I preach this?" The whole of Scripture is wide open and ready for exploration and exposition.

Seventh (we felt that a seventh conviction was numerologically necessary!), a literary approach to the Bible adds freshness and enjoyment to our reading and preaching, along with an antidote to misinterpretation of God's Word. While that's a sentence-full, the three points of this seventh conviction are straightforward. Freshness: if we have never viewed the Bible as literature and as a book that reveals its beauty and truth by literary means, a literary approach to preaching yields fresh insights. Enjoyment: if we can educate ourselves to see the literary qualities of the Bible, we will experience the same pleasure we have when we read Emily Dickinson, Charles Dickens, or J. R. R. Tolkien. Misinterpretation: if we can correctly identify the genre (the book of Jonah is a satire, not a hero story) and literary devices (Proverbs 3:11 is a synonymous parallelism—making the same point two ways, not making two points), we will rightly interpret God's Word for God's people. Which, as a final aside, always bring freshness and enjoyment to all.

THE *END* OF THE INTRODUCTION

One of the most telling (and sadly accurate, in my opinion) statements Ryken makes in his excellent essay on "The Bible as Literature and Expository Preaching" is this: "Many Bible expositors would assent to . . . the literary nature of the Bible, only to ignore it when they stand in the pulpit. Mere assent to the idea that the

Bible is a literary anthology has not produced a literary approach to the Bible."[16]

The two main goals of this book are straightforward: First, we desire to inform and inspire pastors to understand that "attentiveness to the literary dimensions of the Bible should be foregrounded in expository sermons."[17] A literary analysis of the Bible is invaluable to faithful preaching. Stop ignoring the obvious; start embracing the important.[18] Second, we seek to supply a foundation for preachers to move from sermons filled with merely abstract theological propositions and proof-texted moral applications to sermons that are fresh, relevant, interesting, and accurate-to-the-authorial-intention—words on God's Word that relive the human experience and revive a love for God and others. So, embrace the arsenal of analytic tools offered. And take up the delightful task of preaching words of delight to God's (usually) delightful people!

In what follows, we cover preaching narrative (ch. 1), parables (ch. 2), epistles (ch. 3), poetry (ch. 4), proverbs (ch. 5), and visionary writings (ch. 6). Our sequel on preaching discourse, satire, hero stories, law, gospel, prophecy, fables, riddles, maxims, monologues and dialogues, and the like will be out precisely 144,000 days after this book releases. (Let the reader understand.) For this present volume, each chapter will be divided into two parts: the first part will cover how to *read* a specific genre; the second will cover how to *preach* it. Basically, I have taken Lee's material and translated it

---

16 Ryken, "Bible as Literature and Expository Preaching," 44.

17 Ryken, "Bible as Literature and Expository Preaching," 44, 47.

18 "Everything that writers put into their composition is something they regarded as important, including the literary aspects of a text. If literary matters were important to the writers of the Bible, they need to be important to us as readers" and preachers (Ryken, *Literary Introductions to the Books of the Bible*, 10).

so that preachers get the full benefit from it. I have also added my own insights built on his tutelage and my years of pastoral experience. So, if you ever wanted to figure out how Dr. Leland Ryken's lifetime of work on the Bible as literature can help you in your preaching, keep reading!

1

The Greatest Stories Ever Told

Preaching Narrative

SIX QUESTIONS. Answer honestly. First, have you ever heard a preacher use the Bible as a launching pad; that is, a text is read near the start of the sermon, and then, once the preacher gets into his message, the Bible recedes from view and rarely resurfaces? I have seen some preachers lift up the Bible, read a verse, and then say absolutely nothing about the Bible! I assume this doesn't describe you.

Second, have you ever heard a preacher use the Bible as a road map that travels through as many parallel passages as possible; that is, a narrative is read (let's say, from the Synoptics) and then its parallels in the other Gospels are quickly exegeted, then Paul is quoted at length, and finally you earn a gold star for flipping the fastest to everywhere in the Bible but the actual story that was read as the Scripture reading for the day? Instead of understanding a particular narrative within the context of the full narrative, and living in that text for the whole sermon and experiencing an in-depth experience of the story, you are whisked away to a thousand rabbit holes of exegetical curiosity. Been there? Heard that? Might have done that a time or two?

Third, have you ever heard a preacher use the Bible to moralize a text? For example, on a Men's Retreat the story of Judah and Tamar is treated as an exposition on the importance of avoiding sexually immoral women on business trips, and the narrative of Joseph and Potiphar's wife as the follow-up talk on how we can have victory, as Joseph did, over the sexually aggressive woman at work? That will preach. But it is not how those stories should be preached. The story of Judah and Tamar (Genesis 38) derives its meaning, as any biblical narrative does, from the literary whole, namely, the story of Joseph recorded in Genesis 37–50. The story of Judah and Tamar is more about God keeping his promises than about an immoral sex act, and it fits within the story of Joseph in that Joseph saves the lives of Judah's offspring, an offspring from which the Christ came.

Fourth, have you ever heard a preacher use the Bible as a lecture on systematic theology; that is, he gives a doctrinal sermon that is divorced, not from verses in the narrative, but from the narrative itself? For example, the miracle of Jesus walking on water becomes merely a proof text for the doctrine of Jesus's divinity. The story itself is stripped of its textual beauty so that one doctrine can be emphasized. That narrative does confirm that doctrine, but that is not the sole intent of the narrative. It misses the God-woven texture of a story that offers multifaceted truths about God, humanity, discipleship, sin, and salvation.

Fifth, have you ever heard a preacher use the Bible as a sideshow for the slideshow? That is, he uses a detailed PowerPoint presentation or video clips that dominate the sermon? Many churches today fail to recognize the power of a good story and storyteller. There is nothing more riveting than listening to a master teacher work through a masterfully written story about the Master! Artwork or graphics on a slide can help the listener (and looker) follow along and illustrate complex concepts visually, but tech-dominated "preaching" is dominated by the wrong medium. What happens is that most people delight in the interesting images and amusing clips, not the very Word of God.

Sixth, have you ever heard a preacher use the Bible as a starting point to his own imaginative narrative exposé; that is, he pretends to be a character in the story and adds a dozen details to the inspired narrative? For example, when he comes to the detail of Zacchaeus's size, a quarter of the sermon "exegetes" its significance through actual actions. A tree is on stage. The preacher makes himself small by wearing a long robe, dropping to his knees, and scurrying across the stage. He comes to the tree, eyes it, then the congregation. They cheer him on. He climbs the tree. Okay, I'll admit, I have never seen that, but nothing would surprise me today. The point, in question form, is this: why the need to expand in the extreme upon a God-inspired narrative? Is your dramatic interpretation really an improvement on the Spirit's inspiration?

If you answered yes to any or all of the above questions, let me ask you a final question: Do you lament the current state of preaching within Bible-believing churches? I imagine so. Well, one sure remedy to such models of preaching is a serious commitment to the literary nature of the Bible. For think about it: One cannot preach "the-Bible-as-a-launching-pad" sermons, or any of the above examples, and faithfully preach any of the stories of Scripture. Envision a sermon on David and Goliath, the Gerasene demoniac, or the conversion of Saul that begins with a quote from the most popular verse from the text and off the preacher goes on a tangent, never to return to one of the greatest stories ever told.

In this chapter we will explore how to read and preach the most prevalent genre in the Bible.[1] Narrative is not the most important genre just because it is the most prevalent (each genre is essential for a full-orbed preaching ministry), but if you do not understand the basics of this genre, you will be greatly limited. Completely limited! For even the non-narrative parts of the Bible take their place within the overarching metanarrative that unifies the Bible. The central character in the organizing story of the Bible is God, and the central literary (and theological!) concern of the Bible is the characterization (or depiction) of God. The acts of God constitute the plot of the master story of the Bible.[2] And every creature interacts with this divine protagonist. So, of all the chapters in this short book, we invite you to eye and apply this most foundational one.

HOW TO READ BIBLICAL NARRATIVE

In his *MasterClass* video on "Storytelling and Writing," Salman Rushdie states, "We need stories to understand ourselves. We are the only creature that does this unusual thing—of telling each other stories in order to try to understand what kind of creature we are." Later he says, "When a child is born, the first thing a child requires is safety and love. The next thing that the child asks for

---

1 Reflecting on the prevalence of stories in the Bible, Thomas G. Long writes, "There are battle stories, betrayal stories, stories about seduction and treachery in the royal court, stories about farmers and fools, healing stories, violent stories, funny stories and sad ones, stories of death, and stories of resurrection. In fact, stories are so common in Scripture that some students have claimed, understandably but incorrectly, that the Bible is exclusively a narrative collection. This is an exaggeration, of course—there is much non-narrative material in the Bible—but the claim that the Bible is a 'story book' is not far off the mark" (*Preaching and the Literary Forms of the Bible* [Philadelphia: Fortress, 1989], 66).

2 "Although the story of what God does is the primary action in the Bible, it is not the only one, and we should not disparage or minimize the other storylines" (Leland Ryken, *Literary Introductions to the Books of the Bible* [Wheaton, IL: Crossway, 2015], 15).

is 'Tell me a story.'" That is where we start. Human experience. "Tell me a story" is perhaps the most universal human impulse. We live in a story-shaped world, and our lives themselves have a narrative quality about them. We universally resonate with stories! So, why wouldn't we, as preachers, do everything in our power to understand how to handle (even master) this genre? Do you want to connect with your congregation? Of course. Then don't underestimate the power of comprehending and communicating God's uniquely designed stories to people made in his image. You will find no more promising sermon material than the stories God gave to his church and world.

THE COMPONENTS OF A STORY

If you have been to seminary, you will have learned that no principle of biblical hermeneutics is more important than that a written text needs to be approached in terms of the kind of writing that it is. Right? Maybe. And surely you had a whole class on preaching narrative. Right? Wrong. Or, likely wrong. Well, in this chapter, we offer no master class, but we do submit to you a short and hopefully inspirational tutorial. We hope we inspire you to learn more; to build your library, and to actually read what is in your library. But we know that pastors are busy, almost as busy as literary scholars and Bible publishers! So, our *Concise Manual on Preaching Narrative (While Invigorating the Elect and Captivating Converts)* awaits you. We begin with the two foundational steps that you need to take each time you come to a Bible story.

First, know that a story is a story. Be able to identify the genre. If the text in view starts, "A long time ago in a galaxy far, far away," you need to turn off your television, computer, or app. But if it starts, "In those days a decree went out from Caesar Augustus that all the world should be registered," you need to know that a God-breathed story has started and that your congregation is soon to be thoroughly engaged by your skillful retelling. And, if needed, feel free to ask your in-house droid, that is programmed for both protocol and etiquette, "What genre is Luke 2:1?" Both C-3PO and Siri will give you the correct answer. But you are surely not so shallow. You likely listen to Bach as you translate Sunday's text, and sip Intelligentsia Coffee when you turn to form your homiletical outline. Okay, maybe you don't. But you read books like the one in hand because you want to improve your preaching. And you know a story when you see a story.

But are you committed to analyzing a biblical narrative in keeping with the traits of that genre? To do that is the second step. Stories consist of three components—setting, characters, and plot. Each of these needs to be acknowledged and analyzed in our treatment of a biblical narrative. I find such analysis extremely pleasurable, and I often share aspects of my delight in the story with God's people from the pulpit. Because I delight not only in *what* God says to us in his Word but in *how* he has said it, both I and my hearers grow in our knowledge of God and appreciation of how he has chosen to communicate to us. Part of that growth is that together we use and understand terms like setting ("Notice that our passage is set in Jericho"), characters ("Look how Rachel is described"), and plot ("As we see this drama unfold, we come now to its climax—the point of no return"). The terms we all learned in high school English literature class are the right terms to use when reading and presenting the stories of the Bible. By the time I preached through the Gospel of Matthew at New Covenant Church (in Naperville, Illinois), and the Gospel of Mark at Westminster Presbyterian Church (in Elgin,

Illinois), my congregation knew, understood, and used a plethora of literary terms associated with the genre of narrative. Such knowledge is not esoteric; it is immensely practical—as practical as learning what the word "gigabyte" means when buying a cell phone, "audible" when quarterbacking a football team, and "cinematography" when hosting the Oscars.

Setting

Setting is one of the most overlooked but essential aspects of proper exegesis of biblical narratives. But what does it matter that we take careful note of historical ("In the year that King Uzziah died," Isa. 6:1), geographical ("Rehoboam went to Shechem, for all Israel had come to Shechem to make him king," 2 Chron. 10:1), topological ("He went up on the mountain," Matt. 5:1), physical ("Now he was ruddy and had beautiful eyes and was handsome," 1 Sam. 16:12), cultural ("And as Jesus reclined at table," Matt. 9:10), chronological ("When the seven days were almost completed," Acts 21:27), or descriptive ("On an appointed day Herod put on his royal robes, took his seat upon the throne," Acts 12:21) details? First and foremost, if it mattered to the biblical authors, it should matter to us. Put differently, if it mattered to the Holy Spirit, it should matter to the Spirit-filled preacher. If every jot and tittle matters (Matt. 5:18 KJV), surely each detail an inspired storyteller adds to his inspired story contributes to the story.

Second, the setting provides the necessary context to the characters' actions within the narrative. It "enables the action that occurs within it."[3] The more we know about *who* is *where when* and

---

3 Leland Ryken, *How Bible Stories Work: A Guided Study of Biblical Narrative* (Bellingham, WA: Lexham, 2015), 29.

perhaps *why*, the better we will understand *what* is about to happen. Knowing something about the location, climate, nationality of the characters, time of day, season of the year, and so on, helps us make better sense of the story.

Third, the setting ignites and exercises our imaginations, making a story, with its vivid descriptions, come alive. When we read, "for a long time [he] had worn no clothes, and he had not lived in a house but among the tombs" (Luke 8:27), we *see* a terribly sad scene. We visualize the cold, naked man and his dark, eerie shelter. We want a solution to his problem. We want Jesus to step in to save—to clean up this unclean scene.

Fourth, the setting often takes on symbolic overtones and becomes a major part of the message or theme of a story. For example, the informed exegete grasps the intrabiblical allusions of Jesus in "the wilderness" at the start of his ministry, and the fourfold repetition of the word "Passover" when he served the twelve at the Last Supper; and he pieces together the themes that Jesus, as true Israel, succeeds where Israel of old failed, and that, as the Passover Lamb, he is sacrificed so that God might pass over his people, saving them from their sin.[4]

Fifth, the setting often creates the mood or builds an atmosphere. When we read, "And when the sixth hour had come, there was darkness over the whole land" (Mark 15:33), the author has already engaged and prepared his readers for Jesus's dark cry of dereliction ("My God, my God, why have you forsaken me?" v. 34).

---

4 "Again, in the midst of the feeding of the five thousand in the wilderness, Mark pauses to note that the multitude sat down on the 'green grass.' Why does he describe the color of the grass as green but not the sky as blue or the sand as yellow? Is Isaiah's vision of the wilderness in blossom even now being realized?" (Long, *Preaching and the Literary Forms of the Bible*, 78–79).

Characters

Characters are a second component of stories. A character is simply a person in the story. There are major and minor characters, as well as the main character—the protagonist. All the unfolding action of the story spins around the axis of this "first" or "primary" (*prōt-*) "struggler" or "competitor" (*agōnistēs*), and one of the most useful strategies for mastering a story is to regard oneself as the observant traveling companion of the protagonist.[5] Like Christian in Bunyan's *Pilgrim's Progress*, we follow him on his journey until the end.

We get to know the characters in a story by their abilities, traits, roles and relationships, stated or inferred attitudes and emotions, dialogue, actions, titles and names, physical description, gestures, authorial insider information, foils, and responses from other characters.

A good overriding premise is that we should get to know every character in a story as fully as the details in the text enable us to do. For example, in Matthew 15:21–28, the Evangelist gives the woman who approaches Jesus the archaic title "Canaanite" (v. 22). That label, along with the setting of "Tyre and Sidon" (v. 21), the impatient indignation of the apostles ("Send her away, for she is crying out after us," v. 23), and the hesitancy of Christ ("I was sent only to the lost sheep of the house of Israel," v. 24), reveals to the reader her status. This character is an outsider to the people and privileges of Israel. And yet the storyteller so shapes the story that we grow both in sympathy and admiration as the story reaches its climax. As Jesus pronounces, "O woman, great

---

5 Bible stories "center on the struggles of a protagonist, usually hindered or opposed by an antagonist. Supporting characters also appear, but exegetes will focus primarily on the protagonist and antagonist" (Jeffrey D. Arthurs, "Preaching the Old Testament Narratives," in *Preaching the Old Testament*, ed. Scott M. Gibson [Grand Rapids, MI: Baker, 2006], 79).

is your faith" (v. 28), we gladly join in his high commendation. Despite her race (Gentile), gender (woman), and problem (a demon-possessed daughter), we admire her and want to emulate her. And through her movement, confessions, doggedness (!), and postures we get the theological points of the passage. We too should move toward Jesus (she "came" to him, vv. 22, 25), call him "Lord" (vv. 22, 25, 27) and "Son of David" (v. 22), beg him for mercy ("Have mercy on me," v. 22), persist in prayer ("she came" to him again, saying, "Lord, help me," v. 25), and worship him ("she . . . knelt before him," v. 25). We should also be repulsed by her foil—the disciples. We don't want to share in their religious impatience, lack of compassion, narrow view of the kingdom, bigotry, and likely chauvinism.

Plot

Plot is the third component. Aristotle's ancient but still accurate statement that plot is the "soul" of a story in that the action moves the narrative, and that each story has a beginning (an action is introduced), a middle (it progresses toward the appointed goal), and an end (it reaches closure as the issues that have been introduced are resolved) suffices.[6] And each plot is built around one or more conflicts that reach resolution at the conclusion. *Conflict and Resolution* is not only the name of my new 1980s flashback band (we do weddings and Bar mitzvahs), it is the core of grasping and explicating this genre. And the preacher who thinks that it is optional to name the conflicts and trace their progress is, to paraphrase an '80s icon (Mr. T), to be pitied as a fool. The good reader, following Aristotle's advice, needs to see

---

6 Aristotle, *The Rhetoric and the Poetics of Aristotle*, trans. W. Rhys Roberts (New York: Modern Library, 1984), 1450a.

how the individual parts of the plot relate to the whole. The good preacher needs to divide the story, no matter how brief, into its successive units, and name these units accurately. He needs to understand and implement in his study (and most subtly in his sermon) the arc of the story: setting, rising action (including the conflict), climax, and resolution (see diagram 1.1).

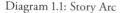

Diagram 1.1: Story Arc

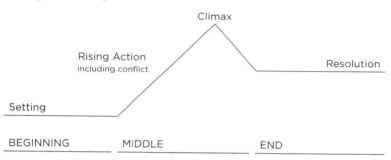

"Exposition" could be called "background," and it usually involves the *setting* being set: some character (Jesus) somewhere (in Cana of Galilee) on perhaps a certain day (someone's wedding day) is about to act (turn water into wine). Take, for example, the story of Abraham's (almost) sacrifice of his son. The background is, "After these things God tested Abraham" (Gen. 22:1). "These things" presumably refers to the birth of Isaac, God's protection of Hagar and Ishmael, and Abraham's treaty with Abimelech (Genesis 21). The fact that God *tests* the man he has called and with whom he has made a covenant introduces an imbalance, a disequilibrium that needs resolution. This pattern is typical of all plots in biblical narratives. So too are the next four stages:

Conflict	God commanded Abraham to sacrifice Isaac, a request surprisingly out of step with the promise of offspring.
Rising action	Father and son journey to the mountain of sacrifice, which includes Isaac carrying the wood to light the fire and asking about the animal for sacrifice, and Abraham constructing an altar, binding his son, and raising the blade for sacrifice.
Climax	The angel of the Lord stops the sacrifice. Abraham has passed the test!
Resolution	God provides an acceptable sacrifice (a ram) and reaffirms his covenant promises to Abraham.

Through this customary structural arrangement, biblical stories, like most stories told around the campfire and found in world literature, are voiced. We go back to the fact that God gave his people stories. And it is through these stories that he *shows* us the truth. For example, the accurate and important theological proposition that God is sovereign is sketched across the final fourteen chapters of the first book of the Bible. The preacher who ignores plot when he walks through the final narrative in Genesis, and then all of Numbers, Joshua, Judges, Ruth, 1 and 2 Samuel, 1 and 2 Kings, 1 and 2 Chronicles, Ezra, Nehemiah, Esther, and Jonah, is indeed the fool. If you want to invite your congregation's "interest and emotional involvement, while at the same time imbuing the events with meaning,"[7] you need to know how, and have a commitment to, "plodding" out the plot.[8]

---

7 Bar-Efrat, *Narrative Art in the Bible* (Sheffield, England, UK: Almond, 1989), 93.

8 Bonus insight for footnote readers: Storytellers tell their stories with beauty and skill using plot devices, such as foreshadowing (the death of John the Baptist in relation to Jesus's death), suspense (what will come of Joseph's dreams?), testing (Abraham's sacrifice of Isaac), poetic justice (the fates of Mordecai and Haman), irony (the taunt, "If you are the Son of

HOW TO PREACH BIBLICAL NARRATIVE

The careful expositor understands that "good narrative is a complex interweaving of characters, plot, and setting presented by the narrator, who speaks from outside the plot, moving it forward by reporting activities, descriptions and dialogue." He also grasps that the biblical narrator is often "*omniscient*, knowing the inner lives of the characters and selectively representing their thoughts, feelings and intentions . . . *omnipresent*, moving easily from one location to another, [and] *omnipotent* in the domain of the story," in that he "conveys a moral and ethical tone, passing judgment on characters and events."[9] Indeed, it is that *tone* that the expositor eyes, picking up on "the author's attitude toward his or her subject." Is his tone "sentimental, optimistic, cynical, bitter, objective, compassionate, irreverent," or a mixture of "sweet sadness, hopeful realism, or understated gratitude"?[10] You decide. More than "you decide," you need to form a sensible sermon. The advice of two doctors (Lee and I) follows, one an octogenarian who has published nearly as many books as there are skyscrapers in Chicago.

We transition from the study to the pulpit, seeking to answer the question, "How do we express in sermon form a biblical narrative's literary features and message?" Put differently, "How does our exegesis of the text's literary features help equip us to reproduce the text's rhetorical impact in our sermons?"[11] Below are eight suggestions for preaching a sermon on a biblical narrative.

God, come down from the cross," Matt. 27:40), and surprise (the Roman centurion who crucified Christ confesses him as "Son of God"), to name a few.

9 Elaine A. Phillips, "Novella, Story, Narrative," in *Dictionary of the Old Testament: Wisdom, Poetry, and Writings*, ed. Tremper Longman III and Peter Enns (Downers Grove, IL: InterVarsity Press, 2008), 492, emphasis mine.

10 Andrew T. Le Peau, *Write Better: A Lifelong Editor on Craft, Art, and Spirituality* (Downers Grove, IL: InterVarsity Press, 2019), 138.

11 See Arthurs, "Preaching the Old Testament Narratives," 73–74.

Pick the Proper Pericope

Pick the proper pericope.[12] This suggestion is obvious and usually easy to do, as most English Bible translations correctly divide the various narratives for you. For example, in the ESV the story of Samson is divided as such:

The Birth of Samson	Judges 13
Samson's Marriage	Judges 14
Samson Defeats the Philistines	Judges 15
Samson and Delilah	Judges 16:1–22
The Death of Samson	Judges 16:23–31

Of course, with any long narrative within Scripture, it is possible to do one sermon and cover the plot. However, it is impossible to do justice to all the important details. Thus, I suggest, for Samson's story, that the expositor does justice to the story only if the sermon series is five sermons. Moreover, if one goes beyond five sermons, the sermons wouldn't fit the five unique plots of each pericope.

That said, there are times, especially in the Gospels, when two or three stories should be told together in one sermon, as that follows best the author's intent. For example, the three short miracle stories in Matthew 8:1–17—the cleansing of a leper, the healing of the centurion's servant, and the cooling of Peter's mother-in-law's fever, along with Jesus's evening ministry where "he cast out the [evil] spirits . . . and healed all who were sick" (Matt. 8:16)—are all intended to make the same point: "This was to fulfill what was spoken by the prophet Isaiah: 'He took our illnesses and bore our

---

12 The Greek word *perikopē* means "section," literally "cutting across." It is a way of talking about a section within a biblical text that is separate from what comes before and after it because it forms a new or different coherent literary unit.

diseases'" (v. 17, quoting Isa. 53:4). Jesus is the prophesied servant whose sufferings defeat disease, death, and the devil. Matthew 8:1–17 should be preached as one sermon.

So too should a "Markan sandwich" (or interpolation) be preached in one sermon. Markan sandwiches are a literary technique that the Evangelist employs, where he "sandwiches one passage into the middle of another with an intentional and discernable theological purpose," emphasizing "the major motifs of the Gospel."[13] He does this, for example, in Mark 5:21–43:

A Jairus pleads with Jesus to save his dying daughter (vv. 21–24)
    B The woman with an issue of blood touches Jesus's garment and is saved (vv. 25–34)
A Jesus heals Jairus's daughter (vv. 35–43)

We see here the typical A-B-A schema of such interpolations. The two stories (A-A and B) should be preached together in one sermon, and the key themes of the extent of Jesus's power, the salvation found in him, and the nature of true faith should be included.

Relive the Story

After picking the proper pericope, our next task is to relive the story. "The stories of the Bible," Ryken writes, "will succeed only to the extent to which we exercise our imaginations and allow ourselves to be transported from our own time and place into another time and place."[14] The great advantage of narrative is its

---

13 James R. Edwards, "Markan Sandwiches: The Significance of Interpolations in Markan Narratives," *Novum Testamentum* 31.3 (1989): 196.

14 Leland Ryken, *Words of Delight: A Literary Introduction to the Bible* (Grand Rapids, MI: Baker, 1992), 53.

power of transport—its ability to lift us out of our own time and place and plant us in another time and place. We are transported there through understanding the setting, characters, and plot. We will come to that next. For now, we immerse ourselves in the story as fully as possible with a central goal in mind: to understand, and then explain, illustrate, and apply the human experience expressed in the biblical narrative.

Stories take human experience as their subject. Truthfulness to life and reality is the particular gift of literature and art, and we need to respect this before we involve ourselves with the other type of truth, namely, ideational truth. Every story is an invitation to share an experience. We share that experience with the characters in the story, first of all, but at another level we share the experience with the author or storyteller. The storyteller remains a presiding presence in the story, and we are aware of that presence. This tour guide uses devices of disclosure to influence how we experience and interpret the events of the story. We need to take our cues from the authorial presence in the story. The storyteller determines everything, including what we are allowed to see and vicariously experience.

Take, for example, the short but significant story of the Tower of Babel (Gen. 11:1–9). The first half narrates the success of the conception and construction of a great tower. While we don't know precisely what it looked like, we can all envision an impressive building that took amazing ingenuity and effort to build. The second half details this advanced civilization's quick downfall. Human language is confused, the project abandoned, the people divided and dispersed. Their gesture of aspiration toward deity is a complete failure. God judges their pride by thwarting their project.

"Stories," as Ryken summarizes, "function by first removing us from our own time and place and then (when we reflect and analyze) sending us back to our own world with a sharper sense of understanding."[15] Indeed! Once we have immersed ourselves in the narrative, we can journey from its world into our own. The Tower of Babel captures the spirit of our age as well as any story in all of Scripture. How's this list for relatable human experiences (and heaps of homiletical material):

- individual and communal aspiration
- the urge for human fame and achievement
- utopian zeal and dreams
- self-reliance and self-sufficiency
- technology and faith in what it can achieve
- the collective pride of the human race
- the urge for permanence
- the urge for material power
- the city as the locus of human civilization
- human inventiveness and creativity
- social cooperation, based on shared dreams and a single language
- architectural feats
- communal idolatry (finding security in a substitute deity)
- linguistic division among people groups
- the abandonment of hopes and dreams[16]

What novelist John Steinbeck wrote of the popularity of the story of Cain (Gen. 4:1–16) could equally be applied to the story of the

15 Ryken, *How Bible Stories Work*, 22.
16 Ryken, *How Bible Stories Work*, 21–22.

Tower of Babel: "this is the best-known story in the world because it is everybody's story . . . the symbol story of the human soul."[17]

After interacting with the themes in the story that correspond with universal (and therefore recognizable) human experience, we seek to share with our congregations our reliving of the storyteller and his story. "The key to prompting empathy in listeners," Jeffrey Arthurs offers, "is to imaginatively reexperience the text in both your study and the pulpit, and then to express those feelings with conviction."[18] We pray that God will use our retelling of the biblical narrative to open the minds, touch the hearts, and enliven the wills of those who hear our voices.

Don't Skip the Setting

Bryan Chapell defines expository preaching as follows: "The main idea of an expository sermon (the topic), the divisions of that idea (the main points), and the development of those divisions (the subpoints) all come from truths the text itself contains. No significant portion of the text is ignored. In other words, expositors willingly stay within the boundaries of a text (and its relevant context) and do not leave until they have surveyed its entirety with their listeners."[19] In your preaching of biblical narratives, can it be said that "no significant portion of the text is ignored"? Would your congregation say that you do not finish the sermon unless

---

17 John Steinbeck, *East of Eden* (New York: Penguin, 1952), 268. "No story has power, nor will last, unless we feel in ourselves that it is true and true of us." From Terry R. Wright, *The Genesis of Fiction: Modern Novelists as Biblical Interpreters* (New York: Routledge, 2007), 62, who quotes from Steinbeck's *Journal of a Novel.*

18 Jeffrey D. Arthurs, *Preaching with Variety: How to Re-Create the Dynamics of Biblical Genres* (Grand Rapids, MI: Kregel, 2007), 98.

19 Bryan Chapell, *Christ-Centered Preaching: Redeeming the Expository Sermon*, 2nd ed. (Grand Rapids, MI: Baker Academic, 2005), 131.

the text has been "surveyed [in] its entirety," *including the setting*? However seemingly mundane (e.g., a setting such as "and the next day"), a commitment to expository preaching sees the setting of each story as significant.

To illustrate the importance of setting, let's walk through the story of the conversion of Zacchaeus. Where is the story set? The first line introduces the hero (Jesus), his first action ("he entered"), the town he entered ("Jericho"), and his reason for entering Jericho ("he . . . was passing through," Luke 19:1). The phrase "passing through" reminds the reader of Jesus's ultimate mission in Jerusalem (he is passing through because his passion is his mission) and it adds an ironic twist. Jesus's mission, as clearly declared in Jesus's final line in this account, is that he "came to seek and to save the lost" (v. 10). Jesus's salvation of Zacchaeus fits perfectly with the metanarrative of the cross. He wasn't just randomly passing through Jericho. He came there on his preordained divine mission to save a certain tax collector. He came to knock down the walls of Zacchaeus's hard heart.[20]

Speaking of that man, notice how Luke, in the setting, quickly moves from the hero, Jesus, to the main character, Zacchaeus. He does this in a way often done in the Gospels to introduce something or someone important: "And behold." Translations that fail to translate the καὶ ἰδοὺ fail to understand the intentionality. The character we are to "behold" (stop and take a good look at) is named (something uncommon in the Synoptics), his occupation stated ("a chief tax collector"), and his financial position within

---

20 Sometimes the setting takes on symbolic value, and that perhaps is the case here. Moreover, certain place settings, such as Jericho, allow the preacher to flesh out some of the details of that location: e.g., give Old Testament background, archaeological details, and possibly contemporary perspectives on the town.

society noted ("he was . . . rich," v. 2). In verse 3, his height (a rare character description in the Bible) is also recorded ("he was small in stature").

Each detail sets us up for actions that occur. Because he was short, Zacchaeus needed to climb a tree to see Jesus. Because he was a chief tax collector, he was despised by his fellow Jews as a greedy traitor who would have defrauded many people ("they all grumbled, 'He [Jesus] has gone in to be the guest of a man who is a sinner,'" v. 7). Because he was rich, his declaration of repentance is remarkable ("Behold, Lord, the half of my goods I give to the poor. And if I have defrauded anyone of anything, I restore it fourfold," v. 8). The detail about Zacchaeus's wealth also serves as a foil to the rich young ruler, who refused to heed Jesus's command. Jesus commanded *that* man to sell everything he owned (18:22); Zacchaeus unwittingly obeys. Perhaps he didn't give away everything, but he must have come close: half to the poor; half to those he had *made* poor ("if I have defrauded . . ."). Finally, his name not only *surprisingly* resurfaces when Jesus calls him by name ("Zacchaeus," 19:5; how did Jesus know his name?), it offers further irony. His name, זכי (Hebrew), means "pure" or "innocent." Obviously, this man was not that! He was a notorious "sinner" (v. 7). But he has, by the end of the story, obtained a purity of heart through actually seeing Jesus. Jesus calls him "a son of Abraham," not merely because he is Jewish but because he, like Abraham, is now justified (declared perfectly innocent) by faith ("And he believed the LORD, and he counted it to him as righteousness," Gen. 15:6; cf. Rom. 4:1–8). Whether this intratextual allusion is intentional or not, the preacher has license to interpret and illustrate Scripture with Scripture.

So, with the example above, do you see how important the setting is or often can be? Don't skip it. Soak it in. Set it forth.

Identify the Characters; Identify with the Characters

Our next task is to focus on the characters in the narrative, to both identify them and then identify *with* them. We suggest five steps.

First, list all the characters in the story. Take Korah's rebellion. Here's the start of that story:

> Now Korah the son of Izhar, son of Kohath, son of Levi, and Dathan and Abiram the sons of Eliab, and On the son of Peleth, sons of Reuben, took men. And they rose up before Moses, with a number of the people of Israel, 250 chiefs of the congregation, chosen from the assembly, well-known men. They assembled themselves together against Moses and against Aaron and said to them, "You have gone too far! For all in the congregation are holy, every one of them, and the LORD is among them. Why then do you exalt yourselves above the assembly of the LORD?" (Num. 16:1–3)

The list of characters includes God (the Lord), five people (Korah, Dathan, Abiram, Moses, and Aaron), and two large groups of people (250 chiefs of the congregation, the people [or congregation] of Israel).

Second, after assembling the cast of characters, divide them into major and minor characters, determining the function of each in the action. Find the central character/s and those arrayed against him/them; that is, label the protagonist/s and antagonist/s. In the above narrative, Korah, Dathan, and Abiram are the antagonists (they "rose up . . . against"), and Moses and Aaron are the protagonists. Another more advanced division would be between what literary-critical scholars call a "stock" character (someone who exhibits only one trait), and a "round" character (someone whose attitudes, actions, and dialogue come across as a real, fully developed person).[21]

Third, observe and analyze each key character. "The starting point for good character analysis is a keen eye for the obvious."[22] The first two steps should take only a few minutes. You can do it. You should do it! This third step takes about a half hour. One way to collect the needed data is to use Cornelis Bennema's chart of character descriptors (table 1.1).[23]

Fourth, after you identify the characters and their traits, seek to identify with them. Here is a checklist that Ryken offers to analyze characters:

- Agency: Who or what does the characterizing in a given instance?
- Mode: Does a given piece of data constitute direct character-izing or indirect characterizing? If the former, is the statement of commentary a piece of objective description or an evalua-tive assessment of a character?
- Within a given piece of data, do you approve or disapprove of what a character does? Overall, is a given character presented positively or negatively in this story?[24]

---

21 Jack D. Kingsbury describes "round" characters as "those who possess a variety of traits, some of which may even conflict, so that their behavior is not necessarily predictable. Round characters are like 'real people.' In Matthew's story, Jesus and the disciples count as round characters" (*Matthew as Story*, 2nd ed. [Philadelphia: Fortress, 1988], 10).

22 Ryken, *How Bible Stories Work*, 67.

23 Cornelis Bennema, *Encountering Jesus: Character Studies in the Gospel of John*, 2nd ed. (Min-neapolis: Fortress, 2014), 38.

24 Ryken, *How Bible Stories Work*, 50–51.

Table 1.1: Cornelis Bennema's Chart of Character Descriptors

Name of Character	
Narrative appearances	
Origin	Birth, gender, ethnicity, nation/city
	Family (ancestors, relatives)
Upbringing	Nurture, education
External goods	Epithets,* reputation
	Age, marital status
	Socioeconomic status, wealth
	Place of residence/operation
	Occupation, positions held
	Group affiliation, friends
Speech and actions	In interaction with the protagonist
	In interaction with other characters
Death	Manner of death, events after death
Character analysis	Complexity [i.e., traits]
	Development
	Inner life
Character classification	Degree of characterization**
Character evaluation	Response to the protagonist
	Role in plot
Character significance	Representative value

*   "An exalted title for a person or thing; a feature of the high style. Examples are 'the Lord of hosts' as a title for God (Ps. 24:10) and 'Darius the Mede' as a title of the Persian king (Dan. 5:31)" (Leland Ryken, "Glossary of Literary Terms and Genres," in *The Literary Study Bible, English Standard Version* [Wheaton, IL: Crossway, 2019], 1979).

** "Characterization," as Kingsbury defines it, "has to do with the way in which an author brings characters to life in a narrative" (*Matthew as Story*, 9).

It is that final question to which we turn next. The goal of the above analysis is "for us to get to know the characters as fully as possible, and then to decide what the author intends us to learn about life and God on the basis of these characters."[25] For each character we should ask, "Am I like him/her? Should I be like him/her? What of his/her story is mine?"

For example, most Christians easily identify with Peter in his threefold denial of Jesus. But do we identify more with Mary or with Martha? The priest, the Levite, or the good Samaritan? Do we identify more with the grumbling onlookers who are repelled because Jesus has "gone in to be the guest of a man who is a sinner," or with Zacchaeus, who joyfully receives Jesus and generously distributes his ill-gotten wealth to those in need? Do we recognize something of Jonah's unmerciful bigotry in our own ministries? Can we say with the oblivious apostles, after Jesus declared that one of them will betray him, "Is it I, Lord?" Below is an example of how I preached on this point in my opening sermon on the Gospel of Mark:

> Mark does not just talk about who Jesus is and what he has done. He also highlights various responses to him. There are wrong responses and right ones. And through the various characters who encounter Jesus, we ourselves enter into the drama. With each character we should ask ourselves, "Should we imitate their response to Jesus or not?"
>
> For example, we should not say about Jesus, as the scribes did, "He is possessed by Beelzebul" (3:22), or join Peter at the

---

25 Ryken, *How Bible Stories Work*, 68. "Storytellers have *devices of disclosure* by which to guide our assessment of a character's experiment in living" (Ryken, *How Bible Stories Work*, 117). For example, in Genesis 13, note the outcome (does something positive or negative happen to the character?), point of view (e.g., the narrator of the story of the separation between Abraham and Lot provides a subtle comment about the land which makes Lot look selfish and Abraham sacrificial), and authorial commentary (e.g., the citizens of Sodom "were wicked, great sinners against the LORD," Gen. 13:13).

transfiguration (9:5) in making Jesus equal with Moses and Elijah (build a tent for each), or follow the rich man in not following Jesus' call (10:17–22), or betray Jesus like Judas did (14:43–46), repeatedly deny Jesus like Peter did (14:66–72), ridicule Jesus as Pilate did (15:9, 26), and mock him like the Roman soldiers (15:16–20), the chief priests, and the scribes (vv. 31–32). But we should follow Jesus like Simon, Andrew, James, and John (1:16–20), and join the leper on our knees before Jesus, saying, "Make me clean" (1:40), and humbly acknowledge, as the father of the demon-possessed boy did, our need for Jesus' help—not only to deliver us from evil but to grow our faith: "We believe; help our unbelief" (see 9:24). We should also see with blind Bartimaeus that Jesus, as the Son of David, is able to cure both physical and spiritual blindness ("Son of David, have mercy on me!"; 10:47), and shout aloud with the crowd, "Hosanna! Blessed is he who comes in the name of the Lord. Blessed is the coming kingdom of our father David! Hosanna in the highest!" (11:9–10). Yes, indeed. Lord, save us! We should, moreover, like the woman who came with an expensive bottle of perfume, pour out a year's wages upon Jesus (14:3–9), and join in the centurion's cry at the cross, "Truly this man was the Son of God!" (15:39).

In 13:14, Mark interjects "Let the reader understand." But Mark wants his readers not just to understand the Olivet Discourse (where we find that interjection). He wants us to understand who Jesus is, what he has done for us, and how we should respond to him. One way that Mark teaches his readers to respond to Jesus is through key characters—respond like him and her and them.[26]

---

26 Douglas Sean O'Donnell, *Mark: Arise and Follow the Son*, forthcoming.

Fifth, as preachers we seek to identify with the characters. "Without sympathetic connection," Arthurs notes, "the sermon will lack credibility."[27] Here is where I suggest a personal testimony that connects with the themes of the text; in your transparency and vulnerability you will also connect with your congregation.[28] For example, in my first sermon in my new calling at Crossway, where I also serve as chaplain, I preached on the sinful woman who anointed Jesus (Luke 7:36–50). Here is how I concluded that brilliant and beautiful story:

With this story laid afresh before us, let me ask you: how will you respond to the grace of God offered in Jesus Christ? Like Simon or like the woman? Like Simon? No. Like the woman? Yes. Have faith in him. Love him. Serve him. And find "peace" and "rest for your souls."

As a few of you know, I came to Christ as a sexual sinner. I grew up in a devout Roman Catholic home where virginity was prized, and where I was taught to wait for marriage. I strongly believed that. I wanted to live out that conviction. And I did so throughout high school. And as a morally pure teenager—by all outward appearances, that is—I looked down on those who were sexually active. I know it's not proper Protestantism anymore to compare a devout Roman Catholic with a Pharisee, but I was more like Simon in this story than you might imagine. I went to church each week and on holy days of obligation, prayed the rosary every day in the month of May, fasted throughout Lent, served as an altar

27 Arthurs, *Preaching with Variety*, 92.
28 Le Peau's advice to writers is true for preachers: "Be vulnerable. Personal stories that show your own weaknesses or mistakes will help your audience identify with you, appreciate you, and open themselves up to what you have to say" (*Write Better*, 64).

boy and Eucharist minister, and was quite seriously considering the monastic life or the priesthood. But then a girl came along. Amazingly, it didn't take much to make me renounce my monkish ways. I lost my virginity. I bought the lie that true love is what justifies sexual intimacy, and if there was ever true love it was this. The feeling of love justified anything and everything I did.

Well, a few months later, my girlfriend told me she was pregnant! At age eighteen my girlfriend was pregnant, and at age nineteen I was the father of a baby boy. And when my boy's mother moved on from me—our true love forever didn't last forever, not even twenty months—God's saving grace moved me toward Christ. I cried—like this woman. Uncontrollably. You should have seen it. You wouldn't have believed the mess. And I prayed, "Jesus, forgive me and clean me up on the inside, for I'm full of lust and pride." And you know what? (The story of salvation hasn't changed.) He forgave me and cleaned me up.

I share that, and I end with that, because I want you to know (as your new chaplain) that when I say—"Be like this woman. Have faith in Christ. Love him. Serve him. Find peace and rest for your souls"—I mean it because I've experienced it. I used to be that, and now I'm this. I've been "washed, sanctified, and justified in the name of the Lord Jesus Christ and by the Spirit of our God" from my religious hypocrisy (like Simon) and my sexual sin (like the woman). Listen, God knows that human beings are self-righteous and sexually sinful. But God has not left us to ourselves. He has sent his Son to forgive the debtor, however great your debt. So, Crossway/Good News Publishers, receive afresh the good news of the cross. Come to the feet (and outstretched hands!) of Jesus Christ. Come to the only one who can say to you today and always, "Your sins are forgiven. . . . go in peace."

Reader, listen! A personal story from your life, attached to a biblical narrative, always proves a powerful combination that engages your hearers and often moves them to the desired attitudes, emotions, and actions. Obviously, you cannot and should not do this in every sermon, but you can and should do it, likely more than you do.

Divide the Plot Sequence

In her book on writing fiction, Anne Lamott writes,

> Plot grows out of character. . . . Let what they say or do reveal who they are, and be involved in their lives, and keep asking yourself, Now what happens? The development of relationship creates plot. Flannery O'Connor, in *Mystery and Manners*, tells how she gave a bunch of her early stories to the old lady who lived down the street, and the woman returned them saying, "Them stories just gone and shown you how some folks *would* do."[29]

That is precisely what plot is: it details what characters will up and do.

So, as Ryken rightly admonishes, "Especially important is the process of identifying the action—dividing the story into units and naming them accurately. Doing this pays big dividends when we move [step six, below] from story to theme."[30] Dividing a plot sequence into its constituent parts is not like writing a report for a postdoctoral seminar on astrophysics. "Anyone can divide a story into its successive units and identify plot conflicts and formulate an accurate statement of the unifying action of a story. All it takes is

---

29 Anne Lamott, *Bird by Bird: Some Instructions on Writing and Life* (New York: Anchor, 1994), 52–53.
30 Ryken, *How Bible Stories Work*, 115.

being convinced that these are the right things to do with a story."[31] The goal of such division is to produce a simple and seeable outline of the story,[32] an exegetical outline that will help serve as the foundation of your homiletical outline. Don't rush the necessary process:

> We should not be in a hurry to get to the religious or moral ideas in a Bible story. . . . In much biblical scholarship, preaching, and Bible study, there is too much time or space devoted to the ideas of the Bible stories and not enough time or space to reliving the story and absorbing the human experiences that are silhouetted with heightened clarity in it.[33]

Let the structure and movement of the text inform the structure and flow of the sermon. And as you retell the story in your sermon, don't take the story out of the story. Keep the plot moving. Don't often interrupt the retelling with a disruptive illustration, unnecessary application, or unimportant aside.

Move from Story to Theme

For any biblical text, one of the preacher's main tasks is to grasp and clearly communicate the ideational truth. This task is easy when preaching an epistle. Paul's proposition is your point. If he writes, "Do not be conformed to this world, but be transformed by the renewal of your mind," your two points of exegesis and application are obvious. But what about a story? Biblical stories offer representational truth, where a theme is disclosed through a

---

31 Ryken, *How Bible Stories Work*, 79.

32 "During the spadework phase of this analysis, it is very useful to draw horizontal lines to divide the sequence into easily seen units" (Ryken, *How Bible Stories Work*, 70).

33 Ryken, *How Bible Stories Work*, 125.

story wherein characters embody realities and the plot illustrates truth. For example, the story of David and Goliath (1 Samuel 17) communicates that "God is mightier than the most intimidating champion his enemies can muster and that he blesses those who step out with fearless faith."[34] Or, in the amnesty of Barabbas and sentencing of Jesus ("So Pilate . . . released for them Barabbas . . . and . . . delivered [Jesus] to be crucified," Mark 15:15), we have the great doctrine of the great exchange in story form.

So, every biblical narrative, like any good story, embodies human experience in such a way as to lead us to relive it along with the characters in the story, but each story also conveys a message or theme. "What is the big idea?" is a question that preachers trained under Haddon Robinson were taught to ask and answer. It is not the only question to ask, but it is an important one, especially as it relates to narratives. Sometimes the big idea is not stated in the text and thus not easily deduced, such as in the story of David and Goliath. (The key, then, is not to allegorize or moralize, but to study, ask learned friends, and pray.) Other times, the narrator himself or a character in his story shares the big idea. This is a big help! Below are four examples where Jesus shares the focused truth of the text:

". . . know that the Son of Man has authority on earth to forgive sins . . ." (Mark 2:10)

"A prophet is not without honor, except in his hometown . . ." (Mark 6:4)

"You go, and do likewise." (Luke 10:37)

---

34 Arthurs, "Preaching the Old Testament Narratives," 77.

"The Son of Man came to seek and to save the lost." (Luke 19:10)

So, if you preach the parable of the good Samaritan (Luke 10) as an allegory about how Jesus, as the ultimate Good Samaritan, paid for all our sins, you've missed the point; or if in your retelling the story of the conversion of Zacchaeus (Luke 19) you think his seeking after Jesus supersedes Jesus's seeking of the lost tax collector, you have the two themes backwards. It is this clearly stated, or carefully deduced, big idea that becomes then the main emphasis of the sermon.

Frame within the Context

To effectively preach Bible narratives, it is foundational to set the story within its historical, theological, and literary context. The story of Ruth is understood and properly applied only when we know something of the connection between the historical setting ("In the days when the judges ruled," Ruth 1:1), Ruth's bitter tragedy (her husband's death, 1:5), her sweet marriage to her redeemer Boaz (4:13), and the promise of the Davidic covenant ("she bore a son. They named him Obed. . . . Obed fathered Jesse, and Jesse fathered David," 4:13, 17, 22; cf. 2 Samuel 7).

Moreover, following the model of apostolic preaching, we should preach every particular narrative in relation to the Bible's metanarrative, the story about God and the salvation of his people that spans from creation to new creation. This big story includes "the covenants with Israel and the nations that were given to Abraham, Moses, and David . . . the sending of Jesus the Messiah and his life, death, and resurrection . . . a coming judgment that all people must face," and the "right response," namely, "believing in Jesus, which means believing in all that has been said about Jesus." When we "preach through any narrative segment of the Bible," Paul House advises, "preachers should keep this sweeping narrative in mind."[35]

Create a Homiletic Outline

How do we put it all together? Whether you preach without notes, with a few Post-its pinned to the pulpit, from a fairly robust outline, or from a full manuscript (the fully sanctified position!), below I offer five arrangements. Each arrangement comes with an example from a recent sermon series that I preached on Mark.

First, follow the story's plot. Move from disequilibrium to resolution, from problem to solution. When I preached on Mark 9:14–29, I gave two points. (It's not a sin to give a two-point sermon!) I started, as the story does, with *the problem* (a demon-possessed son and the disciples' inability to help, vv. 14–24), followed by *the solution* (Jesus's incredible authority over evil, vv. 25–29). Simple enough.

Second, make a point based on each key character. For example, when I preached on Mark 10:46–52, in my introduction I spoke of the climax of this miracle story: Jesus's statement to blind Bartimaeus, "Your faith has made you well," or it could be rendered (as the verb is *sōzō*), "Your faith has saved you." I went on to say, "Saving faith is a key theme here. But there are other themes, and other lessons to be learned in this short but theologically charged text. And, one way to learn all the lessons is to review the three characters in the story: the 'blind beggar' who cries out for help; those who, at first, oppose him ('his disciples and a great crowd,' v. 46); and 'Jesus of Nazareth' (v. 47), the Savior who restores the man's sight." I started, then, with those who opposed the poor

---

35 Paul House, "Written for Our Example: Preaching Old Testament Narratives," in *Preach the Word: Essays on Preaching: In Honor of R. Kent Hughes*, ed. Leland Ryken and Todd Wilson (Wheaton, IL: Crossway, 2007), 36.

man's plea by highlighting the actions and comments from the disciples and the crowd.

Third, use your main applications as points. I have found this strategy successful. Only a small percent of the congregation falls asleep or leaves for the bathroom! You still retell the story. You always retell the story. God forbid you don't retell the story! But you arrange your material to appeal to the "So what?" question that arises in everyone's mind the moment you start your sermon. When I preached Mark 1:21–39, I offered three lessons: we must (1) believe that demons exist and wreak havoc in this world; (2) know that Jesus has come to destroy the works of the devil; and (3) follow Jesus's priorities—prayer and preaching. My sermon on Mark 7:24–37 also featured three lessons: let us be astonished at (1) Jesus's extraordinary authority; (2) the extent of his kingdom; and (3) his eschatological salvation.

Fourth, use key themes to retell the story. Okay, with my example for this suggestion, I move from Mark to Luke, but only because I just preached on Zacchaeus. And besides, variety in writing, as in preaching, is important. Here's my homiletical outline, as I tied it to the text and flow of the story:

Point One	Seeking	"Zacchaeus was *seeking* to see who Jesus was"
Point Two	Receiving	"he . . . *received* him [Jesus] joyfully"
Point Three	Pulling[36]	"The Son of Man came to *seek* and to *save* the lost."

Fifth, be cool like jazz. That is, offer an inducive arrangement. "Don't show the bones" is how I sometimes phrase it. I get the image

---

36 The word "pulling" is not in the text. I use the image based on the context—a rich man is pulled through the eye of the needle (Luke 18:25).

of the jazz musician from the excellent book my new friend Eric Redmond edited. In Charlie Dates's insightful preface, he writes,

> A gift of black preaching to the field of homiletics is its intersection of preaching as science and art. On one hand, preaching has technical elements for exegesis, structure, theological, and doctrinal proclamation. On the other, preaching, like jazz, can move within a structure, an invisible outline, a storytelling that makes the point without necessarily announcing the point. It can invite hearers into the biblical narrative, turn their ears into eyes, and arrest their imagination.[37]

An invisible outline indeed! Don't show the bones. Jazz musicians know their chord structures, but they don't play them in front of you. They use them skillfully. Beautifully. Go and do likewise! As you are retelling the story, add a few riffs. That is, quote the text, retell it in your own words, add an illustration or an application, and then back to the melodic line. You can assert the application (I'm not against that; see my applications-as-points suggestion above), but sometimes suggestion, not assertion, serves your congregation best.[38] As Robinson states, "Narratives are most effective when the audience hears the story and arrives at the speaker's ideas without the ideas being stated directly."[39]

---

37 Charlie E. Dates, "Preface: The Treasure and Potential of African American Preaching," in *Say It! Celebrating Expository Preaching in the African American Tradition*, ed. Eric C. Redmond (Chicago: Moody, 2020), 18.

38 See Sidney Greidanus, *The Modern Preacher and the Ancient Text: Interpreting and Preaching Biblical Literature* (Grand Rapids, MI: Eerdmans, 1988), 225.

39 Haddon W. Robinson, *Biblical Preaching: The Development and Delivery of Expository Messages*, 2nd ed. (Grand Rapids, MI: Baker, 1989), 130.

See table 1.2 for additional ideas for organizing sermons based on narratives.

Table 1.2: Five More Possible Ways to Organize Homiletical Outlines on Narratives

Geographical shifts	Your outline could follow Jesus's movement: "near to Jerusalem" (Mark 11:1), "on the road" to Jerusalem (v. 8), and entering Jerusalem: "And he entered Jerusalem" (v. 11).
Locations	On the beheading of John the Baptist (Mark 6:14–29), you could serve as a tour guide, taking your congregation from (1) the king's headquarters (2) to the prison (3) to the banquet hall (4) to the tomb.
Scenes and themes	Matthew 26:57–75 records two trials. Thus, it offers a twofold outline. As Jesus is on trial before the Sanhedrin for his messiahship ("Tell us if you are the Christ," v. 63), Peter is on trial before a few servants for his discipleship. (The "now" of verse 69 means that the subsequent events occur "at the same time" as Jesus's trial ["now," v. 59].) Matthew's literary artistry is astounding! As Jesus stands on trial inside the high priest's house before the high-ranking religious authorities in Jerusalem and tells the truth, Peter sits outside and repeatedly lies as lowly servant girls question him. He thrice denies Jesus.

Table 1.2 (*continued*)

| Relationship of key words to scenes and themes | Mark 10:13–31 can be preached as a unit, rather than preaching one sermon on Jesus's interaction with the children (vv. 13–16) and another on the rich man's encounter with Jesus (vv. 17–31). These texts belong together because Mark uses three key words to connect the two stories: the word "child/ren" (vv. 13, 14, 15, 24, 29, 30), "enter" (vv. 15, 23, 24, 25), and "kingdom of God" (vv. 14, 15, 23, 24, 25, cf. "gospel" of the kingdom [v. 29 with Matt. 4:23]). Yet more important than those three key words are the shared themes found in these two stories, told in three scenes.

In scene one, children come to Jesus. He receives them. He blesses them. He offers an object lesson: "Truly, I say to you, whoever does not receive the kingdom of God like a child shall not enter it" (10:15). That lesson, then, is played out in the next two scenes.

In scene two, a rich man approaches Jesus. Does he receive the kingdom like a little child? Put differently, is he willing to be totally dependent on Jesus, a dependence that, in his case, would show itself in absolute self-denial in regards to his great possessions? No, he is not willing.

Then, in scene three, Jesus instructs his disciples on the dangers of wealth: "How difficult it will be," he says, "for those who have wealth to enter the kingdom of God!" (v. 23). He then reiterates his point: "*Children* [he calls his disciples], how difficult it is to enter the kingdom of God!" (v. 24). Then, he gives an exaggerated metaphor to explain just how difficult it is: "It is easier for a camel to go through the eye of a needle than for a rich person to enter the kingdom of God" (v. 25). The disciples are astonished. They wonder if anyone can enter the kingdom and experience eternal life, ultimate salvation. Next, Jesus talks about the possibility of an impossibility. God alone can save people! Then, Peter makes an interesting statement to Jesus: "See, we have left everything" (v. 28). Is that statement (which represents a reality) an expression of childlike faith? |

Table 1.2 (*continued*)

Questions	An outline for Mark 9:2–13 could be these four questions. First, what does God say here about Jesus? Second, what is the proper response to that revelation? Third, what does Jesus say about his mission? Fourth, what is the proper response to that revelation?

CONCLUSION

Our goal with this chapter, as with the following chapters, is to equip you with helpful and reliable tools so you might more effectively understand and teach the Bible. And as my coauthor wisely phrases it for every genre, "If the message is embodied in a form, we first need to master the form. The 'how' is the door that opens the 'what' of the utterance."[40] The form in this central chapter is narrative. Aren't you glad God gave us stories! I love stories. Lee loves stories. You love stories. Your congregation loves stories. The unbelieving world loves stories. Such stories God has given, through his inspired scribes, to shape us! They inspire us to action. Inspire us to evangelize the lost through the only One who came to seek and to save the lost.

BUILD YOUR LIBRARY! HELPFUL RESOURCES

Alter, Robert. *The Art of Biblical Narrative*. New York: Basic, 1981.

Greidanus, Sidney. *Preaching Christ from Genesis: Foundations for Expository Sermons*. Grand Rapids, MI: Eerdmans, 2007.

House, Paul. "Written for Our Example: Preaching Old Testament Narratives." Pages 22–37 in *Preach the Word: Essays on Preaching: In Honor of R. Kent Hughes*. Eds. Leland Ryken and Todd Wilson. Wheaton, IL: Crossway, 2007.

40 Ryken, *Literary Introductions to the Books of the Bible*, 10.

Mathewson, Steven D. *The Art of Preaching Old Testament Narrative*. Grand Rapids, MI: Baker, 2002.

Pratt, Richard. *He Gave Us Stories: The Bible Student's Guide to Interpreting Old Testament Narratives*. Brentwood, TN: Wolgemuth & Hyatt, 1990.

Ryken, Leland. "And It Came to Pass: The Bible as God's Storybook." *Bibliotheca Sacra* 147.586 (1990): 131–42.

_____. *How to Read the Bible as Literature*. Grand Rapids, MI: Zondervan, 1984.

_____. *How Bible Stories Work: A Guided Study of Biblical Narrative*. Bellingham, WA: Lexham, 2015.

2

Let Him Who Has Ears Hear

Preaching Parables

THE SENTENCE "He did not speak to them without a parable" (Mark 4:34) has been used as a proof text for the centrality of parables in Jesus's earthly ministry. The problem is that the pronoun "them" (4:2, 33, 34) clearly alludes to the "very large crowd" (v. 1) to whom Jesus taught a few parables on one particular day. Also, Mark records only two full-scale narrative parables in all of his Gospel; the rest of Jesus's teachings can be categorized as appeals (e.g., "The time is fulfilled, and the kingdom of God is at hand; repent and believe in the gospel," 1:15); callings ("Follow me, and I will make you become fishers of men," 1:17); pronouncements ("Son, your sins are forgiven," 2:5); short instructions (8:34–38); and larger discourses (13:5–37), including apocalyptic prophecies (vv. 24–27). Jesus spoke to the crowds and his disciples alike in many literary genres. Moreover, the Sermon on the Mount (Matthew 5–7) and the Upper Room Discourse (John 15–17) contain no parables, and there is no mention of parables when Jesus taught at the synagogues in Nazareth and Capernaum (Luke 4:14–17, 31–37).

That does not mean parables were not central to Jesus's teaching ministry. Jeffrey Arthurs says, "When we come to the parables, we come to the heart of Jesus' ministry. In fact, we come to the heart of Jesus himself—his values and mission."[1] G. P. Anderson adds that "no aspect of his teaching is more memorable and influential than these unassuming similes and vivid stories."[2] These estimations are not exaggerations because, depending on how you define the term *parabolē*,[3] which occurs fifty-two times in the New Testament (fifty of those times in the Synoptics!), the Gospels record up to seventy parables.[4] Arthurs estimates that "approximately 43 percent" of Jesus's "words in Matthew, 16 percent of his words in Mark, and 52 percent of his words in Luke are parables."[5] Anderson lists eleven "Parables in Mark and/or the Triple Tradition [the Synoptics]," nine "Parables common to Matthew and Luke (Q?)," ten "Parables unique to Matthew," and sixteen "Parables unique to Luke."[6]

---

1 Jeffrey D. Arthurs, *Preaching with Variety: How to Re-Create the Dynamics of Biblical Genres* (Grand Rapids, MI: Kregel, 2007), 103.

2 G. P. Anderson, "Parables," in *Dictionary of Jesus and the Gospels*, ed. N. Perrin, Joel B. Green, and J. K. Brown (Downers Grove, IL: IVP Academic, 2013), 651.

3 In Scripture, the term "parable" (*māšāl* in Hebrew ["to be like"]; *parabolē* in Greek ["to throw alongside"]) covers a wide-ranging "cross section of metaphorical or analogical speech" (Craig L. Blomberg, *Preaching the Parables: From Responsible Interpretation to Powerful Proclamation* [Grand Rapids, MI: Baker Academic, 2004], 23).

4 Jesus preached around forty narrative parables. There are only a few narrative, or partly narrative, parables in the Old Testament. See Judg. 9:7–15; 2 Sam. 12:1–4; 2 Kings 14:9–10; Ezek. 17:2–10; Isa. 5:1–7.

5 Arthurs, *Preaching with Variety*, 103. Cf. Klyne R. Snodgrass, *Stories with Intent: A Comprehensive Guide to the Parables of Jesus* (Grand Rapids, MI: Eerdmans, 2008), 22.

6 Anderson, "Parables," 654–55. "John's Gospel is excluded from the inventory, not because it lacks extended metaphors altogether (e.g., Jn 10:1–18; 15:1–8), but because these are arguably of a different type than the parables of the Synoptic Gospels" (656).

If we limit our use of the term to the symbolic narratives Jesus teaches in the Synoptics, the percentage lessens. Jesus doesn't speak a high percentage of the time in parables, even to the crowds. But his parabolic recorded speech is high enough a percentage, and more importantly, high enough in its narrative placement and literary value, for us to spend both a chapter discussing and a lifetime seeking to master it. Thus, the data above and the point just made instructs us on the importance of knowing how to read and preach parables. We turn now to that task.

This chapter is divided into three sections. First, we discuss the literary features or characteristics of parables. Second, we offer ten steps to help you interpret the parables. Third, we add additional suggestions for preaching parables. We may not master the parables, but let us at least stand in awe of the wisdom of our Master, *the master storyteller.*

LITERARY FEATURES OF PARABLES

"The parables of Jesus are at once thoroughly literary."[7] Ryken's obvious insight is sadly too often overlooked. Like the Epistles, preachers can treat parables as if they are genre-less data sources wherein the preacher's purpose is to quickly find the kernel of didactic truth, peal it out of the ten-foot stalk and the soil in which it has grown, and serve the sweet corn to the congregation. Thus, we see the need to start with some of the key literary characteristics of biblical parables.[8]

---

7   Leland Ryken, *Words of Delight: A Literary Introduction to the Bible* (Grand Rapids, MI: Baker, 1992), 403.

8   For further explication on the literary features of the parables, see Leland Ryken, *How to Read the Bible as Literature* (Grand Rapids, MI: Zondervan, 1984), 138–53.

Definition

When Peter asks Jesus to explain a "parable" Jesus taught ("Not what goes into the mouth defiles a man; but what comes out of the mouth, this defiles a man," Matt. 15:11 NKJV), we would likely classify Jesus's proposition more as a proverb than a parable, in that there is no story with double meaning (e.g., a man's mouth symbolizes some spiritual truth). However, Peter's usage of "parable" reflects an understanding of the Hebrew word *māšāl*, which can refer to "a prophetic saying, a proverb, a riddle, a discourse, a poem, a short story, a similitude—almost any kind of pithy maxim or anecdote."[9] To Peter, any aphoristic utterance constitutes a "parable."

The word itself is a combination of the preposition *para* ("beside") and the verb *ballō* ("to cast"), literally meaning to "toss next to," or "to place alongside." That etymology, and the visual it provides, offers a good start to a helpful definition. A parable makes a comparison: God is like the longing and loving father who forgives and embraces a prodigal son who has returned home; the growth of the kingdom of God is like that of a mustard seed. Those two realities are alike in some way, and together they teach theological truths and spiritual lessons. My friend Robert Kinney, when he instructs on this genre for the Charles Simeon Trust, offers this definition: "A parable is a simple and usually narrative story, grounded in the real world, and used to provoke the audience on a spiritual (or moral) matter or even to make a spiritual (or moral) point."

---

9 John MacArthur, *Parables: The Mysteries of God's Kingdom Revealed through the Stories Jesus Told* (Nashville: Nelson, 2015), xxv. In the Septuagint, *parabolē* is used to translate the Hebrew word *māšāl* in thirty of its thirty-four occurrences. *Māšāl* "encompasses a broad range of reference, describing a variety of aphoristic utterances," including oracles, saying, proverbs, and taunts (Anderson, "Parables," 651).

The above definition can be broken down into three points. First, Jesus's parables can be any aphoristic utterance (such as what Peter and the disciples heard above) and simple, short similes ("the kingdom is like"). However, the majority of Jesus's parables are fictional stories.[10] This means we should approach them as we would any narrative, seeking to grasp setting, characterization, and plot.[11] Second, they are grounded in the real world. "They deal," as Ryken puts it, "with the most realistic situations imaginable: a farmer sowing seed, a shepherd caring for sheep, a woman baking bread" (see "Homespun Realism," below).[12] Third, they are told to provoke (or challenge!) Jesus's hearers on a spiritual (or moral) matter or even to make a spiritual (or moral) point. Put differently, they were intended to both shock people into thinking afresh about God and his ways (e.g., can a Samaritan be a good neighbor?) and challenge them to act in accordance with such new knowledge ("Go, and do likewise"). They are secular pictures or stories from everyday life based on shared or seen experiences—fishermen casting their nets, a mother kneading bread for supper, a farmer sowing seed, a man traveling from one town to the next, a shepherd caring for his sheep—that make comparisons in order to communicate kingdom priorities and realities.[13] We might add to the above definition that parables can be understood only by means of God's ear-opening grace

---

10 Parables are "the indisputable example of fiction in the Bible" (Leland Ryken, *Words of Life: A Literary Introduction to the New Testament* [Grand Rapids, MI: Baker, 1987], 61).

11 Some of the parables are complex stories "with a skillfully designed plot, elaboration of setting and dialogue, and subtle characterization" (Ryken, *Words of Life*, 61).

12 Ryken, *Words of Life*, 61.

13 They are "realistic stories, simple in construction and didactic . . . in purpose, that convey religious truth and in which the details often have a significance beyond their literal narrative meaning" (Ryken, *How to Read the Bible as Literature*, 202).

(see "The Purpose of Parables," below), followed by extended mental effort and prayerful wrestling.

Three Types of Parables

There are three types of parables Jesus preaches. First, and continuous with the Hebrew Scriptures' use of *māšāl*, are Jesus's aphorisms ("Can a blind man lead a blind man? Will they not both fall into a pit?" Luke 6:39). Second are similes ("The kingdom of heaven is like treasure hidden in a field," Matt. 13:44). Third are symbolic stories (the parable of the sower). Our focus will be mostly on Jesus's narrative parables.

Simple Short Stories with Profound Timeless Truths

Parables have "the double quality" of "surface simplicity and hidden complexity."[14] The parables exist, as Ryken notes, "on a continuum ranging from the simple to the complex. On the one end of the spectrum is the single metaphor or simile in which Jesus compares the kingdom of heaven to a mustard seed or lost coin or hidden treasure. At the other end is a relatively complex story with a skillfully designed plot, elaboration of setting and dialogue, and subtle characterization."[15] This is true. But it is also true that even the more complex parables tell stories that come across, at first hearing, as stories so simple that even young children can grasp the main characters and the basic plotline.[16] If they can't yet grasp the spiritual lessons, they can literally draw some of Jesus's word

---

14 Leland Ryken, *Jesus the Hero: A Guided Literary Study of the Gospels* (Wooster, OH: Weaver, 2016), 97.

15 Ryken, *Words of Delight*, 403.

16 "All the parables are built around exceedingly simple and vivid images: a little rich boy swilling hogs, a housewife tirelessly searching for a lost penny, a shepherd placing one of his beloved sheep on his shoulders, a hypocritical theologian at prayer, the humiliation of a

pictures. In this way, all of Jesus's parables are ingeniously simple. But even the simplest and shortest parables about a commonplace everyday occurrence—a woman hiding leaven in three measures of flour until the batch was fully leavened (Matt. 13:33; cf. Luke 13:20–21)—communicate weighty truths. The kingdom of God is like that slow-rising leaven. The reign of God through Christ seemed nearly invisible at the time of Jesus's proclamation of this parable. Yet, by the time he returns, the slow but certain growth will have produced an exponentially enormous outcome. As the leaven mixed into fifty pounds of bread will rise enough to feed a hundred people, or a few families for a few months, a number too many to count will become part of Jesus's glorious and everlasting rule. This story, which appears to be merely a snapshot from an ordinary event in everyday life, is a picture of one of the biggest truths in God's big story of salvation.

Homespun Realism

Jesus's parables are *fictional* stories told by a master storyteller who was a keen observer of life in first-century Palestine. But the *truths* contained therein have a homespun realism that certainly appealed to his original readers and appeals to a universal audience because they hold a mirror up to real life. The people of first-century Palestine to whom Jesus preached readily understood the common characters (landowners, farmhands, fathers and sons, embezzlers, widows on a pension, bridegrooms, warring kings, thieves, tax collectors, violent robbers, merchants, innkeepers, priests, etc.); occasions (harvest, weddings, dinner banquets, etc.); items (mustard seeds, unshrunk cloth, pearls, fishing nets, sheep, hidden

---

guest who has worn the wrong dress at a fancy party" (Richard Lischer, *Reading the Parables*, Interpretation [Louisville: Westminster/John Knox, 2014], 11).

treasures, fig trees, etc.); and actions (sowing seed, retaliation of an angry master, weeds growing among wheat, pouring wine into wineskins, baking bread, traveling to a neighboring town, extending wedding invitations, finding a lost coin, etc.). So, the parables are works of fiction, but their "thoroughgoing realism" (as seen above) makes them very different than the works of fantasy fiction that feature "talking animals or haunted forests."[17] This realism is "something that can help make the parables come alive in our imaginations,"[18] and the archetypes (recurrent master images of life and literature)—e.g., lost and found, master and servant, the dangerous journey, the prodigal, the abundant harvest—awaken very deep feelings in the human psyche. Archetypes touch us where we live.

Oral Folk Stories

The biblical parables are oral folk stories. Their realism points to this, as does their composition. "They adhere," as Ryken points out, "to the rules . . . of folk stories through the centuries."[19] Those rules include (1) plot conflict, (2) suspense, (3) contrast or foil, (4) simplicity or the single plot, (5) repetition, especially threefold repetition, (6) end stress (the crucial element comes last, often as a foil to what has preceded), and (7) universality, especially universal character types. On this theme, Arthurs adds this insight:

> These simple folk stories engender . . . memory. Like proverbs, the parables were transmitted from person to person through oral communication. To be permanent they had to be simple,

---

17 Ryken, *Words of Delight*, 404.
18 Ryken, *Jesus the Hero*, 99.
19 Ryken, *Words of Delight*, 405. The list of rules is Ryken's.

brief, with the form of utterance aiding transmission. Thus the parable form allows no digressions, abstractions, or lengthy explanations. The . . . comparison of parables to jokes applies here also. We can remember jokes, even though we don't write them down, because of their brevity and simple form—stock characters, a single conflict, a formulaic rise in action, and a sudden turn or punch line.[20]

Universal Appeal

These divinely inspired folk stories set in first-century Palestine have appealed to billions of people for over two millennia. Part of the appeal is that a good story is a good story no matter the unfamiliar settings, characters, and actions. Another appealing feature is anonymity. Other than Lazarus, no other character is named. This quality, found often in the miracle accounts in the Gospels and other parts of Scripture (e.g., the couple in the Song of Solomon), extends an invitation to the ordinary man and woman and their everyday experiences and emotions.

Delayed-Action Insight

"Jesus' own theory of communication rested on what" Ryken calls "delayed-action insight." Knowing that listeners cannot absorb everything that they hear, Jesus told brief, memorable parables that do not carry all their meaning on the surface. They were intended to be carried away and mulled over for meaning. Like riddles, "they yield their meanings only to those who . . . take the time to ponder them."[21]

---

20 Arthurs, *Preaching with Variety*, 111.
21 Leland Ryken, *Choosing a Bible: Understanding Bible Translation Differences* (Wheaton, IL: Crossway, 2005), 25; cf. Ryken, *Words of Delight*, 406.

From Surface to Symbol

As we mull over the meaning of a particular parable, we realize both that there is a riddle-like quality to Jesus's so-called simple sayings and that without God's help to hear, no matter how long we ponder the puzzle, the pieces won't fit into place (see "The Purpose of Parables," below). That said, even if God gives the gift of faith, we need to labor long and hard to perceive the spiritual realities and second meanings of these simple short stories. We need to double down on the double meanings. Does virtually every detail in the parable have a symbolic meaning, as it does in the parable of the sower, or only the main characters and key actions, as in the parable of the prodigal son? (More on how to answer that question in a moment.)

Safeguarding Symbolism

Double meaning is at the heart of Jesus's parables. There are certainly allegorical, or more safely termed "symbolic" meanings. But, per the questions above, how do we discern what has a second meaning and what does not?

When I served as a lecturer at Queensland Theological College in Brisbane, Australia, I taught a class on the Synoptic Gospels. For my lectures on parables, I started with a personal testimony of my love for church history, which includes writing a master's thesis on John Donne's interpretation of the Song of Solomon. I have great admiration for those Christians who have walked ahead of us, and I tried to reinforce in my students the importance of "walking on the ashes of God's saints"—Donne's term for following in the exegetical footpaths of wise Christians who have gone before us.

That said, after I shared about my appreciation for church history in general and the history of biblical interpretation in particular, I handed out Augustine's commentary on the Good Samaritan (in his *Quaestiones Evangeliorum* 2.19). And without any verbal judgment or facial expressions from me, together we read each line aloud:

A *certain man went down from Jerusalem to Jericho*; Adam himself is meant; *Jerusalem* is the heavenly city of peace, from whose blessedness Adam fell; *Jericho* means the moon, and signifies our mortality, because it is born, waxes, wanes, and dies. *Thieves* are the devil and his angels. *Who stripped him*, namely; of his immortality; *and beat him*, by persuading him to sin; *and left him half-dead*, because in so far as man can understand and know God, he lives, but in so far as he is wasted and oppressed by sin, he is dead; he is therefore called *half-dead*. The *priest* and the *Levite* who saw him and passed by, signify the priesthood and ministry of the Old Testament which could profit nothing for salvation. *Samaritan* means Guardian, and therefore the Lord Himself is signified by this name. The *binding of the wounds* is the restraint of sin. *Oil* is the comfort of good hope; *wine* the exhortation to work with fervent spirit. The *beast* is the flesh in which He deigned to come to us. The being *set upon the beast* is belief in the incarnation of Christ. The *inn* is the Church, where travelers returning to their heavenly country are refreshed after pilgrimage. The *morrow* is after the resurrection of the Lord. The *two pence* are either the two precepts of love, or the promise of this life and of that which is to come. The *innkeeper* is the Apostle (Paul). The supererogatory payment is either his counsel of celibacy, or the fact that he worked with his own hands lest he should be a burden to any of the weaker brethren when the Gospel was new, though it was lawful for him "to live by the gospel."[22]

After each line, there was increased laughter.[23] Afterward, I asked two questions. First, why did you laugh? Or, what is wrong with Augustine's allegorical interpretation that you thought it funny? The class quickly offered correct answers, such as,

- Augustine is allegorizing in arbitrary ways, ways certainly not intended by Jesus or understood by his original audience.
- Augustine finds secret symbolism for nearly every detail, but his determinations don't seem to be made with an objective criterion in mind. How does he know that the "two pence" equals either Jesus's double love command or his promise of life in the present and future? Why limit it to those twofold themes? Why not a dozen other possible interpretations?

Second, I asked, As Christians throughout the centuries followed this method (it dominated the history of interpretation until the late nineteenth century), what do you think the result was? Often, I had to supply the answer, which is, Everyone did what was right in his own eyes! There were vastly different interpretations. I showed examples and then moved on to a PowerPoint slide titled "Contemporary Corrections." I did a brief overview (summarized below),

---

22 Anderson ("Parables," 657) notes that in *On Christian Doctrine* (1.31, 33) Augustine gives a straightforward application of this parable, "to the Christian moral obligation to love neighbor."

23 Ryken labels Augustine's allegories of the parables as laughable, and his "allegorizing of the parable of the Good Samaritan represents this tradition at its frivolous worst" (*Jesus the Hero*, 101–2).

walking from the groundbreaking work of Adolf Jülicher to that of Craig Blomberg.

In his book *Die Gleichnisreden Jesu* (1888), Adolf Jülicher (1857–1938) rejected the Greco-Roman forms of interpretation applied to Jesus's parables, namely, that they should be "treated as elaborate allegories, with almost every detail in each expounded as if it had some second level of spiritual or symbolic significance."[24] He argued that Jesus's parables reflected true-to-life conditions in first-century Palestine and that the details are included to establish realism, not so that analogy might be drawn from each aspect. Rather than treat the parables as metaphor, he argued that they were similes—drawing a comparison between two things so that an analogy might be drawn. To Jülicher, each parable makes one simple point, which usually yields a moralistic maxim.[25] According to Richard Lischer, Jülicher argued "that each parable is a simple, straightforward story with but one point, which he called the *tertium comparationis*, the point of comparison. The *tertium* is the 'third thing' which unites the abstract religious idea and the vivid picture contained in the parable."[26]

---

24 See Blomberg, *Preaching the Parables*, 13, 24.

25 Similarly, Joachim Jeremias (1900–1979) insisted that each parable has only one main point and that any other aspects of the story were mere embellishments intended to make the story memorable.

26 Lischer, *Reading the Parables*, 7. "The problem with Jülicher's [view] . . . is that the single 'points' he substituted for the church's florid allegories tended to be universal maxims or truisms of the lowest common denominator. For example, the parable of the Talents reminds us that a reward must be earned by performance. The parable of the Dishonest Steward enjoins the wise use of the present as the condition of a happy future. The parable of Lazarus and the Rich Man teaches joy in a life of suffering and fear of a life of pleasure. The Good Samaritan represents the ideal of the neighbor . . . who is above all a fellow human being. . . . In his reading, Jesus' lessons tended to confirm what enlightened moderns already believed. The generic approach prompted the British scholar C. W. F. Smith's famous one-liner: 'No one would crucify a teacher who told pleasant stories to enforce prudential morality' (*Jesus of the Parables*, 17)" (7). (Lischer is referencing Smith's *The Jesus of the Parables*, a rev. ed. of which was published by HarperCollins in 1975.)

Nearly a hundred years later (with a number of other important studies in between), Craig Blomberg published his dissertation on the distinctively Lukan parables.[27] He found Jülicher's approach to be artificially limiting and argued that the parables are inherently allegorical in a limited and constrained sense.[28] Blomberg explains his simple but significant thesis as follows: "Following the model of many of the rabbinic parables and of great narrative literature more generally, I argued that Jesus' parables made one main point per main character. . . . The main characters (and often only the main characters) in Jesus' parables do 'stand for something.'"[29] He argues that Jesus's parables draw comparisons between the characters within their stories and either God or the people listening. Thus, he categorizes parables according to the number of characters they involve—triadic (three characters), dyadic (two characters), or monadic (one character). He finds that the majority are triadic but finds a range of structures—for instance, describing a relationship between a master and good and bad servants, or placing a unifying character between a good and a bad example. In his own words, "Interestingly, the forty or so parables of Jesus exhibited only six different structures when one examined the number of main characters in each and the relationships among those characters. Approximately two-thirds of Jesus's narrative parables presented three main characters or groups of characters in a triangular (or what some have called 'monarchic') structure, with a master figure (including kings, fathers, landlords, shepherds, farmers, etc.) interacting with one or more contrasting pairs of subordinates (good and bad servants, sons, tenants, sheep, plants, etc.)."[30]

---

27 Craig Blomberg, "The Tradition History of the Parables Peculiar to Luke's Central Section" (PhD diss., University of Aberdeen, 1982).

28 See Anderson's summary of Blomberg ("Parables," 660).

29 Blomberg, *Preaching the Parables*, 13.

30 Blomberg, *Preaching the Parables*, 15–16.

As someone who has preached nearly two hundred sermons on passages in the Synoptics, and on most of the parables, I find Blomberg's homiletical theory both convincing and extremely helpful. I don't find it limiting, as some do,[31] for I do not believe that the parables are "susceptible to multiple, equally valid interpretations."[32] There is authorial intent, an intent sometimes clearly expressed by Jesus with a summary maxim (see table 2.1). The principle of "end stress" is important because, when employed, Jesus directly informs his listeners of what he takes to be the main point. He also provides a proper lens by which to re-view the details of the parable. For example, the end stresses of the parables of "lost things" trilogy (Luke 15:7, 10, 32) together tell us that there should be celebratory joy whenever anyone repents.[33]

Moreover, Blomberg allows for such "big idea" preaching,[34] and promotes the value of harmonizing the points on each character into one main point. He speaks of Barbara Reid's idea, stating that "the best way this approach [of preaching the big idea] can be harmonized with the multiple points in many parables is to 'discern which of the many points is the main one that the assembly needs to hear at this place and time.'"[35] Blomberg also offers this suggestion and admission:

---

31 "While it is an improvement to expand interpretation so as to assign a 'point' to each character (Blomberg), such an approach, for all its schematic discipline, is still too much indebted to a static view of the parables that requires them to yield 'points,' whether one or several" (Anderson, "Parables," 661).

32 Anderson, "Parables," 662.

33 For a more detailed example of end stress, see "Step Ten (Application)."

34 As noted in chapter 1, finding the "big idea" (a summarizing thought or preaching point for each sermon) was popularized by Haddon W. Robinson, *Biblical Preaching* (Grand Rapids, MI: Baker, 1980).

35 Barbara Reid, *Parables for Preachers* (Collegeville, MN: Liturgical, 1999), 18, summarized by Blomberg, *Preaching the Parables*, 22.

Table 2.1: Examples of End Stress Summary Maxims

Matthew 18:35	So also my heavenly Father will do to every one of you, if you do not forgive your brother from your heart.
Matthew 20:16	So the last will be first, and the first last.
Matthew 21:43	Therefore I tell you, the kingdom of God will be taken away from you and given to a people producing its fruits.
Matthew 22:14	For many are called, but few are chosen.
Matthew 25:13	Watch therefore, for you know neither the day nor the hour.
Matthew 25:46	And these will go away into eternal punishment, but the righteous into eternal life.
Luke 10:37	You go, and do likewise.
Luke 12:21	So is the one who lays up treasure for himself and is not rich toward God.
Luke 14:11	For everyone who exalts himself will be humbled, and he who humbles himself will be exalted.
Luke 15:7	There will be more joy in heaven over one sinner who repents than over ninety-nine righteous persons who need no repentance.
Luke 15:10	Just so, I tell you, there is joy before the angels of God over one sinner who repents.
Luke 15:32	It was fitting to celebrate and be glad, for this your brother was dead, and is alive; he was lost, and is found.

We could suggest other harmonizations as well, most notably by looking for a 'big idea' [or taking the one Jesus gives!] that incorporates elements of all of the points of the passage. . . . Perhaps it is simply due to my lack of creativity or imagination, but I cannot always think of a way to summarize concisely in a simple proposition the three main lessons of a tripartite passage. . . . But if nothing comes to mind after a reasonable period of time, better to preach the full message of the text than to curtail one-half to two-thirds of it.[36]

Subversive Confrontations from an Otherwise Compassionate Savior

There is no denying that Jesus's parables contain "a strong satiric element," and that our Savior's satires are often subversive attacks against his earthly, and deep down demonic, opponents. His sanctified subterfuges often come at the end of the parables, when he submits shocking reversals of expectations. For example, the parable of the good Samaritan would have shocked the phylacteries off the Pharisees when Jesus presented the religious establishment as anti-Leviticus 19:18 and their enemy the Samaritan as acting like the righteous man of Ezekiel 18. And, in the parable of the ten virgins, the late-coming husband, who rejects his bride's closest friends, would have blown off the head coverings of the whole ancient Middle-Eastern world.

The Purpose of Parables

There are at least three reasons why Jesus taught in parables.

First, he did so to communicate effectively. As David Wenham states, "Jesus taught profound theology, yet he did so not in long and complex discourses, but through down-to-earth, real-life stories. . . . Jesus' parables reveal him as a master communicator."[37] Like an illustrative story in our sermons, Jesus's memorable short stories with relatable characters, shocking twists, and odd endings, would have, like any good illustration, stimulated thought and increased attentiveness. "The parables were teaching sessions in

---

36 Blomberg, *Preaching the Parables*, 22.
37 David Wenham, *The Parables of Jesus* (Downers Grove, IL: IVP Academic, 1989), 13.

which Jesus imparted information, as well as storytelling sessions that captivate and entertain us."[38]

Second, Jesus taught in parables to conceal and reveal. Between Jesus's telling and interpretation of the parable of the sower, he answers the disciples' question, "Why do you speak to them in parables?" (Matt. 13:10):

> To you it has been given to know the secrets of the kingdom of heaven, but to them it has not been given. For to the one who has, more will be given, and he will have an abundance, but from the one who has not, even what he has will be taken away. This is why I speak to them in parables, because seeing they do not see, and hearing they do not hear, nor do they understand. (13:11–13)

He supports that claim with a prophecy from Isaiah, which he claims is being fulfilled (see 13:14–15; Isa 6:9–10).[39] Just as Isaiah's ministry was met with stubborn and measured unbelief, Jesus was met, especially in the near context of what is recorded in Matthew 13, with indifference (11:20), misunderstanding (12:46), unbelief (13:58), and hostile opposition (12:10, 14, 24). It might strike us as strange to say that Jesus's "immediate judgment against their unbelief was built right into the form of discourse he used when he taught publicly,"[40] but that is clearly what Jesus said about parables. In fact, the Jewish authorities even understood this, after Jesus's

---

38 Ryken, *Jesus the Hero*, 97.

39 Later, Matthew will interpret Jesus's method of teaching, saying that "all these things Jesus said to the crowds in parables; indeed, he said nothing to them without a parable" (Matt. 13:34) as a fulfillment of Psalm 78:2: "This was to fulfill what was spoken by the prophet: 'I will open my mouth in parables; I will utter what has been hidden since the foundation of the world'" (Matt 13:35).

40 MacArthur, *Parables*, xxi.

telling of the parables of the Two Sons and the Wicked Tenants ("When the chief priests and the Pharisees heard his parables, they perceived that he was speaking about them," Matt. 21:45). To the self-righteous, the mysteries of the kingdom remain hidden (Matt. 11:25);[41] Jesus's parables serve as divine judgments!

For the disciples, however, parables serve a different purpose. Parables do not conceal the truth but reveal it. They are expressions of God's gracious mercy! As I have stated elsewhere,

> To those who persist in unbelief, the mystery of the gospel of the kingdom is not seen, but, to those receptive to what God is doing in Jesus, parables are like looking at stained-glass windows on the inside of a church while the sun pours through. For the twelve, Jesus affirms their unique spiritual privilege: "But blessed are your eyes, for they see, and your ears, for they hear. For truly, I say to you, many prophets and righteous people longed to see what you see, and did not see it, and to hear what you hear, and did not hear it" (13:16–17). "Hear then" (13:18), Jesus says to those disciples who by God's sovereign grace can "see with their eyes and hear with their ears and understand with their heart" (13:15). Indeed, when Jesus finishes his teaching from the boat, he turns to the twelve and asks, "Have you understood all these

---

41 "I thank you, Father, Lord of heaven and earth, that you have hidden these things from the wise and understanding and revealed them to little children" (Matt. 11:25). As John Nolland states, Jesus teaches that "alongside and beyond the active choice and personal responsibility of those who have spurned the message (vv. 20–25) stand the decision of God about the people to whom what is really going on will be revealed and from whom it will be concealed, and the choice of the Son of those to whom he will reveal the Father." Put differently, "That wise and understanding people do not necessarily understand what is going on points to insight in this context as something that *must be divinely bestowed* and cannot be achieved at the merely human level" (*Matthew*, New International Greek Testament Commentary [Grand Rapids, MI: Eerdmans, 2005], 469, 471, emphasis mine).

things?" and they reply, "Yes" (13:51). They have been chosen to be scribes who are being "trained" by Jesus to grasp and give to others the "treasure" of "the kingdom of heaven" (13:52).[42]

Third, Jesus taught in parables to give word-picture summaries of his kingdom ministry. As Wenham explains,

Jesus did not paint vivid, visual pictures of God's love only through his words, but also through his actions. His giving of the bread and wine to his disciples at the last supper was an acted parable, as was his carefully planned entry into Jerusalem on a donkey before the crucifixion. His eating with tax collectors and sinners was an acting-out of the message of the parable of the prodigal son. His miracles, for example his healings, his miraculous feeding of the hungry and his transformation of the water into wine, were pictures of the kingdom of God. . . . Jesus' parables were therefore not just a convenient teaching method which Jesus happened to hit on. They were part and parcel of his whole ministry; they were a forceful and visual demonstration of what he had come to do.[43]

TEN STEPS: FROM STUDY TO SERMON

As mentioned earlier, I served as a lecturer (professor) overseas—in Australia. When I taught a class on the Synoptic Gospels, as part of the class I came up with a lecture humorously titled, "Doug O's Amazing Ten Steps for Mastering Parable Interpretation and Find-

---

42 Douglas Sean O'Donnell, *Matthew*, The Gospel Coalition Bible Commentary (Austin, TX: The Gospel Coalition, 2021), available at https://www.thegospelcoalition.org/commentary/matthew.

43 Wenham, *Parables of Jesus*, 14.

ing Meaning in Life."[44] Using the parable of the wicked tenants in Mark 12:1–9 as our base text, let's walk through those ten steps:

> A man planted a vineyard and put a fence around it and dug a pit for the winepress and built a tower, and leased it to tenants and went into another country. When the season came, he sent a servant to the tenants to get from them some of the fruit of the vineyard. And they took him and beat him and sent him away empty-handed. Again he sent to them another servant, and they struck him on the head and treated him shamefully. And he sent another, and him they killed. And so with many others: some they beat, and some they killed. He had still one other, a beloved son. Finally he sent him to them, saying, "They will respect my son." But those tenants said to one another, "This is the heir. Come, let us kill him, and the inheritance will be ours." And they took him and killed him and threw him out of the vineyard. What will the owner of the vineyard do? He will come and destroy the tenants and give the vineyard to others.

Each step toward interpreting this parable involves answering a question, and the ten questions are divided into four categories: context, observation, meaning, and application. The first three steps have to do with context.

Step One (Context)

First, within the context of the whole narrative of Mark's Gospel, where is this parable found?[45] The parable is found in the last

---

44 These steps assume that Jesus's parables are, as Snodgrass summarizes, "stories with intent."

45 Note also the importance of the Old Testament context, as here Mark is borrowing language and ideas from Isaiah 5:1–7.

section of the book (see table 2.2), set in Jerusalem, which depicts the last week of Jesus's life. This is the second of only two narrative parables in Mark, and its placement is purposeful. Jesus tells this parable to foreshadow his fate.

Table 2.2: An Outline of Mark

1:1–15	Introduction to the Gospel: John the Baptist and Jesus
1:16–3:6	Jesus in Galilee: Ministry and Controversy
3:7–6:6	Jesus in Galilee: Jesus Teaches and Shows His Power
6:7–8:26	Jesus in Galilee: Jesus' Acts Yield a Confession
8:27–10:52	After a Key Confession, Jesus Heads to Jerusalem and Prepares His Disciples for the Suffering That Is to Come
11:1–16:8	In Jerusalem, Jesus Meets Controversy and Rejection, Leading to His Death and Resurrection, as He Also Teaches of Suffering, Judgment, and Vindication*

* Darrell Bock, *Mark*, New Cambridge Bible Commentary (Cambridge: Cambridge University Press, 2015), 36.

Step Two (Context)

Second, what is the preceding context, and does it shed any light on the motive and/or content of the parable? Put differently, was there an issue, teaching, or action that prompted this parable? For example,[46] the parable of the good Samaritan is prompted by Jesus's interaction with a lawyer, who seeks "to put him to the test" (Luke 10:25); by the lawyer's "desiring to justify himself"; and by his second question, "And who is my neighbor?" (v. 29). That context is loaded with important information!

46 Two other examples include Luke 14:7 ("Now he told a parable to those who were invited, when he noticed how they chose the places of honor, saying to them. . . .") and Luke 18:9 ("He also told this parable to some who trusted in themselves that they were righteous, and treated others with contempt").

So too are the details given before the parable of the wicked tenants (Mark 12:1–9; Matt. 21:33–46). In Mark 11:12–25, in a symbolic gesture regarding the temple's spiritual barrenness, Jesus withers a fig tree to its roots. He also enters into the holy place of God's holy people in the holy city and makes a complete commotion, wholly upsetting the exchange of money and purchase of the animals necessary to conduct the Passover sacrifices. In Mark 11:27–28, the temple authorities ("the chief priests and the scribes and the elders") question his authority to do this: "By what authority are you doing these things, or who gave you this authority to do them?" This is the first of four questions of opposition (11:28; 12:14, 19–23, 28). Jesus replies to their opposition to him with defenses of his God-given authority. He also challenges their authority and offers a judgment upon them by speaking in parables ("And he began to speak to them in parables," 12:1). Mark records one of those parables.[47]

Don't overlook the placement of a parable! The preceding context often offers insight into the parable's meaning. Some of Jesus's parables are answers to specific questions—the parable of the unmerciful servant (Matt. 18:23–35) answers Peter's question, "How many times shall I forgive?" Other parables are part of Jesus's argument or explanation (see Matt. 21:28–32) or a response to something that occurred (see Luke 7:36–40).

Step Three (Context)

Third, look at what happens after the parable is told. Is there a reaction to the parable? For example, "Then the disciples came and said to him, 'Do you know that the Pharisees were offended when they heard this saying?'" (Matt. 15:12).

---

47 For another parable Jesus told in this context, see Matthew 21:28–32.

After the parable of the wicked tenants there is a hostile reaction. The authorities "were seeking to arrest him . . . for they perceived that he had told the parable against them" (Mark 12:12). They didn't *immediately* arrest him because, once again, "they feared the people" (v. 12). (The crowd was still pro-Jesus at this time.) "So they left him and went away [for now]" (v. 12). The religious leaders needed to regroup and come up with a better plan to take Jesus down.

In Mark 4:10–12, Jesus explained that to some people parables reveal the mystery of the kingdom and to others they conceal it. Earlier, I suggested that, for those who are receptive to the gospel, the parables are like the shapes and colors of stained-glass windows seen from the inside of a church. Now I'll suggest that, for those who resist the gospel, these same parables are like those same stained-glass windows seen from the outside: grey, lifeless, and meaningless. With their reaction, it is clear that the chief priests, scribes, and elders are standing on the outside. They correctly perceive that the parable is about them (12:12), but they likely do not understand the extent of the judgment Jesus renders against them. "For those outside," Jesus taught, "everything is [told] in parables, so that 'they may indeed see but not perceive, and may indeed hear but not understand, lest they should turn and be forgiven'" (4:11–12; cf. Deut. 29:4; Jer. 5:21; Ezek. 12:2). The religious authorities see and hear that the parable is about them, but they do not perceive and understand that it should lead them to repentance from their hostile rejection of Jesus and to faith in him as their messiah and savior.

So, the context of the parable of the wicked tenants tells us it is a parable of judgment,[48] a story-form pronouncement of judgment by Jesus against those who reject him. These reactions are helpful

---

48 "Robert Capon . . . classifies the parables according to the consecutive periods of Jesus' ministry into which they fall, believing them to correspond to the basic topics of 'kingdom,'

not only in understanding how the original audience responded, but also in understanding how the people under our care might respond as well. Some unbelievers might react with hostility to your sermon on one of Jesus's parables; others might be humbled, made more inquisitive, strengthened in the faith, or even converted.

Step Four (Observation)

From those three questions about the context of parables, we move to further instruction based on observations. The fourth step is to look to see if there is a major contrast made in the parable. If so, note what it is. Also, see if there is any direct discourse. If so, also note who speaks, where in the story, and what is said. These two details often provide clues for unraveling the parable's meaning. Start thinking about how those contrasts and the discourse might aid understanding.

In the parable of the wicked tenants, there is a major contrast between the owner of the vineyard and the wicked tenants. There is no dialogue between those two major characters, but there is self-reflective processing. The owner thinks to himself, "They will respect my son" (Mark 12:6); the tenants think to themselves, "This is the heir. Come, let us kill him, and the inheritance will be ours" (v. 7). Those are two key lines, lines we will return to later.

Step Five (Observation)

Fifth, what would have surprised or shocked the original hearers and readers? The two actions expressed in verses 6 and 7, that we noted just above! It is shocking that the owner, after what had happened to his three servants and more ("with many others," Mark

---

'grace,' and 'judgment,' respectively" (Blomberg, *Preaching the Parables*, 17). This certainly fits the location of Mark's parable of the wicked tenants.

12:5), would risk sending his own "beloved son" (v. 6).[49] Also, the tenants' rationale for killing the son—that they would somehow inherit the vineyards if the son were out of the equation—makes no sense.[50] This is a senseless murder.

The goal in answering this question is to get a sufficient handle on the historical, literary, cultural, religious, social, and linguistic context of first-century Palestine. When I teach on parables, I often ask the class to turn to the parable of the two debtors in Luke 7:41–42:

> A certain moneylender had two debtors. One owed five hundred denarii, and the other fifty. When they could not pay, he cancelled the debt of both. Now which of them will love him more?

I ask, "How much is a denarius?" The term is used eight times in the New Testament (and the plural "denarii" seven times) but is never explained. The students will need to consult a commentary or study Bible, or recall how someone explained the term to them. They will learn that a denarius was the typical day's wages for a common laborer. I then ask, "How does that bit of information help you better understand the parable?"

Next, I have them turn to the parable of the unforgiving servant in Matthew 18:21–35. I start by reminding them of the importance of step two: Jesus's parable is a response to his teaching on church

---

49 "The 'unrealistic' behavior of the landowner and the tenants in the parable corresponds exactly with the 'unrealistic,' but true behavior of the God of Israel [e.g., Heb. 11:35–37]. . . . What some scholars criticize as absurd and unrealistic is in reality the inconceivable 'amazing grace' of God!" (Robert H. Stein, *Mark*, Baker Exegetical Commentary on the New Testament [Grand Rapids, MI: Baker Academic, 2008], 531–32).

50 For answers to the question, "How could the tenants expect to inherit the vineyard?," see Mark L. Strauss, *Mark*, Zondervan Exegetical Commentary on the New Testament (Grand Rapids, MI: Zondervan, 2014), 516.

discipline (the hope that a brother will confess his sins and find forgiveness and restoration) and Jesus's answer to Peter's question, "Lord, how often will my brother sin against me, and I forgive him? As many as seven times?" Jesus teaches that the forgiveness his disciples should offer to other disciples should be limitless ("seventy-seven times," vv. 21–22). That point is reinforced and grounded in God's grace. In the parable, Jesus teaches that those who are forgiven by God must forgive others.

When we come to the parable, I ask about the numbers and remind them to look for what is surprising. The king forgives his indebted servant ten thousand talents. How much is a talent? A talent, we learn, is twenty years' wages. How much, then, is ten thousand talents? That sum represents the largest imaginable amount, as a talent was the highest unit of currency and ten thousand the highest Greek numeral. To offer a comparison, it equals 60,000,000 denarii! Would the servant, or anyone for that matter, be able to pay this astronomical amount? Of course not. Thus, once we have a handle on the numbers, we have a better understanding of the king's generosity. When we read that the king "forgave him the debt" (18:27), we are reading about amazing grace. We grasp the shock of his salvation. We also grasp, as the story progresses and we read that the forgiven man fails to forgive a far lesser debt, the shock of the hardness of the human heart.

Step five can be summarized in two ways. First, "no parable can be . . . unrelated to the milieu in which it has originated or the situation of those who read it."[51] Second, we need to explain Jesus's world to our audience so that they might understand, for example, the difficulty of finding ten lost silver coins in a dark first-century

---

51 Lischer, *Reading the Parables*, 2.

Palestinian home with slits for windows and irregular stones for pavement (Luke 15:8–10), and the shock of Jesus's praise of a tax collector's prayer (18:9–14).

Step Six (Observation)

Sixth, list every person, place, thing, and action in the parable.

The *people* mentioned in the parable of the wicked tenants are the owner of the vineyard, his servants (plus the "many others," Mark 12:5), his son, and the tenants. Also note "the others" in verse 9. The only *place* is the vineyard, mentioned five times. Most of the *things* detailed revolve around the vineyard: a fence, pit, winepress, tower, and fruit (vv. 1–2). Two other things include "the country" that the owner went away to (v. 1) and the "season," indicating the time for harvest or the appointed time to collect the rent (v. 2).

The *actions* include the owner planting, securing, and leasing out his vineyard ("a man . . . planted . . . put . . . dug . . . built . . . leased . . . went away," v. 1). The owner then sends his servants and son to collect payment or produce from the tenants ("he sent a servant," v. 2; "he sent . . . another servant," v. 4; "he sent another" servant, v. 5; "he sent" his son "to them," v. 6). Next, the tenants act violently toward the sent ones ("they took . . . and beat him and sent him away empty-handed," v. 3; "they struck him . . . and treated him shamefully," v. 4; "him they killed," v. 5; "they took him and killed him and threw him out of the vineyard," v. 8). The final action is the owner's threefold promise of coming retribution: "He will *come* and *destroy* the tenants and *give* the vineyard to others" (v. 9).

Steps Seven and Eight (Meaning)

After those six steps comes the seventh and eighth. Here's where the fun begins. We move from context to observations to meaning.

Step seven is: from the list we compiled in step six, who or what has a likely second level of meaning? In other words, the "beloved son" certainly symbolizes someone, and the "fence" likely does not. The son is more than a son; but the fence is just a fence.[52]

Step eight follows: Work out the meaning. On the parable of the prodigal son, Sallie McFague TeSelle writes, "One could paraphrase this parable in the theological assertion, 'God's love knows no bounds,' but to do that would be to miss what the parable can do for our insight into such love. For what *counts* here is not extricating an abstract concept but precisely the opposite, delving into the details of the story itself, letting the metaphor do its job of revealing the new setting for ordinary life. It is the play of the radical images that does the job."[53] I agree, in part. I agree that we

---

52 For example, in my sermon on the parable of the ten virgins, I said, "The difference between the two groups [the foolish and wise] comes out in [Matthew 25] verses 3, 4. The difference is preparedness and lack of preparedness; more specifically, it is preparedness and lack of preparedness for the unexpected. We are told that 'the wise took flasks of oil with their lamps' (v. 4), while the foolish 'took their lamps,' but they 'took no [extra] oil with them' (v. 3). The difference is the extra oil, not merely oil. All ten have oil. Thus, the original oil that runs out can't represent, as some argue, saving faith, good works, or the Holy Spirit, unless we believe that true Christians can lose their salvation, which doesn't fit well with the bridegroom's final words—'I do not know you' (v. 12); that is, 'I never knew you,' not 'I once knew you but now I no longer know you.' I think the oil is oil, and it simply symbolizes preparedness (cf. Luke 12:35, where 'stay dressed for action' [i.e., be prepared] parallels 'keep your lamps burning' [i.e., be prepared]). I know that takes the spiritual beauty out of it. I know an allegory about the extra oil representing the second blessing of the Holy Spirit would give you goose bumps. Sorry to be such a downer. In fact, I think the oil is secondary to the oil-keeper. The focus falls not on the oil but on the person who has oil reserves. So, while I'm sympathetic to those who see the oil as 'good works' (that reading fits Matthew, no doubt—especially the burning lamp being good works in 5:15, 16 and the emphasis of works in the rest of chapter 25) or short-term enthusiasm (like the seed sown upon the rocky soil in the parable of the soils, 13:20, 21) or even 'anything you please' (the 'open' interpretation—fill in whatever might be missing in your life), in the end I say that the oil is oil and the prepared person, not the lamp and oil within, is the emphasis" (Douglas Sean O'Donnell, *Matthew: All Authority in Heaven and on Earth*, Preaching the Word [Wheaton, IL: Crossway, 2013], 730).

53 Quoted in Kenneth E. Bailey, *Finding the Lost* (St. Louis: Concordia, 1992), 18.

must delve into the literary details—metaphors, similes, and the like—and transfer those details of the ancient text to the ordinary life of our people in our specific setting. But that doesn't mean we cannot and should not extricate theological and ethical assertations. Moreover, just because Jesus offers an explicit explanation or interpretation of only two parables—the parable of the sower and the parable of the wheat and weeds—that does not mean that both he and the Evangelists (see Luke 18:1, 9) don't have specific authorial aims.

So, as it relates to the parable of the wicked tenants, here's my stab at the symbolism: The owner is God the Father. His servants are the prophets.[54] The first servant who is killed is possibly John the Baptist (Mark 6:14–29). The son is Jesus (see 1:11; 9:7; 14:61; cf. Gen. 22:2), the Father's last entreaty or God's "final emissary" to rebellious Israel, and the one "to whom the vineyard rightly belonged."[55] The vineyard is Israel ("the vineyard . . . is the house of Israel," Isa. 5:7).[56] The tenants, as revealed at the end of the pericope, are the temple authorities—the chief priests, scribes, and elders. The fruit symbolizes the fruit of repentance that John preached about, the fruits that sprout from having faith,

---

54 For the prophets as "servants," see Jer. 7:25–26; 25:4; Amos 3:7; Zech. 1:6; and on their rejection, see 2 Sam. 10:2–5; 2 Kings 17:7–20; 2 Chron. 24:20–22; 36:15–16; Isa. 3:14; Jer. 12:10; 25:3–7; 26:20–23. See R. T. France, *The Gospel of Mark*, New International Greek Testament Commentary (Grand Rapids, MI: Eerdmans, 2002), 460. Cf. Klyne Snodgrass, *The Parable of the Wicked Tenants: An Inquiry into Parable Interpretation*, Wissenschaftliche Untersuchungen zum Neuen Testament 27 (1983; repr., Eugene, OR: Wipf & Stock, 2011), 78n25.

55 Snodgrass, *Parable of the Wicked Tenants*, 87.

56 "The metaphorical vineyard in the Old Testament does not designate the nation so much as the elect of God and all the privileges that go with this election. . . . Logically it is necessary to understand the vineyard as the privileges entrusted to the people, i.e., the law, the promises, and the working of God in past and present, or as the vineyard is interpreted in Matthew 21,43, the kingdom of God" (Snodgrass, *Parable of the Wicked Tenants*, 75, 76).

namely, a life of prayer to God and forgiveness of others (Mark 11:22–25). The many acts of violence represent persecutions for righteousness, for obeying God's orders. The murder of the son is the cross of Christ. The throwing of his body "out of the vineyard" (12:8) is likely a reference to Jesus's burial. (If not for Joseph of Arimathea, Jesus's body would have been left outside to rot.) The "others" mentioned in verse 9—the vineyard will be given "to others"—could be limited to the new, godly leaders of the early church, who have replaced the bad shepherds of Israel; or it could have a wider scope, representing the elect from among the nations, Jews and Gentiles, those who hear God's word, respond to the gospel in faith, and bear fruit for the kingdom. As Snodgrass suggests, this group is "the true Israel and will replace those who are bound up in the hypocritical established religion and are Israel in name only."[57]

The whole parable, then, is a short summary of the grand story of the Bible. God chose Israel out of the world to be his own people. He cared for and protected them. He sent his prophets to proclaim his word, offer his promises, render his judgments, and predict the future. But so often throughout Israel's history, the leaders of God's people rejected, persecuted, and even killed the prophets. Finally, God so loved his people, even though they had so rebelled against him, that he sent his own beloved Son. But then the unthinkable happened. The irrational. The inexplicable. God's people killed God's own Son. "They took him and killed him and threw him out of the vineyard" (v. 8). He was buried in a borrowed tomb outside of Jerusalem. How then does the story end? Vindication of the rejected but now risen Son! Judgment and salvation. Those who reject Jesus

---

57 Snodgrass, *Parable of the Wicked Tenants*, 93.

will be destroyed (both in AD 70 and forever),[58] while those who accept him will share in his inheritance (both now and forever).

That is the meaning of the parable, and here is Jesus's final metaphoric summary to the Bible experts of his day:

Have you not read this Scripture:

> "'The stone that the builders rejected
> has become the cornerstone;
> this was the Lord's doing,
> and it is marvelous in our eyes'?" (Mark 12:10–11)

Here Jesus quotes from Psalm 118:22–23, the same poem on the lips of the people as Jesus journeyed up to Jerusalem on the colt. In the original context, the poem is about Israel. Yet here in Mark, Jesus applies it to himself, as the ultimate fulfillment of all the promises to and about Israel. He is the stone that the builders (or wicked "tenants") rejected. To them he was a useless stone that did not fit properly into their design. But that stone, upon his death and then formally when every stone of Herod's temple was turned over and destroyed, became the cornerstone—the part that holds everything together—to a new and everlasting structure. This is the permanent foundation stone (1 Cor. 3:11; Eph. 2:20). But while it is an immovable foundation, it is also a living stone, a rock that trips up and crushes down on those who oppose him but saves all who are willing to build upon it (see 1 Pet. 2:6–8). "As it is written [in Isa. 8:14], 'Behold, I am laying in Zion [Jerusalem] a stone of

---

58 Note that the tenants "kill" (Mark 12:5, 7, 8) God's servant and son, but God "destroys" them (v. 9), likely indicating "a more comprehensive and devastating judgment" (Strauss, *Mark*, 516).

stumbling, and a rock of offense; and whoever believes in him will not be put to shame'" (Rom. 9:33; 1 Pet. 2:7).

There is, then, an important connection between the two halves of our text. Jesus does not answer the religious leaders' question at the end of chapter 11 ("By what authority are you doing these things?" Mark 11:28), but he does, in a sense, answer it with his parable at the start of chapter 12. His authority comes from God, his Father. He is his beloved Son. He is the beloved Son that they want to kill, the promised stone that they want to dispose of. He is the heaven-sent Son and stone.[59]

Step Nine (Application)

From meaning we move to applications, the final two steps: C (context), O (observation), M (meaning) and A (application). I hope you're not, by now, in a coma!

Step nine answers the question, "Who are the main characters and what is the point of application for each that Jesus is trying to get across?" We can discern who the main characters are from the actions. Who acts in this parable? The servants and son do what they are told. They are sent by the owner, and they go. They obey. But it is the owner and the tenants who have all the verbs attached to them. The important, and repeated, verb for the owner is the word "sent" (4x). The important, and repeated, verb for the tenants is "killed" (3x). What then are the two points of application? I will make it three, two related to the owner of the vineyard (God), and one to those who reject those he sent.

---

59 "The parable may . . . be seen as an implicit answer to the question about the source of his authority in the previous episode, which Jesus refused to answer (11:33). His authority comes from his Father, who is the vineyard's owner, and he has been sent to claim what is rightfully his" (Strauss, *Mark*, 509).

First, know and appreciate that God is longsuffering. Think again about what Jesus teaches about his Father in this parable. God carefully cultivates this vineyard. Then, his chosen people take care of it. When he sends his select servants, the holy prophets, to see how the work is going, those that he first sends are brutally beaten. At this point, if I were God, I would stop there. My patience would be exhausted. The day of retribution is now at hand! But this is not what God does. Here "the Lord is patient toward" them; he does not desire that "any should perish, but that all should reach repentance" (2 Pet. 3:9). The God of the universe is lovingly longsuffering. He sends more servants. What a demonstration of patience! The phrases from the parable "he sent to them another servant" (Mark 12:4), and "he sent another" (v. 5), and then, the little detail that he sent "many others" (v. 5) writes in large print—like a banner following the Goodyear blimp—"God is Patient." And just when you think his people have exhausted his patience, he sends and sacrifices his own beloved Son. Oh, the loving longsuffering of God. Know it. Appreciate it. Praise God for being a patient God.

Second, grasp, and be saddened by, human depravity. Due to Adam's sin, we are all born spiritually blind, ignorant, and wicked. Totally depraved. We are not as bad as we could be, but we are tainted in every part of our being—our minds (we don't think rightly), our hearts (we don't feel rightly), and our wills (we don't do what is right).[60] We are not too different from the

---

60 As Michael Horton, *For Calvinism* (Grand Rapids, MI: Zondervan, 2011), 41, states, "The 'total' in total depravity refers to its extensiveness, not intensiveness: that is, to the all-encompassing scope of our fallenness. It does not mean that we are as bad as we can possibly be, but that we are all guilty and corrupt to such an extent that there is no hope of pulling ourselves together, brushing ourselves off, and striving (with the help of grace) to overcome God's judgment and our own rebellion." For more on this theme, see Douglas

religious leaders in our passage. "There but for the grace of God, go I." For some, that popular saying can be trite, but for us it should not be. We should rejoice in the grace of God, knowing and appreciating what we have been saved from—from thinking, feeling, and acting against God the way the Sanhedrin thought, felt, and acted.

Third, rejoice that God is just. Usually, this parable is labeled the parable of the wicked tenants. But it could be called the parable of the patient but just master, because the focus of Jesus's teaching is not on the rebels but on his righteous Father. God judges those who do not receive his Son. God judges those who reject his Son.[61] Like the fruitless fig tree and the spiritually barren temple,[62] in Jesus the old regime is over. God has come. In his justice, he has destroyed the temple and its wicked leaders. And he has given his vineyard to others, believers from among the nations.

Step Ten (Application)

We come finally to the tenth step, where we seek to explain how the ideas embedded in the story apply both *then* (in Jesus's day) and *now* (to us today); and, the question we seek to answer is, If you had to summarize the central application or key theme of this parable, what would it be? Remember, it must be related in some way to Jesus and his kingdom—its coming, its proclamation,

---

Sean O'Donnell, "'If You, Then, Who Are Evil': Sin in the Synoptic Gospels and Acts," in *Ruined Sinners to Reclaim*, ed. David Gibson and Jonathan Gibson (Wheaton, IL: Crossway, forthcoming).

61 This is a "judgment parable" that "asserts that, contrary to appearances, God will judge and will achieve his purposes, and people will be held accountable" (Snodgrass, *Stories with Intent*, 297–98).

62 "The parable of the vineyard was, in fact, the spoken form of the parable of the fig-tree which Jesus had 'told' in the previous chapter" (Sinclair B. Ferguson, *Let's Study Mark* [1999; repr., Carlisle, PA: Banner of Truth Trust, 2016], 188).

participation in it, how to get in, the kind of things that keep you out, encouragement to persevere in it, etc. The parables cannot be separated from Christ and his kingdom.[63] So, look to see if Jesus features as one of the characters. Also, look at the end to see if Jesus gives you the answer, as our Lord often gives the punch of the parable at the end.

In the parable of the wicked tenants, Jesus is one of the characters. He is the "son" who faithfully obeyed the will of his Father and was killed. So what? The final and main application, found in Jesus's own summary of the parable (Mark 12:10–11), is twofold. First, we are not to reject the sent Son ("beloved son," v. 6) and foundation stone ("the stone," v. 10), but receive him. We are to welcome him, build upon him, give him the fruits of our labors. Second, we should not only receive him but marvel in the whole grand plan of salvation. With humility and joy, we should say and sing, "This was the Lord's doing [this whole plan that is played out here], and it is marvelous in our eyes" (v. 11).

The point of this final step, if it is not clear from the explanation and illustration above, is that every parable has a connection to the gospel. So, when you preach, don't moralize (e.g., the point of the parable of the talents is that God rewards hard work; so, work

---

63 To C. H. Dodd, "the kingdom of God stands at the center of Jesus' proclamation" (quoted in Anderson, "Parables," 658). Blomberg and Lischer agree. Blomberg writes (*Preaching the Parables*, 23), "All of the parables impinge on Jesus' understanding of the 'kingdom of God,' whether that expression explicitly appears in the context of any given passage or not. For Jesus, the 'kingdom' referred more to a power than to a place, more to a rule or reign than to a realm. In short, it referred to God's 'kingship,' taking on new and greater dimensions on earth, inaugurated with Christ's first coming but to be consummated only at his second" (cf. Blomberg, *Interpreting the Parables* [Downers Grove, IL: InterVarsity Press, 1990], 296–313). Lischer adds (*Reading the Parables*, 20), "Even parables that do not explicitly reference the kingdom, like the Pharisee and the Tax Collector, or the Good Samaritan, are widely considered to be narrative illustrations of life in the kingdom of God."

hard!).[64] Moreover, because the parables describe various parts of the gospel of the kingdom—the rule of Christ inaugurated in the incarnation and consummated in the second coming—set your sermons within the context of the whole gospel story (death and resurrection of Christ) and response (repentance, faith, and obedience). The parables feature what the whole of the New Testament covers: gospel need, gospel proclamation, gospel response, and gospel ethics. In your preaching, follow Jesus's pattern.

ADDITIONAL SUGGESTIONS FOR PREACHING PARABLES

These ten steps, if followed, will set your sermon on sure hermeneutical ground. Below are eight suggestions to help your homiletics soar. Or, at least get off the ground.

First, share what is truly important. If you are clearly given the main point of a parable in the text, or you have painstakingly discerned it in your study, share it with God's people from the start and throughout. For example, Luke tells us in Luke 18:1 that Jesus taught the parable of the persistent widow "to the effect that they [his disciples] ought always to pray and not lose heart." You need to unpack the symbolic relationship between the unrighteous judge and God and the widow and God's elect, but not at the expense of sharing the point of those two characters' actions. The sermon should be dominated by what is truly important, not by all the possible interpretations or twenty minutes of unraveling the symbolic details.

Second, take time to explain. You need to get to the point (see above), but not at the expense of making sure that all the important

---

64 This does not mean that we should shy away from preaching "basic Christian doctrine and *morality*" from the parables. See Ryken, *Words of Delight*, 403, emphasis mine.

details in the parable are explicated. In most settings, we are up against two obstacles: (1) people who don't use or hear parables on a regular basis, or at all, and (2) most biblical parables are "notoriously puzzling" and their "meaning is rarely transparent."[65] Be patient. Explain slowly and clearly. Illustrate.

Third, contemporize. One way to explain and illustrate is to retell a parable, or part of a parable, as a paraphrase and/or with a relevant and accessible story from today. As Blomberg advocates, "it will be both easy and helpful to include some modern equivalent to the biblical story in an introduction, in one or more illustrations interspersed within the body, or in a conclusion to the message. These contemporizations should work to recreate the original dynamic, force, or effect of Jesus' original story. It is not true that narratives cannot (or should not) be paraphrased propositionally; it is true that good exposition should not do *just* that."[66]

Fourth, feel free to group parables together by themes. For example, when I preached on Matthew 13, I divided the material into three sermons. I covered the purpose of parables (13:10–17, with verses 34–35, 51–52), the parable of the sower (13:1–9, 18–23, with verses 57–58), and the other seven short parables (13:24–33, 36–50). I justified grouping the seven parables together because they all shared three themes (growth, judgment, and gain).

Fifth, don't harmonize. "Occasionally variants of the same story appear to make different points, for example, the parable of the lost sheep (Matt. 18:10–14 and Luke 15:3–10) or the parable of the great feast (Matt. 22:1–14 and Luke 14:16–24)."[67] Let them

---

65 Lischer, *Reading the Parables*, 4.
66 Blomberg, *Preaching the Parables*, 24–25.
67 Lischer, *Reading the Parables*, 11.

make those different points. Blomberg states the suggestion this way: "Especially in a series of sermons working their way through large portions of one specific Gospel, messages on parables that are parallel in other Gospels should stress something of what is unique to the specific version of the parable at hand."[68]

Sixth, don't shy away from some shock therapy! Arthurs puts it this way: "Don't disarm Jesus' land mines,"[69] which are "explosive but concealed."[70] I favor that shock therapy analogy because, while there is a concealed but explosive element to Jesus's prophetic parabolic punches, shock therapy, as used by psychiatric professionals, can have positive results. We don't want our people blown to pieces by our preaching! But we do want to let God's provocative word shock their spiritual sensibilities. Related, and continuing with a medical analogy, seek to shock both the head and heart. Shock therapy aims for the head; a defibrillator aims for the heart. For example, when Nathan told David the parable about the rich man and the lamb, it outraged David. But it wasn't until the prophet proclaimed, "You are the man!" that David's head then heart were shocked back to spiritual health. Don't be afraid to deliver the life-saving shock found in many of the Bible's parables.

Seventh, use Jesus's calls to listen! In Mark, Jesus begins the parable of the sower with this exhortation: "Listen! Behold, a sower went out to sow" (Mark 4:3). A dozen times, Jesus calls his listeners to "hear" (e.g., "Hear another parable," Matt. 21:33),[71] and twice to "hear and understand" (15:10; Mark 7:14). Repeatedly throughout my sermons, especially those on parables, I use

---

the same or similar terminology. I might say, "Now, listen to this!" or "Do you understand what Jesus is saying?" or "see or observe [behold!] how Jesus contrasts this with that."

Eighth, have fun! As Ryken suggests, "If we can use the label 'fun genre' without irreverence, the parables of Jesus certainly merit that epithet. They are a delight to read, study, and teach."[72]

CONCLUSION

Warren Wiersbe defined a parable as "a picture that becomes a mirror and then a window," in that "we gaze at the scene [or see the story] in the parable, we see ourselves; then we see truth."[73] We also see Jesus! As Lischer states, "Unlike other stories from antiquity, the parables of Jesus are integrally related to the character and mission of their teller. One can enjoy an Aesopian fable or a rabbinic story without much biographical or contextual background. The parables of Jesus, on the other hand, do not stand alone as individual stories but are woven into a larger narrative."[74] Whatever mistakes we make in reading and preaching the parables, let us not make the mistake of not making much of Jesus. He is the sower of the good seed of the gospel, the heaven-sent Son, the bridegroom of his church, the king upon his glorious throne, the final judge of all people everywhere, and so much more!

BUILD YOUR LIBRARY! HELPFUL RESOURCES

Blomberg, Craig L. *Interpreting the Parables*. Downers Grove, IL: InterVarsity, 1990.

---

72 Ryken, *Jesus the Hero*, 97.
73 Quoted in Arthurs, *Preaching with Variety*, 104. From Warren Wiersbe, *Teaching and Preaching with Imagination: The Quest for Biblical Ministry* (Wheaton, IL: Victor, 1994), 164.
74 Lischer, *Reading the Parables*, 5.

_____. *Preaching the Parables: From Responsible Interpretation to Powerful Proclamation*. Grand Rapids, MI: Baker Academic, 2004.

Ryken, Leland, James C. Wilhoit, and Tremper Longman III, eds. "Parable." In *Dictionary of Biblical Imagery*, 623–24. Downers Grove, IL: InterVarsity, 1998.

Snodgrass, Klyne R. *Stories with Intent: A Comprehensive Guide to the Parables of Jesus*. Grand Rapids, MI: Eerdmans, 2008.

Wenham, David. *The Parables of Jesus*. Downers Grove, IL: IVP Academic, 1989.

3

Love Letters

Preaching Epistles

WHEN I WAS IN COLLEGE and courting my future wife, she went on a class trip to the Holy Land. For nearly five weeks, we wrote many letters to each other. Each letter would arrive a week or so after it was mailed. What a joy to open and read them! Each word was the only connection we had to each other. Phone calls were too expensive then, and email was a new and unavailable technology. While most young couples in love today don't write and mail handwritten letters to each other, most of us understand how the epistolary genre works. Especially pastors! Every pastor, young and old, has written a letter of some sort and for some reason—to the congregation, a shut-in, new parents, a grieving soul.

And every pastor has preached from the New Testament Epistles; and, "in some evangelical circles, preachers find it hard to conceive of preaching from anything other than the Epistles." The reason for this fixation is that "the Epistles are ostensibly the most idea-laden section of the Bible."[1] But, as important as the expression of ideas is to this genre, the New Testament Epistles are more than straightforward expository prose or short treatises of systematic theology. The Epistles are actually very literary documents, and literary analysis is an important key to unlocking their meaning and beauty. Put plainly, preachers preach from the Epistles but don't often preach them as epistles. As Ryken states, "The epistles are typically approached in a manner that is not in keeping with the kind of writing they are. . . . Although exposition of theology and exhortation to godly living are the purposes that moved the writers of the epistles, they wrote with such an amazing grasp of literary technique that to ignore this aspect of the epistles is to distort them. In fact, any in-depth analysis of *what* the epistles communicate leads naturally to an awareness of *how* they communicate that content."[2] This chapter tackles both *how* Epistles communicate and how we as preachers should communicate their theologically and literarily rich content to our congregations.

HOW TO READ BIBLICAL EPISTLES

Before we define the epistolary genre, let's start by stating what the New Testament Epistles are *not*. First, they are not sermons. Though each epistle was written by an evangelist to a congregation or individual Christian and contains theological content and moral exhortations, an epistle has a different form and contains different elements. Just read an epistle aloud, and you will sense the difference.

1 Leland Ryken, "The Bible as Literature and Expository Preaching," in *Preach the Word: Essays on Preaching: In Honor of R. Kent Hughes*, ed. Leland Ryken and Todd Wilson (Wheaton, IL: Crossway, 2007), 51.

2 Leland Ryken, *Letters of Grace and Beauty: A Guided Literary Study of the New Testament Epistles* (Wooster, OH: Weaver, 2016), 17.

Second, epistles are not treatises or essays. While at times and in certain epistles New Testament authors offer a condensed and complex theological argument (most notably Romans and Hebrews), they are far removed from David Hume's essay against miracles or Jonathan Edwards's treatise explaining free will. Theological treaties and essays have a single thesis, and each part supports that thesis. There is a unity to the Epistles but not that type of unity. For example, in Romans, Paul covers a number of topics, such as the righteousness of God, justification by faith, divine election, brotherly love, and submitting to the government. These topics are all related, but there is not the seamless coherence from paragraph to paragraph and thought to thought that one would find in an essay or treatise.

Key Characteristics

What, then, *are* the New Testament Epistles? What characterizes them? We offer six key characteristics.

First, they are letters, both in general terms and in more specific terms of epistolary conventions in the classical world in which the New Testament letters were written. So, like most letters we write, they contain an author, recipient, reason for writing, and often a personal greeting. Moreover, as letters, they are a form of communication between two parties. The Roman author Seneca, living at approximately the same time as the New Testament authors, wrote to his friend Lucilius that his letters "should be just what my conversation would be if you and I were sitting in one another's company or taking walks together."[3] Letters were (and are!) perhaps the closest substitute for a friend's presence.[4] "I had

---

3 Seneca, *Moral Letters to Lucilius*, Letter 75.

4 Heikki Koskenniemi (*Studien zur Idee Phraseologie des griechischen Briefes*) summarizes that presence "as *philphronēsis* ('friendly relationship'), the extending of oneself that occurs when

much to write you," writes the aged apostle John ("the elder") to his dear friend Gaius ("the beloved . . . whom I love in truth"), "but I would rather not write with pen and ink. I hope to see you soon, and we will talk face to face" (3 John 1, 13–14). The New Testament Epistles are also often autobiographical. For example, notice the word "I" above. Personal pronouns abound! Paul uses "I" seventy-one times in Galatians, 120 times in Romans, and 169 times in 2 Corinthians. "Me," "my," or "mine" are used sixty times in 2 Corinthians. What differs from our usual personal correspondences are that epistles are (a) public documents, (b) more formal in vocabulary and literary structure and style (covered in the next section),[5] and (c) didactic.[6]

Second, the New Testament Epistles are *occasional* and *ad hoc* pieces: they arose from specific circumstances and were written for particular purposes.[7] For example, 1 Corinthians was written due to disunity within the Corinthian church, and Paul covers various topics because he is answering specific needs and issues raised within the believing community at a particular moment in time. In this way, the Epistles are not far removed from the email a pastor might get from a concerned congregant who asks clarification about a point in the recent sermon, the status of a youth pastor search, or why a

---

we talk; *Parousia* ('presence'), the reviving of relationship between separated friends; and *homilia* ('dialogue'), the continuance of a conversation." The epistolary "style is as close to conversation as written language can come, and the result is vitality" (Jeffrey D. Arthurs, *Preaching with Variety: How to Re-Create the Dynamics of Biblical Genres* [Grand Rapids, MI: Kregel, 2007], 153 [quoting Koskenniemi], 164).

5   "The New Testament epistles are rhetorically embellished and sophisticated in technique" (Ryken, *Letters of Grace and Beauty*, 14).

6   "The content [of an epistle] resembles that of a teaching ('didactic') document more than a letter that conveys only personal news and feelings" (Ryken, *Letters of Grace and Beauty*, 14).

7   The occasional nature of the Epistles explains why we find a diversity of themes within one letter, as well as an often-informal flow of thought and both personal notes and public news.

budget item was cut. Indeed, the inspired epistles in the Bible are not scholarly treatments of a theological topic, but pastoral responses to specific situations within specific Christian communities. In fact, some letters—like Paul's correspondence to the Corinthian church—could be described as "communication in relational midstream."[8]

That said, while the Epistles are penned as responses to particular circumstances of particular Christians in a particular ancient city or region, they are inspired documents that possess enduring implications and applications to the church universal and throughout the ages. As Thomas Long notes,

> Even though Paul's letters contain many personal, specific, and even fleeting personal references, it is clear that most were composed to be read to the whole worshiping congregation, perhaps over and over again (see 1 Thess. 5:27). In short, the letters of the New Testament are like almost all other letters: connected to a specific set of circumstances but inherently capable of speaking beyond those immediate conditions.[9]

Like the Gospels, the Epistles were designed for wide circulation and "largely intended for public audiences (even when the original recipient was a single person like Timothy)."[10] Moreover, "the authors show an awareness that they were writing for posterity, and not only for the immediate recipients of their letters."[11]

---

8 Jeannine K. Brown, *Introducing Biblical Hermeneutics: Scripture as Communication* (Grand Rapids, MI: Baker Academic, 2007), 151. Brown says this of the New Testament Epistles as a whole.

9 Thomas G. Long, *Preaching and the Literary Forms of the Bible* (Philadelphia: Fortress, 1989), 110.

10 Ryken, *Letters of Grace and Beauty*, 14.

11 Ryken, *Letters of Grace and Beauty*, 14.

Whether the letter would be categorized as a personal,[12] family,[13] teaching,[14] missionary,[15] or administrative letter,[16] every letter in the New Testament is a circular letter; that is, an epistle that was written to be read aloud in the church meeting and then circulated to other churches around the Mediterranean world. As Ryken rightly writes, "These letters . . . are church documents addressed to whole congregations and ultimately to the church worldwide."[17] For example, the letter to Philemon is addressed to an individual, and yet the opening salutation acknowledges others ("the church in your house," Philem. 2); and 1 Corinthians was written "to the church of God that is in Corinth," but also for all Christians everywhere—"together with all those who in every place call upon the name of our Lord Jesus Christ" (1 Cor. 1:2).

Third, the New Testament Epistles Christianized the Greco-Roman epistolary form. The standard three-part epistolary form prevalent in the ancient classical world includes a formal *introduction* (a salutation noting the sender and recipient, offering a greeting, and often addressing a specific issue or issues); followed by the *body* of the letter, which conveys special relevant and desired information while maintaining a personal-relational correspondence;

---

12 E.g., "To Timothy, my true child in the faith" (1 Tim. 1:2). "None of the New Testament epistles is only a personal letter but in some of them the writer shares a large amount of personal information and personal feelings" (Ryken, *Letters of Grace and Beauty*, 26).

13 The New Testament Epistles use the language and emotional tone of a family letter: e.g., "to Apphia our sister" (Philem. 2).

14 A teaching or didactic letter, like Romans, contains "a preponderance of theological exposition" (Ryken, *Letters of Grace and Beauty*, 27).

15 Romans would also classify as a missionary letter in that it is written by a missionary about his mission, and includes his future travel plans.

16 E.g., the Pastoral Epistles can function as an instruction manual from an experienced evangelist and church planter to his subordinates.

17 Ryken, *Letters of Grace and Beauty*, 24.

and ending with a prescribed *conclusion* (often featuring personal notes, a final wish, prayer, or blessing, and perhaps travel plans).[18]

Beyond these familiar conventions, when compared to Greek and Roman letters of the era the New Testament Epistles are distinctive in that they add two unique elements to the standard epistolary three-part structure: a theological thanksgiving and a list of ethical exhortations. For example, Ephesians contains a long thanksgiving to the God of Jesus Christ for the spiritual riches that the believers in Ephesus possess, followed by a prayer for their spiritual welfare (1:3–23), and a longer paraenesis (4:17–6:20; see discussion below).

They are also, and obviously (as witnessed above), Christian letters from a Christian leader to a Christian community and, thus, more Christian, theologically nuanced, and religious than any extant Hellenistic letter. Ephesians opens not with the common "greetings" (*chairein*) but with Paul's usual *charis kai eirēnē*: "*Grace* to you and *peace* from God our Father and the Lord Jesus Christ" (1:2),[19] and it closes with a Godward and Christ-centered *benediction* ("*Peace* be to the brothers, and love with faith, from God the Father and the Lord Jesus Christ. *Grace* be with all who love our Lord Jesus Christ with love incorruptible," Eph. 6:23–24). Other ways in which Greco-Roman epistolary conventions were modified and Christianized include:

- Opening epithets (titles) and mentions of coauthors. For example, in Galatians 1:1–2, Paul labels himself "an apostle," with a clarification of that apostleship ("not from men nor

---

18   See P. T. O'Brien, "Letters, Letter Forms," in *Dictionary of Paul and His Letters*, ed. Gerald F. Hawthorne, Ralph P. Martin, and Daniel Reid (Downers Grove, IL: InterVarsity Press, 1993), 550–53.

19   "The openings of the classical letters of the time are *perfunctory*, but the openings of the New Testament epistles are *profound*" (Ryken, *Letters of Grace and Beauty*, 48, emphasis mine).

through man, but through Jesus Christ and God the Father, who raised him from the dead") and that he has penned the letter with the help of others ("and all the brothers who are with me").[20] In 1 Thessalonians 1:1, Paul clarifies two of the others (from "Paul, Silvanus, and Timothy").

- Prayers of thanksgiving.[21] For example, the authors of 1 Thessalonians continue with a nine-verse prayer of thanksgiving, which begins, "We give thanks to God always for all of you, constantly mentioning you in our prayers" (v. 2) and is full of profound theological truths, including God's election ("brothers loved by God . . . he has chosen you," v. 4), regeneration ("our gospel came to you . . . in power and in the Holy Spirit and with full conviction," v. 5), repentance and faith ("you turned to God from idols to serve the living and true God," v. 9; "your faith in God," v. 8), and a brilliant summary of the Christian life ("your work of faith and labor of love and steadfastness of hope in our Lord Jesus Christ," v. 3) and the gospel ("his Son from heaven, whom he raised from the dead, Jesus who delivers us from the wrath to come," v. 10).

- Conclusions that include warnings ("From now on let no one cause me trouble") and benedictions ("The grace of our Lord Jesus Christ be with your spirit, brothers. Amen," Gal. 6:17, 18).

---

20 Throughout the New Testament Epistles, expressions of familiar relations turn into statements of "partnership in the gospel" (Phil. 1:5) with other believers from around the world.

21 "Classical letters did sometimes include a brief statement of thanks to the gods for deliverance from calamity, but it was so cursory and superficial that it cannot be regarded as the model on which New Testament writers built their magnificent thanksgivings. They in effect produced something new, growing out of their revolutionary new life in Christ. . . . In contrast to the classical letters of the same era, the epistles do not praise God for physical health but triumphantly sound a spiritual note. . . . The spiritual focus is couched in theological and liturgical vocabulary—God, Christ, hope, mercy, faith, redemption, and such like" (Ryken, *Letters of Grace and Beauty*, 55, 57).

• Length. Paul's letters average 2,500 words; Cicero's 295 and Seneca's 955.[22]

Fourth, the New Testament Epistles incorporate many other genres or subgenres, including instruction or exposition, encomium,[23] autobiography and personal news, praise, rebuke, requests, brief liturgical or creedal affirmations,[24] lyrical poems or hymn fragments,[25] diatribe, church manuals, proverbs, travelogues, apocalyptic visions, virtue-and-vice lists, prayers, doxologies, benedictions, and paraenesis. Paraenesis, which will be discussed further in the second half of this chapter, is a list of ethical instructions and/or exhortations customarily found near the end of an epistle. For example, 2 Corinthians concludes with five commands: "Finally, brothers, rejoice. Aim for restoration, comfort one another, agree with one another, live in peace," followed by a promise: "and the God of love and peace will be with you" (2 Cor. 13:11).

The Epistles also use many figures of speech, such as hyperbole (1 Cor. 15:31); question-answer constructions (Rom. 6:15); rhetorical questions (Rom. 8:31–35); aphorisms (1 Cor. 13:8);[26]

22 Arthurs, *Preaching with Variety*, 157.

23 An encomium is "a poem or prose piece that praises either an abstract quality or a general character type. . . . There are two encomia in the epistles: 1 Corinthians 13 in praise of love, and Hebrews 11 in praise of faith" (Ryken, *Letters of Grace and Beauty*, 93).

24 "Based on Old Testament creedal formulas like the *Shema*, the apostle Paul . . . formulated a number of mini-creeds (some based on the *Shema* itself—e.g., Rom. 3:29–30; 1 Cor. 8:4–6) to preserve and protect orthodoxy and to promote the 'one faith' (Eph. 4:5) in Jesus as 'Lord of all' (Acts 10:36)" (R. Kent Hughes and Douglas Sean O'Donnell, *The Pastor's Book: A Comprehensive and Practical Guide to Pastoral Ministry* [Wheaton, IL: Crossway, 2015], 320). Paul's apostolic "creeds" would include Rom. 1:1–5; 10:9; 1 Cor. 15:3–7; Phil. 2:6–11; Col. 1:15–20.

25 Phil. 2:5–11; Col. 1:15–20; 1 Tim. 3:16; perhaps John 1:1–5, 9–11; Rom. 10:9ff.; 1 Cor. 12:3; Eph. 5:14; 1 Tim. 2:5–6; Heb. 1:3; 1 Pet. 3:18c–19, 22.

26 Ryken defines aphorisms as memorable sayings that rivet our attention and live in our memory. Some memorable one-liners in Philippians would include 1:21; 2:12; 3:13–14; 4:7; 4:11.

dramatic apostrophes (1 Cor. 15:55); memorable personifications (James 1:15); pithy, noteworthy assertions (Rom. 8:37); and paradox (2 Cor. 6:8–10, see below): believers are treated

> as imposters, and yet are true;
> as unknown, and yet well known;
> as dying, and behold, we live;
> as punished, and yet not killed;
> as sorrowful, yet always rejoicing;
> as poor, yet making many rich;
> as having nothing, and yet possessing everything. (2 Cor. 6:8–10)

Moreover, the Epistles abound with metaphorical images that help explain and illustrate their message and persuade their readers. For example, Peter appeals to his audience's imagination when he warns the church to stay away from false teachers, by calling them "waterless springs and mists driven by a storm" and describing their coming judgment as "the gloom of utter darkness" (2 Pet. 2:17). They "promise . . . freedom" though they are "slaves of corruption" (v. 19). Their apostasy from orthodoxy resembles a washed pig returning "to wallow in the mire" (v. 22).

Fifth, the New Testament Epistles use both plain and high style, and this intermingling makes the Epistles unique. The aspects of plain style include short sentences and clauses, common vocabulary, frequent use of staccato effect rather than smooth rhythm, and absence of figurative language and rhetorical forms.[27] It is the Epistles' plain style, with its clarity and simplicity, that helps readers understand what is being said. The Epistles' high

---

27 See Ryken, *Letters of Grace and Beauty*, 103.

(or elevated or exalted) style compels us to "take up and read" them again and again, imbibing the beauty of their literary art. As Ryken comments,

> Eloquence is part of the artistry that we can admire in the epistles. . . . The high style of the epistles fires our emotions and makes our imagination soar. We feel elevated and swept along. The eloquent style is one reason we find the epistles so memorable and why the phrases stick in our minds so that it is almost impossible to forget them.

Later he counsels, "They are highly literary compositions and need to be approached as such."[28] In the second half of this chapter we will touch on eloquence in preaching. For now, it is important to note aspects of high style, such as

- long sentences
- parallelism and balance of clauses or phrases
- repetition (in several forms)
- tendency toward exalted vocabulary
- regularity of rhythm (we hear the rise and fall of language in cadence)
- rhetorical forms such as antithesis, paradox, and epithet (an exalted title for a person or thing)
- figurative language (especially metaphor and allusion)[29]

In *Letters of Grace and Beauty*, Ryken offers 2 Corinthians 6:4–10 and 1 Timothy 6:13–16 as two examples of high style:

28 Ryken, *Letters of Grace and Beauty*, 102, 110.
29 Ryken, *Letters of Grace and Beauty*, 100–101.

but as servants of God we commend ourselves in every way: by great endurance, in afflictions, hardships, calamities, beatings, imprisonments, riots, labors, sleepless nights, hunger; by purity, knowledge, patience, kindness, the Holy Spirit, genuine love; by truthful speech, and the power of God; with the weapons of righteousness for the right hand and for the left; through honor and dishonor, through slander and praise. We are treated as impostors, and yet are true; as unknown, and yet well known; as dying, and behold, we live; as punished, and yet not killed; as sorrowful, yet always rejoicing; as poor, yet making many rich; as having nothing, yet possessing everything. (2 Cor. 6:4–10)

Ryken comments, "This is a 'fireworks' passage that incorporates all of the traits listed above. First, the entire passage . . . consists of only two sentences, as the phrases keep piling up. The effect is exaltation. Repetition and parallelism or balances of phrases permeate the entire passage. Antithesis and paradox are present. The rhythm of words and phrases produces a cadence of rising and falling language. The vocabulary tends toward the formal and exalted. Metaphor makes an appearance with 'weapons of righteousness.'"[30]

And then, from 1 Timothy:

I charge you in the presence of God, who gives life to all things, and of Christ Jesus, who in his testimony before Pontius Pilate made the good confession, to keep the commandment unstained and free from reproach until the appearing of our Lord Jesus Christ, which he will display at the proper time—he who is the blessed and only Sovereign, the King of kings and Lord of lords,

---

30 Ryken, *Letters of Grace and Beauty*, 101.

who alone has immortality, who dwells in unapproachable light, whom no one has ever seen or can see. To him be honor and eternal dominion. Amen. (1 Tim. 6:13–16)

Ryken comments, "All of the features of the high style are present here: long, flowing sentence structure; parallelism of clauses; exalted language; stately epithets (titles); allusion (reference to past history); regularity of rhythm (technically called cadence); and metaphor (keeping a commandment unstained)."[31]

In *Words of Delight*,[32] Ryken highlights, with his structural layout, Paul's patterned rhetoric of Romans 8:38–39, 1 Corinthians 15:42–44, and Philippians 4:8. See and savor these highly patterned phrases!

For I am sure that neither death,
          nor life,
          nor angels,
          nor rulers,
          nor things present
          nor things to come,
          nor powers,
          nor height
          nor depth,
          nor anything else in all creation,
will be able to separate us
    from the love of God
    in Christ Jesus our Lord. (Rom. 8:38–39)

---

31 Ryken, *Letters of Grace and Beauty*, 102.
32 Leland Ryken, *Words of Delight: A Literary Introduction to the Bible* (Grand Rapids, MI: Baker, 1992), 437–38.

What is sown is perishable;
> what is raised is imperishable.

It is sown in dishonor;
> it is raised in glory.

It is sown in weakness;
> it is raised in power.

It is sown a natural body;
> it is raised a spiritual body. (1 Cor. 15:42–44)

Finally, brothers,
> whatever is true,
> whatever is honorable,
> whatever is just,
> whatever is pure,
> whatever is lovely,
> whatever is commendable,

if there is any excellence,
> if there is anything worthy of praise,

think about these things.[33] (Phil. 4:8)

With the above examples, who can doubt that the apostle Paul, under the inspiration of God, wrote with eloquence? Moreover, as Ryken comments, "The exalted and highly patterned style" in the above passages are not simply rhetorical embellishments, but are "part of the meaning. The Epistles are affective as well as intellectual. Their style conveys an ecstasy and an emotional conviction that are

---

33 "The very *forms* of biblical writing are inspired, and to the fullest extent possible the forms of the original need to be carried into the syntax and structure of the receptor language" (Leland Ryken, *The Word of God in English: Criteria for Excellence in Bible Translation* [Wheaton, IL: Crossway, 2002], 130).

an important part of their meaning."[34] For example, notice how the structure and style of the creedal affirmations of 1 Timothy 3:16 make the message vibrant and memorable:

Great indeed, we confess, is the mystery of godliness:
He was manifested in the flesh [incarnation],
> vindicated by the Spirit [death],
> seen by angels [resurrection],
> proclaimed among the nations,
> believed on in the world [Pentecost and its aftermath],
> taken up in glory [ascension].

Sixth, the New Testament Epistles were written to persuade. For example, I have no doubt that Paul wrote Romans to convince his audience that "the obedience of faith" (Rom. 1:5; 16:26) in Jesus must be embraced, and that Peter wrote 2 Peter to persuade Christians to "grow in the grace and knowledge of [their] Lord and Savior Jesus Christ" (3:18; cf. 1:2). And, while at times the Epistles are "disjointed in structure and wide-ranging in topics,"[35] there is discernible intent and inherent logic to each letter. The most obvious example comes in 1 John. The aged apostle, who is often circular in his thoughts and themes, makes explicit his intentions for writing: "that which we have seen and heard we proclaim also to you, *so that* **you too may have fellowship with us**; and indeed our fellowship is with the Father and with his Son Jesus Christ. And we are writing these things *so that* **our joy may be complete**" (1 John 1:3–4). Here, John, who is not as linear or logical in his

---

34 Ryken, *Words of Delight*, 438.
35 Ryken, *Letters of Grace and Beauty*, 18.

reasoning as Paul, is quite explicit. (And notice that he has a few big ideas to express, not just one.)

HOW TO PREACH BIBLICAL EPISTLES

Of all the genres in the Bible, the epistle is closest in form and substance to a sermon.[36] Moreover, if you were trained in an evangelical seminary in the last fifty years, finding the "big idea," understanding the logical argument and structural flow, and offering relevant and personal illustrations, are part of the marrow that runs through your homiletical bones. You are confident when preaching this genre. You likely preached from Paul for your first sermon and for seventy percent of your sermons since. So, there is no reason for our advice, right? We imagine, or at least hope, you are now saying, "Wrong!" You bought this book for a reason, and before you give us two stars and a bad review with a header that reads, "Tell me what I don't know," allow us to instruct. Or, at least take some advice on how to explain, illustrate, and apply the Epistles.

Read Aloud a Lot

Step back from preaching for a moment and think about the Sunday service and how the Epistles can be used every Lord's Day to exalt the Lord and edify and encourage the saints. One obvious way to use the Epistles every Sunday is at the end of the service. Give a good word (a benediction) to your good (in Christ!) people.[37] Bless them with God's Word as they leave the sanctuary to live as

---

36 The epistle is "a mode of communication that is like speech. As such, it is extremely supple, incorporating other genres within its framework and combining appeals from logos, pathos, and ethos. Epistles are like speech in four ways: they employ various small forms, argue with linear logic, cite or allude often, and are composed for the ear" (Arthurs, *Preaching with Variety*, 158).

37 For examples, see Hughes and O'Donnell, *Pastor's Book*, 310–13.

God's holy people in their sin city, sinful enough countryside, and every region in between.[38] Another way to use the Epistles is during a congregational prayer, if you have one. (It's a good idea to have one!)[39] A third, but certainly not final, way to employ the Epistles is to read them before the sermon and also as much as you can.

Paul assumed that his letters would be read aloud in the church and throughout the churches. In 1 Timothy 4:13 he exhorts Timothy to "devote [himself] to the public reading of Scripture." In 1 Thessalonians 5:27 his language is stronger: "I put you under oath before the Lord to have this letter read to all the brothers." And in Colossians 4:16 he instructs, "When this letter has been read among you, have it also read in the church of the Laodiceans; and see that you also read the letter from Laodicea."[40] Does your church read aloud God's inspired letters? Do you read God's perfect Word before you preach your imperfect words? Have you ever thought of devoting a whole service to reading? One Saturday morning I came down with a high fever. I also came up with a plan. I called Pastor Andrew Fulton, my right-hand man, and croaked over the phone, "Just read 2 Peter, give three exhortations, and allow others to share their thoughts." Andrew told me that it was a great success and that I should never come back to work, or something like that.[41]

---

38 For two examples, see Hughes and O'Donnell, *Pastor's Book*, 306–9.

39 In a traditional Presbyterian service, we often employ the Epistles for the Confession of Sin and Assurance of Pardon. For example, I recently visited Covenant Presbyterian Church of Chicago, who, for their confession, used Romans 8:5–8; assurance, Romans 8:34–35, 37; and benediction, Romans 15:5–7.

40 Notice that the book of Revelation, including the seven letters to seven different churches (Revelation 2–3), was to be read aloud (see Rev. 1:3)!

41 This is not far removed from Luke's description in Acts 13:15 ("After the reading from the Law and the Prophets, the rulers of the synagogue sent a message to them, saying, 'Brothers, if you have any word of encouragement for the people, say it'") and the first aspect of Justin Martyr's description of the early Christian gatherings (*First Apology*, 67): "On the day called Sunday there is a gathering together in the same place of all who live in a given

My over-the-phone exhortation is no match for Reading Services at Grace Evangelical Free Church in La Mirada, where my college mentor still schools me in the School of Christ. This southern California congregation, where my oldest daughter now blooms (Lily of Biola is her saint's name!), takes time to read through books of the Bible in public services. They actually read through Acts in four hours one Sabbath rest. Question: Does your church read aloud God's letters? If not, a good place to start is with Nehemiah 8 or Luke 4:16–21.[42] Reenact with your people what God's people, under both the old and new covenants, did, and have done throughout Christian history.[43]

There is a place for atomistic sermons on deeply theological texts (like Martyn Lloyd-Jones's 366 sermons on Romans, preached over twelve years). But, in general, the best way to do justice to the epistolary genre is to read it and preach it as a letter! As good as Lloyd-Jones's fifty-minute sermons are, I doubt that many in his congregation remembered by sermon sixteen that he was actually preaching on a relatively short letter that takes, on average, an hour to read aloud.

Take Serial Exposition Seriously

For many years, Lee and I had the privilege of sitting under the preaching ministry of Kent Hughes. In his twenty-seven years at

---

city or rural district. The memoirs of the apostles or the writings of the prophets are read, as long as time permits. Then when the reader ceases, the president in a discourse admonishes and urges the imitation of these good things."

42 See Hughes and O'Donnell, *Pastor's Book*, 38–44; O'Donnell, "The Scripture-Saturated Worship Service," March 9, 2021, available at https://www.pastortheologians.com/sermons; and O'Donnell, "The Bible's Use in Preaching and Public Worship," in *The Pastor's Bible* (Wheaton, IL: Crossway, 2016), x–xii.

43 See "Table 1. The Basic Liturgies of the Western Church," in Hughes and O'Donnell, *Pastor's Book*, 49.

College Church in Wheaton, Illinois, Kent modeled serial exposition of books of the Bible. What that does for the congregation is reinforce a high view of Scripture. Only someone who truly believes that "all Scripture"—even the seemingly insignificant sections—"is breathed out by God" and is the God-ordained means for his people's sanctification ("profitable for teaching, for reproof, for correction, and for training in righteousness," 2 Tim. 3:16) will preach *all* of God's Word. Moreover, only someone who values an epistle as an epistle will preach every greeting and thanksgiving, personal aside, household code, and long list of names found in the final greetings. In my nearly three decades of preaching, two of my most significant sermons (in the sense of edifying and equipping my congregation) came from my careful expositions of the ends of Colossians and 2 Timothy, where Paul lists nearly thirty people. Those long lists are theologically significant and incredibly applicable. Does your congregational know that?

Pick and Preach the Most Relevant Epistle

Before you decide the biblical text for your next sermon series, ask yourself, and have your leaders ask as well, "What does our church need to hear?" As it relates to the Epistles, if your congregation comes from a legalistic background and continues to wrestle with the relationship between their salvation and good works, preach Romans or Galatians. If many of your congregants view grace as cheap and good works as an unnecessary part of the Christian life, preach Titus or James. If you don't know what to preach, preach the letters to the seven churches. When I preached through Revelation 2–3, I began with Revelation 1 (the glorious Christ) and ended with Revelation 4–5 (the worthiness of the Father and the Son). The letters in between cover just about everything positive and negative that you will find in your church, and they help diagnose problems you have (or will encounter) and offer inspired solutions.

Find and Follow the Flow

About once a year I lead a workshop on biblical exposition for the Charles Simeon Trust. In the lesson on Structure, we instruct that every text has a structure, the structure will reveal an emphasis, and the emphasis must shape our message. That principle holds true for all genres. What is especially important as it relates to preaching epistles effectively, is another related principle: every paragraph has a flow of thought, so find that flow and follow it in your sermon.

Jeannine Brown offers three steps to finding the flow of the author's argument: (1) isolate the individual ideas of the passage, (2) identify the connecting words between clauses (the conjunctions and prepositions), and (3) identify explicitly the relationships among the ideas you have found.[44] For example, with Hebrews 4:12 (see diagram 3.1), notice how I began, at the top left, with the explanatory conjunction ("for"). Below that conjunction is the statement of the main theme/clause ("the word of God is"). God's word is described in five ways, with two words ("living," "active") and three phrases ("sharper than any two-edged sword," "piercing to the division of," and "discerning" or "able to discern"), each connected by the conjunction "and." Then, the final two phrases are further divided: the word pierces the soul, spirit, joint, and marrow; and, it is able to discern the thoughts and intentions of the heart.

---

44 Brown, *Introducing Biblical Hermeneutics*, 155. This is called by various names: arcing, phrasing, block-diagramming, and tracing the logic.

Diagram 3.1: Diagram of Hebrews 4:12

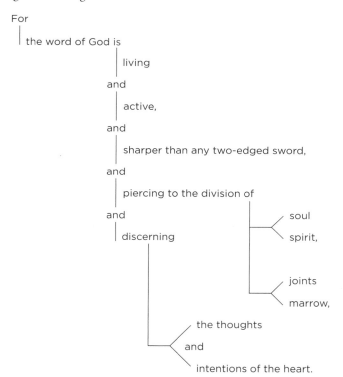

Oftentimes the structural flow, or points of the author's argument, can be used for your homiletical outline. For example, below is an excerpt from a recent sermon I preached on Colossians 1:15–23:

The text before us can be divided nicely into two parts. The first part focuses on Christ; the second on Christians. The first part (vv. 15–20) repeats the pronouns he, his, him, and himself, in reference to Christ, thirteen times. Let's call these verses "He Is." The second part (vv. 21–23) still speaks about Jesus—what his death accomplishes (v. 22)—but the focus falls on Christians, the church's response to the person and work of Jesus. Verse 21 begins, "And you [plural]"; verse 22 uses the phrase "to present you"; verse 23 says, "if indeed you." So, let's call this second section, "And You."

After dividing the text into two simple, memorable, and derived-directly-from-the-text points, I further divided verses 15–20:

For the first section—"He is"—I thought about organizing the material by just following Paul's repetition of the phrase "he is." "He is" (verse 15) "the image of the invisible God." "He is" (verse 17) "before all things." "He is" (verse 18a) "the head of the body, the church." And, "he is" (verse 18b) "the beginning, the firstborn from the dead." However, once I read Dick Lucas's excellent commentary on Colossians, I decided that his homiletical outline was better, as it more memorably summarizes Paul's main points. Lucas labels verses 15–18 *Christ Supreme*. He breaks down that heading into two points: Christ supreme in creation (vv. 15–17) and Christ supreme in the church, the new creation (v. 18). Then, he labels verses 19–20 *Christ Sufficient*. He also breaks down that heading into two points. Christ is sufficient in his person, God with us (v. 19); and Christ is sufficient in his work, God for us (v. 20).[45]

Often, the very points of the author's argument can be used for your outline. Allow me to illustrate. When I preached on Colossians 3:5–14, I ordered my sermon, as any observant and sane pastor would do, around the two main imperatives: put off and put on.

---

45 Dick Lucas, *The Message of Colossians and Philemon*, The Bible Speaks Today (Downers Grove, IL: InterVarsity Press, 1980), 46.

Paul's own outline is obvious: In verse 9, he says, "Put off the old self." Earlier in verse 5, he says, "Put to death," and in verse 8, "put them [certain sins] all away." Christians are to put off certain things, certain sins, certain ungodly attitudes and actions. Those are verses 5–9. In verses 10–14, Paul employs the language of "put on." Verse 10: "put on the new self." Verse 12: "Put on . . . compassionate hearts" and so on. Verse 14: "Put on love."

In Ephesians 5:18–21, after Paul offers a command ("do not get drunk with wine") and the reason to heed that command ("for that is debauchery"), he introduces the main clause: "but be filled with the Spirit." In the following verse he answers the question, "What are some specific ways to be Spirit-filled, and/or to express that the Spirit is at work?" Paul introduces four subordinate or supporting clauses:

(a) addressing one another in psalms and hymns and spiritual songs
(b) singing and making melody to the Lord with your heart[46]
(c) giving thanks always and for everything to God the Father
(d) submitting to one another out of reverence for Christ.

A similar structure is found in Hebrews 12:1–2. The main clause is, "let us run with endurance the race that is set before us." That is supported by the clause before it and two clauses after it:

(a) having so great a cloud of witnesses surrounding us
(b) laying aside every encumbrance and the entangling sin
(c) fixing our eyes on Jesus, the author and perfecter of our faith[47]

---

46 It is possible that "singing" is supporting "addressing one another in psalms." Are they commanded to speak God's lyrics and then sing them, or are the two activities essentially one?
47 David Alan Black's translation, in *Learn to Read New Testament Greek*, 3rd ed. (Nashville: B&H, 2009), 206.

The author of Hebrews then digs deep, as the preacher then should do, into Jesus: "who for the joy that was set before him endured the cross, despising the shame, and is seated at the right hand of the throne of God." The main exhortation is "you all run," but the sermon is useless to motivate our people to persevere if the sermon fails to focus on Jesus, whom we should fix our eyes on.[48] In his suggested sermon on this text, David Alan Black offers the title "Run to Win!" and a theme ("the Christian is called upon to follow the example of Jesus into a life of submission and obedience"). His alliterative homiletic outline follows: (1) Our Encouragement ("having so great a cloud of witnesses"), (2) Our Entanglements ("laying aside every encumbrance"), and (3) Our Example ("fixing our eyes on Jesus").[49]

Bridge the Background

My friend and coworker Justin Taylor writes a popular blog called "Between Two Worlds," where he expertly navigates from the issues in our world to the biblical worldview and vice versa. John Stott labeled his book on preaching with the same title. I won't say who came up with the phrase first, but Stott's subtitle might offer a clue: *The Art of Preaching in the Twentieth Century*. As preachers, for each and every sermon, we must offer a bridge from our congregation to the cross, from the world of our text to the world we live in.

This does not mean that our first sermon on every epistle begins with an outline:

Who is writing?
When?

---

48 As Black (*Learn to Read New Testament Greek*, 207) highlights, the chiastic structure of the text centers on the phrase "fixing our eyes on Jesus, the author and perfecter of faith."
49 Black, *Learn to Read New Testament Greek*, 207.

From where?

To whom?

Why?

"Boring" is the cry not only of the teenager who texts while you explain the text, but also of the Fundamentals major from the University of Chicago and the student from the Torrey Great Books Program at Biola.

That said, you need to say something about the background. For example, if you are preaching on 1 Corinthians 7 and you fail to mention that the chapter begins with some historical background ("Now concerning the matter about which you wrote . . .") and then the entire chapter offers imperatives on marriage and sex, you have missed the obvious. "Paul is obviously replying to a topic that has been raised in a letter from the Corinthian church."[50] You need to travel to Corinth before you go to Chicago (or whatever your hometown is). It is tempting to preach, for example, 1 Corinthians 13 as a love poem dropped from heaven and not set within any original earthly context. But if we preach that text as an ode to love we fail to do justice to its message. Once we understand that it is a rebuke set within Paul's discussion on spiritual gifts, we grasp how to properly preach it.[51]

---

50 Ryken, *Letters of Grace and Beauty*, 34.

51 In her section titled "Reconstructing the Social Setting of the Epistles," Brown writes that we need to do "the historical grunt work that will help us hear the text in its original social setting instead of imposing our own setting onto the text without much thought." She further advises, "After attending to the setting of an epistle by reading the letter itself, we can look to broader geographical, political, cultural, and religious information to assist in reconstructing the social context. Part of the religious background will be provided by the overarching story of the Old Testament and its climactic moment in Jesus the Messiah" (*Introducing Biblical Hermeneutics*, 153).

Little Words, Big Theological Punch

Preach the "big idea," if you can find it. But certainly, don't overlook the little words that pack a big theological punch. Put differently, take time to carefully explain the details. For example, when I preached on Colossians 1:16–17, I pointed out the repetition of "all things" in the poetic pericope, along with the importance of the prepositions "by" and "through" and "for" and "in." Jesus is the creator. All things were created *by* him and *through* him. He is also the sustainer and goal of creation. All things hold together *in* him and were created *for* him.

Give God's People God

In *The Supremacy of God in Preaching*, John Piper writes, "People are starving for the greatness of God, but most of them don't even know it."[52] You need to know it! And you need to preach their greatest need—God. This is certainly what the inspired apostolic authors did. They fed God's people God. Each epistle, from start to finish, is God-centered and God-saturated. For example, in Romans, "God" is mentioned 162 times, and in each chapter and preaching pericope. Romans is a God-centered epistle! If you fail to mention God in every sermon as a main theme, you fail to preach Romans as God designed it to be preached.

As part of my job at Crossway, I am asked to review potential authors for Bible projects. Recently, I reviewed Tara-Leigh Cobble's podcast *The Bible Recap*. One of the components of her daily podcast covering the whole Bible in a year she calls "God Shot." Her "God Shot" was created in reaction to the usual end of a Bible study question about personal application, "How should we live in light of what we have learned?" Instead, with a desire to take

---

52 John Piper, *The Supremacy of God in Preaching* (Grand Rapids, MI: Baker, 2004), 1.

away all the to-do-isms and leave her listeners with a picture of God, she asked questions like, "What is your picture of God and his character from this day's reading? What does God do or say, love or hate, in this passage? What motivates God to do what he does?" What a wonderful focus! And what splendid questions. When you preach God's Word to God's people, do you preach God? Do you tell them who he is and what he has done for them in Christ? It's what they most need! People—your people and all people—are starving for the greatness of God.

Give God's People God's Gospel (or, Evangelize the Elect!)

The New Testament Epistles were not written by systematic theologians. Every letter arose from an ecclesial situation. That said, and as was said above, that does not mean there is no theology in the Epistles. As Arthurs aptly summaries, "While stressing the fact that epistles are pastoral theology, let's not downplay the fact that they are theology. Taken together, they create a profound worldview—a way of understanding self, family, society, evil, temptation, salvation, authority, morality, and the future. That theological worldview provides answers to even the most mundane questions."[53] Pastor, you are a pastor theologian. In each sermon, give your people the theoretical and practical theology they need to know to live as his people in his world. And on the top of the list of theological truths they need to understand, and be weekly reminded of, is God's gospel.

Not only do the Epistles contain the clearest definitions of the gospel (see below); their authors (who are writing to Christians) assume that Christians need to hear the gospel.[54] In Romans 1:1–5 and 1 Corinthians 15:1–5, Paul reiterates this message:

---

53 Arthurs, *Preaching with Variety*, 155.
54 The word "gospel" is used in thirteen of the twenty-one epistolary letters in the Christian Scriptures.

Paul, a servant of Christ Jesus, called to be an apostle, set apart for *the gospel* of God, which he promised beforehand through his prophets in the holy Scriptures, concerning his Son, who was descended from David according to the flesh and was declared to be the Son of God in power according to the Spirit of holiness by his resurrection from the dead, Jesus Christ our Lord, through whom we have received grace and apostleship to bring about the obedience of faith for the sake of his name among all the nations . . . (Rom. 1:1–5)[55]

Now I would remind you, brothers, of *the gospel* I preached to you, which you received, in which you stand, and by which you are being saved, if you hold fast to the word I preached to you—unless you believed in vain. For I delivered to you as of first importance what I also received: that Christ died for our sins in accordance with the Scriptures, that he was buried, that he was raised on the third day in accordance with the Scriptures, and that he appeared to Cephas, then to the twelve. (1 Cor. 15:1–5)

As noted above and in the table below, to faithfully preach the Epistles we must regularly proclaim the gospel of Jesus Christ. That gospel focuses on the Lord Jesus's sacrificial death and glorious resurrection that results in the forgiveness of sin and the hope of eternal life for all who repent and believe, and it leads to a life marked by living daily in ways that are worthy of the gospel. If we fail to preach the gospel, we misinterpret the Bible, miss the

---

55 The origin of the gospel is God, the attestation of the gospel is Scripture, the substance of the gospel is Jesus Christ, the scope of the gospel is all the nations, the purpose of the gospel is the obedience of faith, the goal of the gospel is the honor of Christ's name. From John Stott, *Romans: God's Good News for the World* (Downers Grove, IL: InterVarsity Press, 1994), 46–54.

opportunity to reach unbelievers, and offer a moralistic message that will lead to self-loathing and discouragement.

Diagram 3.2: A Visual Representation of the Gospel[56]

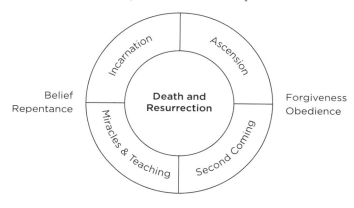

Ground the Imperatives in the Indicatives

In 1623, the English Puritan William Ames published a short book on systematic theology, called *The Marrow of Sacred Divinity.* When Harvard was founded a decade later, this book was used in the classroom to train young divinity students. Ames defined theology as *Theologia est Scientia vivendo Deo*, which can be translated, "Theology is the knowledge of how to live in the presence of God."[57] I think if Paul were ever to pen a definition of theology, his would come close to that. For, to the great apostle, Christian theology was never divorced from Christian living, and Christian living was never divorced from the presence and power of God. Theology by itself, as Timothy George has said, leads to an "arid

---

56 Created by the Charles Simeon Trust for their instructors. Printed with permission.

57 Timothy George, "Foreword," in Todd Wilson and Gerald L. Hiestand, *Becoming a Pastor Theologian: New Possibilities for Church Leadership* (Downers Grove, IL: IVP Academic, 2016).

intellectualism," and ethics by itself leads to "sterile activism or sentimental fluff."[58]

The imperatives—the commands, rebukes, and exhortations—that we find in the Epistles are always grounded in the person and work of God. For example, it is in light of God's grace in the gospel of our Lord Jesus Christ ("I appeal to you therefore, brothers, by the mercies of God") that we offer "spiritual worship," that is, that we offer our whole selves to God ("to present your bodies as a living sacrifice," Rom. 12:1). Other examples abound. See, e.g., table 3.1.

Table 3.1: Examples of Indicatives and Imperatives in the Epistles

Indicative	Imperative	Reference
. . . because he first loved us	We love	1 John 4:19
For the grace of God has appeared . . .	training us to renounce ungodliness and worldly passions, and to live self-controlled, upright, and godly lives in the present age	Titus 2:11–12
[As] God's chosen ones, holy and beloved [and] as the Lord has forgiven you . . .	so you also must forgive	Col. 3:12–13

Throughout the Epistles, our ethical actions are motivated by God's gospel. I label it "gospel ethics."[59] "Paraenesis" is the more technical term. "Paraenesis," as Ryken summaries, "establishes that belief or doctrine must work itself out in our action." It also

58 George, "Foreword."

59 See Douglas Sean O'Donnell, *The Beginning and End of Wisdom: Preaching Christ from the First and Last Chapters of Proverbs, Ecclesiastes, and Job* (Wheaton, IL: Crossway, 2011), 120–24.

"shows that morality or ethics is an indispensable part of the Christian life."[60]

Therefore, because our godliness flows from God and his gospel, it is crucial that we preach imperatives to our congregations grounded in the indicatives. Here is how I followed this principle when I preached Colossians 3:5–14:

Note the word "therefore." I won't use the cliché question, "What's the therefore there for?" I just won't. But I will answer that question. The "therefore" is there for a reason. The reason is to transition the reader from theology to ethics, or from the indicative (here is what God has done for us in Christ through the Spirit) to the imperative (here is how we should respond). This is Paul's pattern throughout his epistles. For example, in Ephesians 4:1, with a "therefore," he transitions from lofty theology to down-to-earth, practical implications. "I therefore . . . urge you to walk in a manner worthy of the calling to which you have been called." So, the "therefore" in Paul's writings, especially the key ones that happen mid-letter, should move our minds back to the motivation presented beforehand. Why should we put off certain bad behaviors and put on certain good ones? Simple. Colossians 1–2 and a bit of 3, where we read about Christ, who is the creator and sustainer of the universe, came as a man, died for our sins, and rose for our justification, and he now (as he has ascended to heaven) rules in power and will soon return as the judge of all people. You see, we put off and

---

60 Ryken, *Letters of Grace and Beauty*, 69. For an excellent summary on paraenesis in the Epistles, see Leland Ryken, Philip Ryken, and James Wilhoit, *Ryken's Bible Handbook: A Guide to Reading and Studying the Bible* (Carol Stream, IL: Tyndale, 2005), 504.

put on because through faith we are united to him (we are "in" and "with" Christ).

In a later sermon, I summarize the letter as follows:

HE IS: Paul talks about the person of Jesus. For example, in Colossians 1:18 he writes, "And he is the head of the body, the church. He is the beginning, the firstborn from the dead, that in everything he might be preeminent."

HE HAS: Paul talks not just about the person of Jesus, but the works of Jesus (what Jesus has done for us). For example, in 1:13, "He has delivered us from the domain of darkness and transferred us to the kingdom of his beloved Son."

IN HIM: Paul talks not just about the person and works of Jesus, but also how that knowledge of him ought to change believers. For example, in 2:6, we read, "Therefore, as you received Christ Jesus the Lord, so walk in him."

It is crucial that we preach imperatives to our congregations grounded in the indicatives. It is also imperative that we preach imperatives! Period.

Preach to Persuade

In 1969, when Martyn Lloyd-Jones lectured at Westminster Theological Seminary on preaching, he answered the question, "What is preaching?" with the memorable answer (an emblem of his own ministry): "Logic on fire." Before that simple, profound, and true definition, he said, "Light without heat never affected anybody.

It is no use to anybody. Heat without light is no good. You must have light and heat."

Many preachers today have heat, but they fail to argue a point logically. Give your congregation some light. Logical light. When is the last time you preached with the intent to "*move* [God's people under your care] to assent intellectually" to something taught in God's Word? When Paul wrote with his characteristic heat and light, seeking "to persuade his readers not to revert to the 'works righteousness' of Judaism but to accept salvation as a free gift," do you match his warmth and lucidity?[61] You may not match it, but do you strike a match next to it?

Supplement with Stories

The suggestion here is simple but often overlooked, or ignored: regularly supplement your exegesis of the Epistles with narrative illustrations. This is important to do because few people can stay with a sustained logical argument or a detailed persuasive discourse for thirty to forty minutes straight. The older I get, and the more sermons I preach, the more I am convinced that I need to tell more stories and I need to tell those stories well.

Share Your Own Story

One of the stories I need to tell especially well is my own story. You need to do the same. Why? The Epistles are filled with autobiography. My take is that, the reason the authors, especially Paul, talk so much about themselves is to offer an ideal to emulate. Minister and author Phillips Brooks spoke of preaching as truth communicated through personality. When we personally testify that we believe and

---

61 Ryken, *Letters of Grace and Beauty*, 77, 78.

have experienced the truth of the text we are preaching, and when we share our own failures and sorrows, we elicit our audiences' attention and empathy. For example, when Julius Kim shared at the 2021 Gospel Coalition National Conference about how he almost died from COVID-19 and how he breathed out what he thought would be his last prayer, I was riveted. I listened carefully to the point he tied to his experience. Autobiography offers ethos, that is, sharing the intimate details of one's life (autobiography) can create credibility (ethos). Indeed, ethos draws our hearers to listen to us, trust us, and be drawn to the truth we are communicating.

From Me to You

The Epistles are filled with first- *and* second-person pronouns, followed by specific praises and rebukes. Follow that pattern in your preaching. Follow this pattern too: Paul writes that God's message ("from God") comes "to me for you" (Col. 1:25). Of course, you and I don't have apostolic authority, but this apostolic outline can still help us when we address our people.

When I preached on Colossians 1:24–2:5 (and yes, that is the only proper division of the text), I gave this transition into my three applications: "Now, with all that said from Paul to the Colossians, let me say this to you . . ." And then I proposed these three applications. First, you must reject any messenger who does not suffer for the gospel and will not preach the necessity of suffering. Second, you must understand the Spirit-designed formula for church growth: power + preaching + persecution = growth. Third, you must take part in the plan. Then, I interlaced some autobiography:

About a month ago, my wife was having a very hard week of ministry. As I listened to her, I wasn't sure what to say. I wasn't sure if I should say anything. But then, I decided I would give her one word of counsel. With a depth of sincerity and love for her, and a genuine desire to be of some practical help, I simply said in a serious, quiet, tender word, "Pick up your cross." That's all I said, and that was all she needed to hear.

I returned to the people, saying,

> My brothers and sisters, the call of the Christian life is not the call to embrace ease and entertainment. No, the call is to self-denial. The call is to follow Jesus. The call is to suffer with him so we might be more like him. The church, as Christ's body, must continue to participate in the sufferings of Christ.

Listen, Brothers

Related to the tip and language above, here's another simple, practical suggestion. How should you address the congregation when you preach? Do you call them "church" or "friends"? I suggest you regularly employ the language of the Epistles—call God's people "brothers and sisters," "saints," and "children [of God, or in the faith]." I also frequently use the vocatives "listen" and "hear," commands Jesus used in his sermons, discourses, and short teachings.

Related to that, when an epistle addresses a specific audience, such as in the household codes, I advise you to take some time to do the same. When I preached on Colossians 3:15–4:1, a sermon I titled "Jesus Is Lord of the House," I preached this:

> C. S. Lewis once wrote, "If the home is to be the means of grace it must be a place of rules . . . the alternative to rule is not freedom but the unconstitutional (and often unconscious) tyranny

of the most selfish member." Children can be selfish—little tyrants—by not obeying their parents. Fathers can be selfish—big tyrants—by provoking their children. To that truth we turn next. "Fathers," Paul writes in Colossians 3:21, "do not provoke your children, lest they become discouraged." The "father" and not the mother, some argue, might be specifically singled out because this is a more prevalent sin for men than for women. I don't think that is the case. I have found that mothers can be as tyrannical as fathers! I think "fathers" are singled out because they are to lead in disciplining and instructing the children and because each relationship has the father at the center of the web of relationships within the home (wife/husband; children/father; slaves/master)—the husband, father, and master are the same person.

Now, what is so remarkable about this command is how revolutionary it was. There is a section in ancient Roman law called "the Power of the Father" which details how a "father could do anything he wanted with his children. He could sell them, turn them into slaves, even take their lives."[62] So, for Paul to admonish fathers to "not provoke" their children, so they won't become "discouraged," not only calls Christian fathers to love their children but it shows how much Christianity valued children.

Then, I drilled down on the dads:

Fathers, let me ask you, how are we doing with this command? Do you irritate your kids by constantly deriding them? Do you put them down more than you build them up? Are you like a

---

62 R. Kent Hughes, *Colossians and Philemon: The Supremacy of Christ*, Preaching the Word (Wheaton, IL: Crossway, 1989), 123.

dripping faucet, constantly trickling down criticism? Do you offer words of encouragement and praise? Have you burdened your children with too many rules or overly strict ones? Do you always say "no" and never "yes"? Do you give your children conflicting messages or inconsistent discipline? Are you capricious, unpredictable? Do you spend time with your children or are you too busy for them and too distant from them? Are you usually grouchy and irritable around your children?

Kent Hughes shares about "a cartoon in which the boss is grouchy toward his employee, who in turn comes home and is irritable with his children. His son, in turn, kicks the dog. The dog runs down the street and bites the first person he sees—the boss!"[63] Fathers, you're the boss! If you don't want the dog to bite you, don't bite and devour your children. Don't "provoke *or* irritate *or* exasperate your children [with demands that are trivial or unreasonable or humiliating or abusive; nor by favoritism or indifference]—don't "break their spirts," or they will "lose heart *and* become discouraged *or* unmotivated" (AMP).

Cross-References

Here I offer another short and simple suggestion: use cross-references wisely and sparingly. If your congregation flips from your main text to a hundred other texts, how will they remember the text's main exhortations? That said, people like movement. Make them flip at least once. Have them do something physical so they can stay with you mentally. Here's an example, another from Colossians. When I preached on Colossians 1:15–20 I had my congregation focus on the phrases "by him all things were created,"

---

63 Hughes, *Colossians and Philemon*, 126.

"all things were created through him," "he is before all things," and "in him all things hold together," by turning to God's rebuke to Job in Job 38–41. I asked, "How many people, places, and things in creation were created by him?" I answered, "All things." I then illustrated, and used the rhetorical art of repetition:

> How about different universes, if they exist? "All things." How about the sun and moon and stars? "All things." How about sheep, camels, oxen, donkeys, lions, moths, bears, eagles, fish, cattle, cobras, falcons, ravens, jackals, ostriches, goats, horses, deer, locusts, hawks, and sea monsters?

I ended, "And those are just a few of the creatures named in the book of Job. The extent of his creation is seemingly inexhaustible! All things."

(An Aside on) Eloquence

Augustine famously wrote of preaching, "Make the truth plain, make it pleasing, make it moving." No preacher today doubts that we should make the truth of the text we are preaching plain or clear. But do you also believe the second and third parts of Augustine's advice? That is, do you believe the sermon should be pleasing— pleasing to the ear, senses, intellect? Moreover, do you believe that the sermon should be moving—that it should affect affections? Jonathan Edwards wrote that the goal of his sermons was to raise the affections as high as possible so long as the affections were raised to that level by the truth. Is that your goal in preaching? I have no doubt that you care about the truth when you preach, but do you care about how that truth is communicated? Do you preach both substantive and stylistically beautiful sermons?

And *should you*? In John Piper's excellent essay "Is There Christian Eloquence? Clear Words and the Wonder of the Cross," later published as "Lest the Cross Be Emptied of Its Power: The Perils of Christian Eloquence," Piper begins, "Should we use our natural powers in choosing words, with a view to making them as compelling as we can? Should we try to be eloquent?"[64] That question is raised because of what Paul writes in 1 Corinthians 2:1: "I, when I came to you, brothers, did not come proclaiming to you the testimony of God with lofty speech or wisdom," or as the NIV translates the final phrase, "eloquence or human wisdom." Earlier, in 1:17, Paul writes, "Christ did not send me to baptize but to preach the gospel, and *not with words of eloquent wisdom* [or "cleverness of speech," NASB], lest the cross of Christ be emptied of its power." Obviously then, one can speak in such a way that it annuls the life-changing power of the message of the cross. Piper then adds his commentary and a question on these two texts: "Is Paul saying that the pursuit of impact on others through word selection, word arrangement, and word delivery preempts Christ's power and belittles the glory of the cross?" Piper answers that question, saying, "No." We do not usurp the role of the Spirit or the power of the cross when we choose and arrange and deliver words in ways that have the greatest rhetorical impact. Piper can say that, and I agree with him, for two reasons:

First, "the eloquence Paul is rejecting [in Corinth] is not so much any particular language conventions, but the exploitations of language to exalt self and belittle or ignore the crucified Lord."[65] First Corinthians 2:1 ("I, when I came to you, brothers, did not

---

64 John Piper, *Expository Exultation: Christian Preaching as Worship* (Wheaton, IL: Crossway, 2018), 139.

65 Piper, *Expository Exultation*, 147.

come proclaiming to you the testimony of God with lofty speech or wisdom") is followed by 1 Corinthians 2:2, "For I decided to know nothing among you except Jesus Christ and him crucified." There is evil eloquence and holy eloquence. The sophists,[66] when they spoke, used carefully crafted words to exalt themselves. That is evil eloquence.[67] Paul, when he spoke, used carefully crafted words to exalt Christ. There are few words more eloquent in the Bible than what Paul pens in 1 Corinthians 1:18–25. Right after Paul says, "For Christ did not send me to baptize but to preach the gospel, and not with words of eloquent wisdom, lest the cross of Christ be emptied of its power," Paul's rhetorical powers are on full display:

For the word of the cross is folly to those who are perishing, but [contrast] to us who are being saved it is the power of God [irony]. For it is written [a quotation from an authoritative text to support his point],

"I will destroy the wisdom of the wise,
and the discernment of the discerning I will thwart."

Where [the use of word repetition and four rhetorical questions] is the one who is wise? Where is the scribe? Where is the debater of this age? Has [another rhetorical question, staring not with "where" but "has," for emphasis] not God made foolish

---

66 Piper, *Expository Exultation*, 145. Piper cites Bruce Winter, who thinks the sophists form the historical "backdrop of what Paul says about his own speech and how he ministered in Corinth" (Winter, *Philo and Paul among the Sophists: Alexandrian and Corinthian Responses to a Julio-Claudian Movement*, 2nd ed. [Grand Rapids, MI: Eerdmans, 2002], 253–54).

67 "We must beware," Augustine entreated, "of the man who abounds in eloquent nonsense" (*On Christian Doctrine*, 4.4.6).

the wisdom of the world? For since [Paul is making an argument, he is seeking to persuade—how?—through repetition of key words, irony, paradox, wordplay], in the wisdom of God, the world did not know God through wisdom, it pleased God through the folly of what we preach to save those who believe. For Jews demand signs and Greeks seek wisdom, but [contrast] we preach Christ crucified, a stumbling block [imagery] to Jews and folly to Gentiles, but to those who are called, both Jews and Greeks, Christ the power of God and the wisdom of God. For the foolishness of God is wiser than men, and [parallelism, paradox] the weakness of God is stronger than men.

What Alistair Wilson said about Paul's beautiful and memorable poem in Colossians 1:15–17 can be said here as well: "Paul is so captivated by the wonder of the person and work of Jesus that the expressions of his thought in writing are raised to new heights."[68] Wilson adds, "Paul has given considerable thought not only to what he wants to say but also to how he wants to say it. Paul's consideration of the deep truths of the Scriptures and the events of Christ's life and death have led him to express these truths in an 'exalted' manner."[69]

To the sophists, eloquence was "an end in itself," that is, they communicated not so that truth might be understood and embraced, but so that people might marvel over their stylistic sophistication. When they spoke, they received the glory—the praise from people. When Paul spoke (or wrote), it was the opposite. He presented the truth of the gospel "with overwhelming weight of

---

68 Alistair Wilson, "Colossians," ESV Expository Commentary (Wheaton, IL: Crossway, 2018), 220.

69 Wilson, *Colossians*, 223.

argument" and "with such intenseness of feeling,"[70] that the listeners' heads, hearts, and hands were stimulated to think, touched to the depths of the soul, and moved to act.

Therefore, we can answer no to the question, "Is Paul saying that the pursuit of impact on others through word selection, word arrangement, and word delivery preempts Christ's power and belittles the glory of the cross?" We can answer no because, first, "the eloquence Paul is rejecting is not so much any particular language conventions, but the exploitations of language to exalt self and belittle or ignore the crucified Lord."[71]

Second, as has already been illustrated above, we can dismiss this concern because the Bible itself—especially the Epistles—is full of literary eloquence.[72] John Donne said, "The Holy Ghost in penning the Scriptures delights himself, not only with a propriety [a modest politeness of language], but with a delicacy, and harmony, and melody of language; with height of Metaphors, and other figures [of speech], which may work greater impressions upon the Readers."[73] Not only is "the Bible filled with every manner of literary device to add impact to the language,"[74] but it claims to be eloquent and invites us to emulate its eloquence. In Ecclesiastes 12:9–10, Qoheleth is not only called a "wise" teacher who "imparted knowledge to the people," but it is also said of him, "He pondered and searched out and *set in order* many proverbs. The Teacher searched to find just the right words, and what he wrote was upright and

---

70 As was said of Jonathan Edwards (see Piper, *Expository Exultation*, 142).

71 Piper, *Expository Exultation*, 147.

72 As Ryken explains, "The elements of artistic form include . . . pattern or design, unity, theme or central focus, balance, contrast, unified progression, recurrence or rhythm, and variation" (*Words of Delight*, 187; cf. 91).

73 Quoted in, Piper, *Expository Exultation*, 140.

74 Piper, *Expository Exultation*, 148–49.

true" (NIV). Or, as the ESV puts it, "The Preacher sought to find *words of delight*, and uprightly he wrote words of truth." The words of truth are words of delight. Also, Proverbs 25:7 states, "A word fitly spoken is like apples of gold in a setting of silver"—what a beautiful image, said beautifully.

Therefore, following what is stated above, what is the benefit to finding just the right words (finding those golden apples) and arranging those words in such a way (upon a setting of silver) that invites your congregation to better understand, apply, and enjoy God's Word? Again, I return to Piper's article. To that question or the question "Why give any attention to maximizing the impact of our language?" Piper gives five reasons for using "artistic, surprising, provocative, or aesthetically pleasing language."[75] We do so in order to,

1. keep interest
2. gain sympathy
3. awaken sensitivity
4. speak memorably
5. increase power

Holy eloquence—crafting intentional artistic language to explain and illustrate biblical truth—usually keeps "people awake and focused" because it creates interest (turns the brain on) and rouses the emotions (warms the heart). Of course, to talk about how a bridegroom is like the rising sun does not convert anyone, but it does help people listen better to you when you turn from that memorable and vivid image to the gospel. As Piper himself puts it, Christian eloquence "is not the *decisive* factor in salvation

---

75 Piper, *Expository Exultation*, 150.

or sanctification; God is. But faith comes by hearing, and hearing by the word. That word in the Bible is pervasively eloquent—words are put together in a way to give great impact. And God invites us to create our own eloquent phrases for *his* name's sake, not ours. And in the mystery of his sovereign grace, he will glorify himself in the hearts of others sometimes in spite of, and sometimes because of [!], the words we have chosen. In that way, he will keep us humble and get all the glory for himself."[76]

CONCLUSION

In 2012, I developed a preacher-training program called 20/12. One Sunday night a month for 12 months a young preacher preaches for 20 minutes. One of the young men, John Higgins,[77] preached a sermon on the end of 2 Timothy. I have tried diligently not to borrow too much from my then-intern's fine sermon. I will, however, conclude by borrowing a thought and a quote from where he began:

If you were commissioned by God to communicate the existence, attributes, and actions of God to the world, how would you do it? Some of us would perhaps communicate using complex language—something along the lines of abstruse philosophical talk or quasi-mathematical diagrams; others of us would produce something more artistic—perhaps a captivating film, or a massive painted mosaic. God thought that the most appropriate way to communicate himself to the world was through his Son—flesh and bones and blood like us—and through a book, a book that contains epistles (how extraordinarily ordinary!)—real time and place and people and circumstances letters, such as a letter from a

---

76 Piper, *Expository Exultation*, 154.
77 On John's YouTube channel (www.youtube.com/c/TheBibleisArt) he offers helpful resources on understanding the Bible as literature.

former Jewish Pharisee sitting in a Roman prison to a young, timid, half-Jewish/half-Gentile/fully-Christian man residing and reading it in a relatively small ancient Greek city.

C. S. Lewis tells of two different and complementary descriptions of why the teapot is boiling: First, you could describe it in terms of thermodynamics and condensation; or second, you could simply say, "The teapot is boiling because Mrs. Lewis wants some tea." Both explanations are true; however, the second one is better for most situations. God talks *teapot talk* to us. Yes, that heavenly unseen being has chosen to reveal his all-glorious self to us earthly, less-than-all-glorious beings in seemingly earthly, less-than-glorious ways—a baby through a birth canal, the washing of feet, bread and wine, three nails through a wooden cross, a letter from one friend to another, warm cloaks, and old scrolls and parchments.

As preachers of all of God's Word, we need to appreciate all of God's Word and understand that each and every aspect of each and every epistle in the divinely inspired New Testament is a blessing from God to his people, a blessing to be handled with care and love and admiration for the Giver of all good gifts.

BUILD YOUR LIBRARY! HELPFUL RESOURCES

O'Brien, P. T. "Letters, Letter Forms." Pages 550–53 in *Dictionary of Paul and His Letters*. Edited by Gerald F. Hawthorne, Ralph P. Martin, and Daniel Reid. Downers Grove, IL: InterVarsity, 1993.

Piper, John. *Expository Exultation: Christian Preaching as Worship*. Wheaton, IL: Crossway, 2018.

Ryken, Leland. *Letters of Grace and Beauty: A Guided Literary Study of the New Testament Epistles*. Wooster, OH: Weaver, 2016.

Schreiner, Thomas R. *Interpreting the Pauline Epistles*. 2nd ed. Grand Rapids, MI: Baker Academic, 2011.

4

The Beauty of the Simple

Preaching Poetry

YEARS AGO, I was asked by a large church in the Chicago suburbs to give a talk to their pastoral staff, ministry residents, and interns on preaching biblical poetry. I began that talk by asking everyone to grab their Bibles and close their eyes. Once everyone's eyes were closed, I said, "Now, flip open your Bible and place your finger anywhere on the page." Then I gave the command to open their eyes and look down at the page. I asked, "Are any of you pointing to a poem?" Fifteen out of twenty-one (71 percent of them) nodded.

The point of this odd exercise was, of course, to point out the obvious: the Bible is full of poems. It is not 71 percent poems, but it is a good one-third.[1] The Psalms, the Song of Solomon, Proverbs, and Lamentations are completely poetic. Job, Ecclesiastes, and the prophets are mainly poetic. Then, throughout the Old Testament

---

1   "Next to narrative, poetry is the largest genre in the Bible. We cannot avoid it if we tried" (Leland Ryken, *Sweeter Than Honey, Richer Than Gold: A Guided Study of Biblical Poetry*, Reading the Bible as Literature [Bellingham, WA: Lexham, 2015], 11).

narratives, there are lyrical poems, such as Lamech's "Song of the Sword" (Gen. 4:17–26) and David's swan song (his last words, in 2 Samuel 22); didactic poems, such as psalms that teach an attribute of God (e.g., his steadfast love); and poems based on salvific events (e.g., the songs of Moses and Deborah).[2] And in the New Testament, there is the Christ hymn of John's prologue, Luke's four nativity poems, the poetic portions of Jesus's Sermon on the Mount (the Beatitudes, the Lord's Prayer, and the discourse on anxiety),[3] and the poetic praises in Revelation, to name a few of the many poems or poetic portions.[4] This fact—that God's Word is filled with poetry—reveals two truths. First, God has chosen to reveal something of his person and plan through poetry. Second, if we seek to communicate better God's revealed wisdom and works, then we need to appreciate biblical poetry and understand how it works.

2   Throughout the Bible, including critical moments in salvation history, poems are provided to express praise for promises and provisions. E.g., the songs found in Ex. 15:1b–18; Deut. 32:1–43; Judg. 5:1b–31; 1 Sam. 2:1–10; 2 Sam. 22:2–51; Hab. 3:2–19; Luke 1:46–55, 68–79; and Rev. 15:3–4. For other notable poetic texts, see Gen. 4:23–24; 49:2–27; Num. 21:14–15, 27–30; 23:7–10, 18–24; 24:3–9, 15–24; Josh. 10:12–14; Phil. 2:5–11; Col. 1:15–20; 1 Tim. 3:16; and possibly John 1:1–5, 9–11; 1 Cor. 12:3; Eph. 5:14; 2 Tim. 2:5–6; Heb. 1:3; 1 Pet. 3:18c–19. The sayings and discourses of Jesus, along with many verses in the New Testament Epistles, are permeated by poetic language (e.g., "You are the salt of the earth," Matt. 5:13; "the tongue is a fire," James 3:6). So too are a majority of Old Testament prophetic discourses embodied in poetic form.

3   As Ryken points out, "Some of Jesus' orations are so patterned and so replete with parallel phrases and clauses that they could be printed as poems" (Leland Ryken, *Jesus the Hero: A Guided Literary Study of the Gospels*, Reading the Bible as Literature [Wooster, OH: Weaver, 2016], 118). He offers Matthew 7:7–8 as an example:

> Ask, and it will be given to you;
>   seek, and you will find;
>   knock, and it will be opened to you.

4   "Additionally, we find interspersed passages of poetry, or passages that employ figures of speech, in virtually all parts of the Bible" (Leland Ryken, *A Complete Handbook of Literary Forms in the Bible* [Wheaton, IL: Crossway, 2014], 152).

I quoted the following excerpt in the introduction, but it is worth quoting again, especially in the context of introducing this genre. In a letter to a friend, Martin Luther wrote, "I am persuaded that without knowledge of literature pure theology cannot at all endure. . . . Certainly it is my desire that there shall be *as many poets* and rhetoricians *as possible*, because I see that by these studies, as by no other means, people are wonderfully fitted for the grasping of sacred truth and for handling it skillfully and happily. . . . Therefore I beg of you that at my request (if that has any weight) you will *urge your young people to be diligent in the study of poetry* and rhetoric."[5] I couldn't agree more with Luther's observation and admonition. Especially today, as our culture is so image-oriented (or image-dominated!), preachers need to teach their congregations how to understand and apply the images and ideas of the God-inspired poems. As seminarians learn the fundamentals of the biblical languages, so every preacher should be competent in the basics of biblical poetry. To that end, in this chapter we will, first, seek to understand how to read biblical poetry and, second, how to preach it.

HOW TO READ BIBLICAL POETRY

Step One: Structure

In seeking to understand how to read a biblical poem, we must first uncover the basic structure of the whole poem and structures within the poem. The biblical authors would agree with Richard Moulton's statement that "art, ultimately, is organization."[6] The

---

5   Martin Luther, "Letter to Eoban Hess, 29 March 1523," in *Luthers Briefwechsel*, in D. Martin Luthers Werke, 120 vols. (Weimar, Germany: Böhlhaus, 1883–2009), 3:50, emphasis mine.

6   Richard G. Moulton, *Literary Study of the Bible* (Boston: Heath, 1898), 150.

Bible's poems are well-organized, and parallelisms are the basic organizing form of Jewish poetic art.

Parallelisms

Every poem in every language uses various forms of repetition. English poetry, for example, frequently uses repetition of sound (e.g., ending syllables rhyme), meter (recurring rhythmical patterns), along with repetitions of themes (e.g., refrains). The ancient poems found in the Bible employ the repetition of parallel words and thoughts in a structured way. This distinctive feature of Hebrew poetry is called parallelism. In parallelism, there is a rhythmical balancing of lines, in that "all or part of the second line matches or is parallel to something in the first line."[7] There is also often a similar grammatical structure and the same syntax in these "thought couplets," as Ryken correctly calls them.[8]

Ideas are often arranged to reflect either similar (traditionally called a *synonymous* parallel) or opposite (*antithetic*) ideas. In a synonymous parallel, the second half-line is similar to the first. The idea is echoed.[9] Below are two examples. The words underlined, italicized, and in bold highlight the obvious similarities.

> But let <u>justice</u> *roll down* like **waters,**
> and <u>righteousness</u> like an *ever-flowing* **stream.**
> (Amos 5:24)

---

7 Ryken, *Sweeter Than Honey, Richer Than Gold*, 70.

8 Ryken, *Sweeter Than Honey, Richer Than Gold*, 69.

9 Parallelism, as C. S. Lewis defines it, is "the practice of saying the same thing twice in different words." By the phrase "the same thing" Lewis does not mean that the second line is the same as the first; but that the second "makes no logical addition" and instead "echoes, with variation, the first" (*Reflections on the Psalms* [New York: Harcourt, Brace, & World, 1958], 3, 5).

Ask, and it *will be given* to **you**;
Seek, and **you** *will find*;
Knock, and it *will be opened* to **you**. (Matt. 7:7)

Thus, if you were preaching on Jesus's instruction on prayer, you would not turn the one point of Matthew 7:7 into three points (e.g., prayer first involves asking, then seeking, and finally knocking).

An antithetic parallelism contrasts two ideas. Notice, in the words underlined, italicized, and in bold below, how the second line is opposite to the first:

A wise son makes a *glad* **father**,
    but a foolish son is a *sorrow* to his **mother**. (Prov. 10:1b)

Whoever goes about *slandering* **reveals secrets**,
    but he who is *trustworthy* in spirit **keeps a thing covered**.
    (Prov. 11:13)

Synthetic parallels advance an idea or develop a thought; that is, each successive line builds synthetically or climactically on the one before it.[10] Note the progression of thought in Proverbs 3:7:

---

10 "*Synthetic parallelism* should be thought of as *growing parallelism* or *expanding parallelism*. The second line completes something that was introduced in the first line. Here is an example:

    These all look to you,
        To give them their food in due season. (Ps. 104:27)

The second line completes the first, but strictly speaking there is nothing in the second line that parallels anything in the first line. The second line simply completes the thought that began in the first line" (Ryken, *Sweeter Than Honey, Richer Than Gold*, 72). I sometimes use the example from Psalm 40:3: "He put a new song in my mouth, [what kind of song?] a song of praise to our God."

Be not wise in your own eyes;
    fear the LORD, and turn away from evil.

First, we are exhorted not to be "wise in [our] own eyes." Then, the first part of the second half-line explains that thought by giving the alternative, "fear the LORD." Finally, the second part of the second half-line adds to that thought, explaining a central component of fearing God, namely, to "turn away from evil."

Another type of parallelism is a "stairstep" structure, where the last word or concept introduces the next line:

In him was *life*,
    and the *life* was the <u>light</u> of men.
The <u>light</u> shines in the **darkness**,
    and the **darkness** has not overcome it. (John 1:4–5)

Whoever receives this child in my name *receives me*,
    and whoever *receives me* receives him who sent me.
        (Luke 9:48)

Other parallelisms include climactic (where the second half of a verse completes the start of the sentence and then enhances the idea),[11] emblematic (an initial metaphor is completed and explained in the second line), and alternate (verses with an ABAB

11 "The tip-off for climactic parallelism is that the second line repeats part of the first line verbatim and then adds to it. Almost always the first line leaves the thought incomplete—dangling in midair until the second line completes it [e.g., Ps. 96:7]. But occasionally the thought is already complete at the end of the first line, and the repetition of a phrase or clause in the second line is simply a pleasing artistic effect and also a way of highlighting something:

In you our fathers trusted;
    they trusted, and you delivered them. (Ps. 22:4)

pattern—the third line echoes the first and the fourth echoes the second):

Climactic	Ascribe to the LORD, O families of the peoples, ascribe to the LORD glory and strength! (Ps. 96:7)
Emblematic	As a deer pants for flowing streams, so pants my soul for you, O God. (42:1)
Alternate	A. For as high as the heavens are above the earth, B. so great is his steadfast love toward those who fear him; A'. as far as the east is from the west, B'. so far does he remove our transgressions from us. (103:11–12)

Parallelism is an essential component of the artistry and beauty of biblical poetry. "Parallelism," writes C. S. Lewis, "is a very pure example of what all . . . art involves."[12] It incarnates the essence of artistry.[13]

Chiasms

Beyond the parallelisms found in successive individual lines, there are the ultimate parallel poetic structures: chiasms. The term *chiasm* derives its name from the Greek letter *chi*, because the basic

---

The repetition of the verb 'trusted' focuses our attention on it and enhances the meaning beyond what would have been achieved if the poet had simply gone on with 'and you delivered them'" (Ryken, *Sweeter Than Honey, Richer Than Gold*, 72–73).

12 Lewis, *Reflections on the Psalms*, 3–4.

13 "If the message were all that mattered in the Bible, we would be left wondering whether the biblical poets did not have anything better to do with their time than putting their utterances into the form of poetic parallelism and inventing apt metaphors. Biblical example leads us to conclude that in God's economy they did not have anything better to do than to be artistic to the glory of God" (Leland Ryken, *Triumph of the Imagination* [Downers Grove, IL: InterVarsity Press, 1979], 41).

form resembles the left half of that letter (X). The first, humorous, example (table 4.1) is my own. When read left to right, top to bottom, the first theme (A) is repeated (A') as the last, and the middle theme (B and B') appears twice in succession.

Table 4.1: A Simple Chiasm

A. The poems in the Bible
    B. are not all chiasms.
    B'. There are not chiasms
A'. in every Scriptural poem.

In more complex chiasms, the middle theme appears only once (not twice) at the center (e.g., the example in table 4.2, from Prov. 31:10–31). Thus, chiasms found in biblical poetry can have a simple ABBA pattern or something more complex, such as the ABCDEFGFEDCBA of this second chiasm. The center point of the poem is its thematic point. In the case of Proverbs 31:10–31, verse 23 centers a young man's attention on the importance of finding an excellent wife.

Table 4.2: A Complex Chiasm: Proverbs 31:10–31

A. The high value of an excellent wife (v. 10)
  B. Her husband's benefits (vv. 11–12)
    C. Her industrious work (vv. 13–19)
      D. Her doing kindness (v. 20)
        E. Fearless [of the present] (v. 21a)
          F. Clothing her household and herself (vv. 21b–22)
            G. Her husband's renowned respect (v. 23)
          F'. Clothing herself and others (vv. 24–25a)
        E'. Fearless [of the future] (v. 25b)
      D'. Her teaching kindness (v. 26)
    C'. Her industrious work (v. 27)
  B'. Her husband's (and children's) praise (vv. 28–29)
A'. The high value of an excellent wife (vv. 30–31)

Obviously, the biblical authors were artists,[14] men and women who loved to use shape and symmetry to express their ideas eloquently and impactfully. A congregation can be inspired when they learn of such beautiful forms and facts.

Other Forms of Poetry

Other structural forms of poetry include acrostics (poems organized by using the successive letters from the Hebrew alphabet), inclusios (poems that begin and end with the same phrase), five-part laments (invocation, complaint, supplication, statement of confidence in God, and vow to praise God),[15] and three-part praises.

Many biblical poems are structured in three parts: introduction to the topic or central experience (which might be an emotion, like the joy of deliverance); development of this announced theme; and resolution, or rounding out the poem on a note of closure. Psalm 1 illustrates these structural considerations well. The topic is the godly person, and the theme is the blessedness of the godly person, as announced in the opening line. A workable outline is to divide the material into three main variations: an introductory portrait of the godly person as seen in acts of avoidance and positive actions (Ps. 1:1–2); further description of the productive life of the godly person, highlighted by the introduction of the wicked as a foil (vv. 3–4); concluding commendation of the godly person by asserting his or her eternal reward, again as contrasted to the end of the wicked (vv. 5–6). Verse 6 can also be viewed as the summarizing conclusion of a general three-part pattern.

14 "Poetry combines truth and beauty in a higher concentration than other genres." It is "abundantly artistic" (Ryken, *Sweeter Than Honey, Richer Than Gold*, 16, 17).

15 For further detail on the five elements of laments, see Leland Ryken, *Words of Delight: A Literary Introduction to the Bible*, 2nd ed. (Grand Rapids, MI: Baker Academic, 1992), 240–41.

In addition to sequential structure, most poems are organized around one or more contrasts. In Psalm 1, we find a central contrast between the godly and the wicked, or between the two ways, but also more localized contrasts between a productive harvest and the worthless chaff of harvested grain, and between final condemnation and eternal reward. Identifying these contrasts is key to properly understanding and applying the text.

Simple but Beautiful

While some of the above structural forms may seem complex, we should keep in mind that they are not as complex as many of the basic forms of Western poetry that most of us were taught in high school English class (e.g., a sonnet or an ode). In fact, they are quite simple. They are simple but beautiful. God delights, so it seems, in "the beauty of the simple,"[16] for most of the poems in our Bibles have simple structures, use simple images,[17] and often convey simple (but important) theological truths, all quite beautifully.

Step Two: Poetic Devices

The first step in reading a biblical poem is to uncover the skeletal structure of the whole poem (e.g., three parts, a chiasm) and struc-

---

16 Ryken, *Words of Delight*, 201.

17 "The biblical poets on the whole were inclined to draw on a body of more or less familiar images without consciously striving for originality of invention in their imagery" (Robert Alter, "Ancient Hebrew Poetry," in *The Literary Guide to the Bible*, ed. Robert Alter and Frank Kermode [Cambridge, MA: Harvard University, 1987], 517). "The most unliterary believer can understand that God is a rock, refuge, shepherd, or king. The simplest reader can imagine a pillow drenched with tears. Anyone can identify with drowning in grief, or imagine what it would feel like to be surrounded by lions or trapped in a cave. All of us know the pleasures of the table" (Kenneth J. Langley, *How to Preach the Psalms*, Preaching Biblical Literature [Dallas: Fontes, 2021], 32).

tures within the poem (e.g., parallel lines, contrasts). The second step is to understand the poetic devices.

If the poetic forms discussed above can be likened to the frame of a painting, the poetic devices then are the painting itself. Devices such as alliteration, apostrophes, assonance, hyperboles, metaphors, personifications, and similes add color and texture to a poem. And, like the frame/painting combination, no matter how artistic the frame might be, it is the painting and not the frame that is the focus. Our job in preaching poetry is to recognize these devices, understand what they connote, and explain the picture the poet has painted through them.

While it would be beneficial if we understood (and remembered how to spell and pronounce!) every possible poetic device—*epiphora* (repetition of final sounds or words), *paronomasia* (wordplay, including puns), *figura etymologica* (variation on word roots, often including names), *metonymy* ("naming something by means of something else with which it is closely associated"),[18] *synecdoche* ("using part of something to signify the whole phenomenon"),[19] or *merism* ("naming two opposites with the intention that we interpret these polar opposites as together encompassing everything between as well as at the poles")[20]—it is enough that we preachers know the most common ones. Following are the ones that I rank (in order of importance) the most necessary to understand. You

---

18 Ryken, *Sweeter Than Honey, Richer Than Gold*, 58. For example, when the prophet Nathan tells King David that "the sword shall never depart from your house" (2 Sam. 12:10), the image of a "sword" symbolizes violence and "house" symbolizes David's offspring.

19 Ryken, *Sweeter Than Honey, Richer Than Gold*, 58. For example, in the petition in the Lord's Prayer "give us this day our daily bread" (Matt. 6:11), the word "bread" represents whatever food and water is needed to sustain life.

20 Ryken, *Sweeter Than Honey, Richer Than Gold*, 59. For example, when David writes "You know when I sit down and when I rise up" (Ps. 139:2), he means that God knows everything about all that he does.

actually need to know what these mean if you are to handle the Bible with competency. These poetic devices are used "for dramatic effect and delight, to surprise and sustain interest, to stir emotion and aid memory, and to say a lot with a little."[21]

Metaphor and Simile

"Success in dealing with the poetry of the Bible rests especially" on understanding imagery,[22] as images are "the most prevalent thing that we encounter when we read poetry."[23] We need to understand the imagery before we try to explain, illustrate, and apply the poem.[24] The images found in metaphors and similes are pervasive in poetry. "A metaphor," Ryken explains, "is an *implied* assertion of correspondence. A simile is an *explicit* assertion of correspondence that uses the formula 'like' or 'as.' The statement 'you are all children of light' (1 Thess. 5:5) is a metaphor because it implies a comparison between how believers live and light. The statement that 'the path of the righteous is like the light of dawn' (Prov. 4:18) is a simile because it uses the formula 'like.'"[25] What metaphors and similes share is the principle of comparison: level A (the literal reference—"you are the salt of the earth," Matt. 5:13) corresponds to level B (the actual subjects and their actions—Christ's disciples and their good works).[26] They also share the principle of indirection, in that the comparison is not literally true ("the name of the

---

21 Langley, *How to Preach the Psalms*, 58.

22 Ryken, *Sweeter Than Honey, Richer Than Gold*, 21.

23 Ryken, *Sweeter Than Honey, Richer Than Gold*, 32.

24 See Leland Ryken, "Metaphor in the Psalms," *Christianity and Literature* 21.3 (1982): 13–19.

25 Ryken, *Sweeter Than Honey*, 35. "The essential principle of both metaphor and simile is analogy or correspondence, as one thing is compared to another to illuminate it" (Ryken, *Jesus the Hero*, 114).

26 "The word 'metaphor' is based on two Greek words (*meta* and *pherein*) meaning 'to carry over.' That is the essential transaction: having fully experienced the image at level A, we

LORD is a strong tower," Prov. 18:10; "the enemies of the LORD . . . vanish—like smoke," Ps. 37:20). Our job is to ask and answer the questions, "How is A (God's name) like B (a strong tower)?" and "How is A (God's enemies) like B (smoke)?"

Metaphors and similes are images that make ideas concrete, precise, memorable, lively, and engaging. When you read the metaphor, their "tongues are sharp swords" (Ps. 57:4), it gets you to stop and think—to engage in the idea.[27] Similes function similarly: "He is like a tree planted by streams of water" (Ps. 1:3). Similes use *like* or *as* to compare this with that. Metaphors assert with poetic license that this *is* that, transferring meaning from one thing to another: "Your word is a lamp to my feet" (Ps. 119:105). The point of such pictures is for the reader to sense better the truth presented. It is fine to say, "My soul feels at peace and secure," but how much better to say, "I have calmed and quieted my soul, like a weaned child with its mother" (Ps. 131:2). It is romantic enough to tell your wife, "I enjoy kissing you," but imagine how she'd respond to the poetic description, "Your lips drip nectar, my bride; honey and milk are under your tongue" (Song 4:11).

Do not underestimate the importance of imagery! Ryken argues convincingly that understanding and interpreting imagery—most notably metaphor and simile—is the most important task in explaining biblical poetry.[28] He concludes that the prime function

---

need to carry over those meanings to level B, which is the actual subject of the statement" (Ryken, *Jesus the Hero*, 114).

27 "Striking language can tease the mind into fresh insight" (Langley, *How to Preach the Psalms*, 76).

28 See Ryken's concluding remarks in *Words of Delight*, 180. See also Leland Ryken, James C. Wilhoit, and Tremper Longman III, eds., *Dictionary of Biblical Imagery* (Downers Grove, IL: IVP Academic, 1998).

of parallelism is artistic beauty and enjoyment,[29] while imagery is where the ideas come to life. If you understand the imagery, you will understand the ideas.

Personification

Personification consists of attributing human qualities to something nonhuman. For example, in the Song of Deborah, the poet writes, "Asher [the tribe, not the person] sat still at the coast of the sea" (Judg. 5:17). In the five examples below, notice how (in order) cities, body parts, abstractions, emotions, and forces of nature are given human attributes, emotions, and physical features:

- "God is in the midst of her [Jerusalem]; she shall not be moved" (Ps. 46:5)
- "their tongue struts through the earth" (Ps. 73:9)
- "righteousness and peace kiss each other" (Ps. 85:10)
- "Weeping may tarry for the night" (Ps. 30:5)
- "the meadows clothe themselves with flocks" (Ps. 65:13)

Apostrophe

Apostrophe is the device that generates strong emotions and a sense of excitement by using direct address to someone or something not present, speaking to it as though it were there. Psalm 148 features a string of them! "Praise him, sun and moon" (v. 3) is one. What C. S. Lewis said of biblical symbols is apropos for apostrophes, namely, that "people who take [them] . . . literally might as well think that when Christ told us to be like doves, He meant that we were to lay eggs."[30]

---

29 Ryken, *Words of Delight*, 183.
30 C. S. Lewis, *Mere Christianity* (1952; repr., Glasgow: HarperCollins, 1986), 119.

Hyperbole

Hyperbole is a "conscious exaggeration for the sake of effect," usually emotional effect. It is "the most nonliteral figure of speech,"[31] as the following two examples demonstrate: the shepherd's saying in the Song of Solomon, "You are altogether beautiful, my love; there is no flaw in you" (Song 4:7); and Jesus's teaching after the rich ruler walked away, that, "It is easier for a camel to go through the eye of a needle than for a rich person to enter the kingdom of God" (Matt. 19:24). Why did the wisdom sage and our Lord Jesus, the very embodiment of wisdom, use hyperbole? Ryken offers three reasons: First, to express strong feeling about a subject; second, as an effective way to express a strong conviction; third, to compel attention.[32]

Paradox

Paradox can be defined as "an apparent contradiction that, upon analysis, is seen to express a truth."[33] We are familiar with the many paradoxes in Jesus's teachings, such as "whoever would save his life will lose it, but whoever loses his life for my sake will find it" (Matt. 16:25), and in Paul's writings ("When I am weak, then I am strong," 2 Cor. 12:10). We also find many paradoxes in poetry, such as "The meek shall inherit the land" (Ps. 37:11). Paradox is subversive. "It undermines conventional ways of thinking and defies the 'wisdom' of the world."[34] It jolts readers and listeners alike out of their complacency. It teaches them to ponder the riddles of life and the afterlife.

---

31 Ryken, *Sweeter Than Honey, Richer Than Gold*, 50.
32 Ryken, *Sweeter Than Honey, Richer Than Gold*, 51.
33 Ryken, *Sweeter Than Honey, Richer Than Gold*, 56.
34 Ryken, *Complete Handbook of Literary Forms in the Bible*, 141.

Allusions

There are thousands of allusions in the biblical poems. "An allusion is a reference to past literature or history."[35] In Moses's Song, the lines "The floods stood up in a heap; / the deeps congealed in the heart of the sea" (Ex. 15:8) is an allusion to Israel's crossing the Red Sea. Obviously, the more we know about the event alluded to, the better we understand the poet's meaning.[36] "Simply by naming the previous literary passage or historical event, the poet unleashes a whole set of meanings associated with this previous thing. When we read in Psalm 136:10 that God 'struck down the firstborn of Egypt,' the poet taps into the entire story of the tenth plague. Without the allusion, the poem praising God would be thinner in meanings."[37]

Other Poetic Devices

Other poetic devices worth knowing would be obvious only if you understood the biblical languages. However, today there are many resources to help those unfamiliar with Greek, Hebrew, and Aramaic. For example, good commentaries on the Bible will point out these features. Here are some common poetic devices involving sound:

- *Wordplay.* Playful turns of phrases. In Jesus's fourth woe to the scribes and Pharisees, he labels the religious leaders "blind guides" and accuses them of "straining out a gnat and

---

35 Ryken, *Sweeter Than Honey, Richer Than Gold*, 62.

36 "Does the psalm make an allusion which was instantly familiar to its first hearers, but which is lost in our generation? The sermon might need a story or word picture that resurrects the referent for the congregation" (Langley, *How to Preach the Psalms*, 68).

37 Ryken, *Sweeter Than Honey, Richer Than Gold*, 63.

swallowing a camel!" (Matt. 23:24). These animals are used not only because of "their relative size disparity," but because "the terms for a camel (*gamlā*) and a gnat (*galmā*) sound very similar in Aramaic, which was Jesus' mother tongue."[38] Here's an example of wordplay from a biblical poem:

> The flowers appear on the earth,
>   the time of singing has come,
> and the voice of the turtledove
>   is heard in our land. (Song 2:12)

The word translated "singing" bears two different meanings. It can mean "singing," which fits with the songbird in the final line, or "pruning," which fits with the flowers metaphor.

- *Alliteration.* Alliteration is the occurrence of the same letter or sound at the beginning of adjacent or closely connected words. "The Song of Songs, which is Solomon's" (Song 1:1) is a good example in English. In Hebrew, the repetition here is called *consonance*, where the repeated *sh* sound in Hebrew in the initial consonants is apparent (*shir hashirim asher lishlomoh*). That *sh* sound followed by the *r* sound emphasizes the Hebrew word for "song" (*shir*).[39]

- *Assonance.* Assonance is another alliterative technique, that "employs the same or similar vowel (rather than consonant) sounds in accented positions."[40] For example, in the Aaronic

---

38 Jeannine K. Brown, *Introducing Biblical Hermeneutics: Scripture as Communication* (Grand Rapids, MI: Baker Academic, 2007), 145.

39 See Douglas Sean O'Donnell, *The Song of Solomon: An Invitation to Intimacy*, Preaching the Word (Wheaton, IL: Crossway, 2012), 17.

40 C. Hassell Bullock, *An Introduction to the Old Testament Poetic Books* (Chicago: Moody, 1988), 40.

blessing (Num. 6:24–26) the *sh* sound in Hebrew is heard at the end of a number of words. An example in English can be found in this simple nursery rhyme, which features a number the poetic devices including alliteration (the p-words) and assonance (the o-sound):

> Pease porridge hot, pease porridge cold,
> Pease porridge in the pot, nine days old;
> Some like it hot, some like it cold,
> Some like it in the pot, nine days old.

See the frame. Grasp its form, function, and even its beauty. But focus on the picture—the color, texture, and themes that the poetic devices above enhance.

Step Three: Emotion

In a recent blog article, my first answer to the question, "What are some tips for reading biblical poetry?" was "Feel it!" I continued, "God intended the awesome imagery of these inspired poems to engage our hearts. So, let them do just that. For example, after a recent sermon I preached on Psalm 23, I asked the congregation to answer this discussion question at home: 'Poetry should be felt in the heart, not just understood in the head. Was there a moment in the sermon, as the text was being explained or illustrated, when you got emotional? If so, what emotion did you feel and why?'"[41]

In a similar vein, Ryken writes, "Images not only embody connotations [meaning]; they also frequently awaken emotions. Poetry is a more affective (emotional) type of discourse than ordinary

---

41 Douglas Sean O'Donnell, "5 Questions about the Psalms," August 6, 2020, available at https://www.crossway.org/articles/5-questions-about-the-psalms/.

discourse. Naming the feelings that are evoked by an image is a genuine and important type of literary commentary on a poem."[42] Take Psalm 59:14–15, for example. As David recounts, "when Saul sent men to watch his house in order to kill him" (superscription), what feelings do the following images evoke?

> Each evening they come back,
>   howling like dogs
>   and prowling about the city.
> They wander about for food
>   and growl if they do not get their fill.

The answer should include "fear, helplessness, confinement, terror, disgust, and outrage" over being confined by wicked men surrounding his house.[43]

All of the images above (from just the beginning of this psalm!) give more than "cognitive content"; they offer "an emotive impact," that is, they help us both understand and feel, and thus participate cognitively and emotionally with the picture they paint.[44] For example, when the psalmist uses the metaphor of a weaned child in her mother's arms to symbolize the state of his soul under God's

---

42 Ryken, *Sweeter Than Honey, Richer Than Gold*, 27. "The chief identifying trait of lyric poetry is its affective element. . . . Sometimes they address our emotions directly by naming them: fear (Pss 2:11–12 and 5:7), joy (5:11; 21:6; 100:2), awe, (Pss 8, 139), peace (4:8), comfort (119:76), contrition (51:17; 119:71), relief from distress (4:1; 20:1), confidence (27:3; 46:2–3), and hope (42:5) are among the emotions modeled, commended, or commanded in the Psalter. So is love for God's Word: 'O how I love your law!' (119:97); 'I delight in your decrees' (119:16). . . . The psalmists acknowledge and express depression (32:3–4), broken heartedness (34:18), soul weariness (119:28), anger (109:1–3, 6–12), anxiety (12:1; 22:21), keen longing (143:7) and deep sorrow (Pss 6 and 88)" (Langley, *How to Preach the Psalms*, 12).

43 Ryken, *Sweeter Than Honey, Richer Than Gold*, 28.

44 Brown, *Introducing Biblical Hermeneutics*, 143.

care, it helps us understand something of the intimacy of our relationship with God, and it helps us feel, Lord willing, closer to the Lord. As Jeannine Brown summarizes nicely,

> Images engage our feelings as well as inspire our thinking. Some images intend to comfort ("The Lord is my shepherd"; Ps. 23:1), others alarm ("Roaring lions tearing their prey open with their mouths wide against me"; Ps. 22:13). Metaphors often raise our ire or startle us. In addition, by using sound and form creatively and with care, poets woo us and captivate us. Poetry draws us into a place of responsiveness with our whole being. Poetry is meta-cognitive; it does more, not less, than communicate on a cognitive level.[45]

Langley adds, "Poetry knows that man does not live by propositions alone. It tries, more self-consciously than prose, to change us by moving our emotions, gripping our imaginations, and addressing our sense of beauty. . . . Preachers, therefore, will want to figure out how sermons on poetic texts can engage affective, imaginative, and aesthetic sense, and will ask whether the literary features of the poems themselves may hold clues as to how such sermons might shape themselves."[46]

HOW TO PREACH BIBLICAL POETRY

I agree with Douglas Stuart's simple suggestion: "If the passage is poetic, analyze it accordingly."[47] So, yes, we should look for any

---

45 Brown, *Introducing Biblical Hermeneutics*, 148.
46 Langley, *How to Preach the Psalms*, 11.
47 Douglas Stuart, *Old Testament Exegesis: A Handbook for Students and Pastors*, 3rd ed. (Louisville: Westminster, 2001), 19.

possible parallelisms, chiasms, key-word repetitions, and more subtle characteristics such as governing metaphors and changes in metaphors. However, not everything we see in a biblical poem should be preached in a sermon. Below are eight suggestions for preaching a prose sermon on a biblical poem.[48]

Pick Poetic Portions Properly

How's that for an absolutely awesome alliteration? Concerning how to choose a pericope, Duane Garrett advises, "Select a portion of the text that has structural integrity."[49] The example Garrett gives comes from Psalm 119. Due to that poem's length, he suggests preaching on one of the twenty-two sections, e.g., the *beth* verses (vv. 9–16), or at least one section at a time. When I preached Psalm 119, I did so in three sermons, dividing the poem thematically, based on images and key words: (1) knowing God's Word, (2) loving God's Word, and (3) obeying God's Word. I took verse 32 as the summary verse: "I will run in the way of your commandments when you enlarge my heart!" I think both methods can work—either selecting the poetic unit or taking your cue from the imagery and allowing that imagery to lead you to similar ideas found throughout the poem.

Let the Form Inform

In his book *Expositional Preaching: How We Speak God's Word Today*, David Helm defines expositional preaching as "empowered preaching that rightfully submits the shape and emphasis of the sermon to the shape and emphasis of a biblical text." Put differently, he states

---

48 Some of these suggestions can be found in Douglas Sean O'Donnell, *The Beginning and End of Wisdom: Preaching Christ from the First and Last Chapters of Proverbs, Ecclesiastes, and Job* (Wheaton, IL: Crossway, 2011), 148–51.

49 Duane A. Garrett, "Preaching from the Psalms and Proverbs," in *Preaching the Old Testament*, ed. Scott M. Gibson (Grand Rapids, MI: Baker, 2006), 102.

that "when it comes to preaching . . . every text has a structure, the structure reveals the emphasis," and our sermons "should be rightfully submitted to the shape and emphasis of the text."[50] Unlike a *narrative*, where the structure can be found by focusing on the shift in scenes and/or characters, along with the typical parts of a plot (setting, conflict, climax, and resolution), a *poem* demands that we look for "repetitions of words or even entire stanzas . . . changes in imagery . . . [and/or] shifts in person or point of view."[51]

Take, for example, Psalm 19. How has King David organized this poem? David has organized his thought with a threefold structure:

Verses 1–6	David's praise of God's revelation in creation
Verses 7–11	David's praise of God's revelation in the law
Verses 12–14	David's response to divine revelation

When I preached Psalm 19, my homiletic outline was as follows:

Verses 1–6	The heavens speak (general revelation)
Verses 7–11	The Scriptures speak (special revelation)
Verses 12–14	How we should listen (responding to the two voices)

However, a poem's structure does not necessarily make for a good sermon outline. For example, a sermon on Job 28 can be outlined based on the refrain (vv. 12 and 20), or it can be outlined based on key theological words (vv. 1–22 speak of man's pursuit of wisdom; then, in vv. 23–28, God with his wisdom enters and

---

50 David R. Helm, *Expositional Preaching: How We Speak God's Word Today* (Wheaton, IL: Crossway, 2014), 52.

51 Helm, *Expositional Preaching*, 56. "What the poets give us is not narrative but narrativity—which is to say, the narrative development of metaphor" (Robert Alter, *The Art of Biblical Poetry* [New York: Harper-Collins, 1985], 39).

answers the refrain's dilemma, "Where shall wisdom be found?"). When I preached Job 28, the poetic form *informed*, but the three theological themes *formed* my outline:

Verses 1–11   The wisdom of man
Verses 12–22   The inaccessibility of man's wisdom
Verses 23–28   The wisdom of God

Similarly, when I preached on Proverbs 31:10–31, I did not present a sermon outline based on the poem's chiastic (6 points, followed by a seventh main point!) or acrostic (22 points!) structure. Rather, my structure played off the themes that open (finding an excellent wife) and close (praise for that wife) the poem. Thus, the congregation walked through the text by answering first the question, "What should a man look for in a wife?" ("beauty marks," like trust and industry), and second, "How does a woman earn the praise of the world around her?" (by serving others).[52]

This is also true for many of the poems we find in the New Testament. The structure of most poems can be used for the homiletical outline. For example, when I preached on 1 Corinthians 13, I organized the text as follows:

Verses 1–3   The preeminence of love
Verses 4–7   The power of love[53]
Verses 8–13   The permanence of love

---

52 This sermon can be found in O'Donnell, *Beginning and End of Wisdom*, 47–60.
53 However, when I preached this sermon, I preached verses 4–7 last, both for emphasis and to conclude with the Christological connection. I spoke of the power of the cross (see 1 Cor. 1:17–18) as the power to save and unite. The church can live in loving harmony only if Christ-like/the cross-of-Christ-like love permeates the church, a love that is not envious, arrogant, irritable, or selfishly insistent.

However, the preaching structure for other poems should be adjusted to better cover the material. For example, when I preached on the Beatitudes (Matt. 5:3–10), I divided the poem thematically based on the grammatical changes. That is, I noticed that there are eight beatitudes,[54] but I also noticed that the first and last blessings conclude with the identical phrase "for theirs is the kingdom of heaven" (vv. 3, 10). I also took note of future promises—"for they shall . . ." (vv. 4, 5, 6, 7, 8, 9). Thus, my three points for this poem were (1) a broken blessedness, which covered the phrases "the poor in spirit," "those who mourn," "the meek," and "those who hunger and thirst for righteousness" (vv. 3–6); (2) a future blessedness, which covered the second halves of verses 4–9; and (3) a selfless blessedness, which revisited each beatitude, showing how the focus for each beatitude is God- and/or others-centered.[55]

So, as demonstrated above, the poetic form informs, but it does not necessarily give you a sermon outline. This is because, as Garrett well summarizes, "what works well in a poem may not work well in a speech."[56]

Uncover the Core Content

"We have never adequately grasped a poem if we do not, after analysis, formulate the big idea of the poem."[57] There are four ways to uncover the big idea or unifying theme of a poem.

First, identify the subgenre. Is this a love song, a poem of praise, hymn of thanksgiving, a lament, etc.?

Second, if possible, identify the historical context. Is the poet addressing God in prayer? Is he coping with slander? Is the implied

---

54 The word "blessed" is repeated nine times, but the final two comprise one beatitude.
55 Douglas Sean O'Donnell, *Matthew: All Authority in Heaven and on Earth*, Preaching the Word (Wheaton, IL: Crossway, 2013), 109–16.
56 Garrett, "Preaching from the Psalms and Proverbs," 103.
57 Ryken, *Sweeter Than Honey, Richer Than Gold*, 85.

situation one of worship in the temple, or a shepherd's care for sheep during the course of a typical day?

Third, see what the poet says at the start and stop of the poem. For example, the opening lines of Psalm 1 introduce its theme (the blessing of the righteous), the foil (the wicked), and even the structure (the righteous versus the wicked). Likewise, the final line of Psalm 46 offers an excellent summary of the poem: "The LORD of hosts is with us; the God of Jacob is our fortress" (v. 11).

Fourth, look for refrains and repetitions. Some biblical poems have a refrain, which is a phrase or sentence that appears at least twice. This should be easy to find, and once found, one may assume such repetition reveals the poem's theme. The most obvious example would be the refrain (repeated twenty-six times, at the end of each verse) in Psalm 136, "His steadfast love endures forever."[58] Other examples include Psalms 42–43 (42:5–6a, 11; 43:5): "Why are you cast down, O my soul, and why are you in turmoil within me? Hope in God; for I shall again praise him, my salvation and my God"; and the Song of Solomon (2:7; 3:5; 8:4): "I adjure you, O daughters of Jerusalem . . . that you not stir up or awaken love until it pleases." The Song of Solomon uses both a strict refrain (2:7; 3:5; 8:4) and a variant refrain (2:16 is inverted in 6:3 and abbreviated in 7:10). Other biblical poems have repeated words, key words, which function in the same way as refrains, such as "voice" (seven times) in Psalm 29, "all" (seventeen times) in Psalm 145, and "vanity" (more than thirty times) in Ecclesiastes.

Other kinds of repetition include "*inclusio*, beginning and ending the poem with the same word or motif (Psalms 8, 118, 136,

---

58 Refrains can be found from beginning to end (as in Psalm 136). They can also be found in the middle (see Psalms 39:5, 11; 67:3, 5), and at the middle and the end (see Psalms 46:7, 11; 49:12, 20; 57:5, 11; 80:7, 19; 99:5, 9).

and the 'Halleluiah' psalms 146–150); *apostrophe*, as in Psalms 115:9–11 and 118:2–4, with the only variation being the names inserted in the repeated phrase; *anaphora*, in which a key word or phrase is repeated with incremental advance in thought with each repetition (the 'How many?' of Psalm 3 and the 'How long?' of Psalm 13); and *echo*, as in Psalm 130:6, with its plaintive lines:

"My soul waits for the Lord
    more than watchmen wait for the morning,
    more than watchmen wait for the morning."[59]

Take Psalm 23. Ryken summarizes the theme of this famous psalm as "the contentment that comes from resting in the sufficiency of God's providence." That unifying theme ("the literary motif that unites the entire poem and to which all the parts relate") is supported by various pictures of provision: "noontime rest in an oasis-type place (lying down in green pastures); leading the sheep in safe paths during the course of the day; protecting sheep from fear in dangerous places on the path; finding strips of grass for grazing (the prepared table); protecting the sheep from predators and poisonous plants (the enemies of v. 5); dealing with scratches or cuts and attending to fevered sheep (the anointed head and overflowing cup); and safety overnight in the sheepfold (the metaphoric 'house' at the end of the poem)."[60]

An Acronym for Analysis (Or Rather: Sunday Exposition and Exhortation!)

DOA. This acronym does not mean "dead on arrival" (although the idea is close to DOD "dead on delivery") but rather "don't

---

59 Langley, *How to Preach the Psalms*, 62–63.
60 Ryken, *Sweeter Than Honey, Richer Than Gold*, 82, 92–93.

over-analyze." That is, don't over-analyze *in* your sermon. Analyze the poetry in the study, but don't analyze every aspect of it from the pulpit. After all, this is a sermon. And sermons should be clear and interesting, and there are few things more ambiguous and boring than listening to lectures on poetry. Would you rather see Macbeth acted out on stage or hear an erudite academic talk about the thane of Glamis's 146 lines?

Matthew Arnold wrote, "The language of the Bible is fluid . . . and literary, not rigid, fixed, scientific."[61] He is right. The Bible is not a mind-numbing, high-minded scientific journal. (No offense to the scientific community!) It is living literature. Thus, we must show its liveliness. This means we should not "mechanically grind every poem," showing our congregations every structural form and poetic device.[62] Apply aesthetic minimalism to preaching poetry— "less is more" or "less is better."[63] Hide that ugly radiator in the floorboards. Strip the poem down to its most fundamental features, thus highlighting that beautiful simplicity. Always point out what is important (e.g., the acrostic structure of Psalm 119), but only point out what you think is most relevant to the point of the poem.

Allow the Imagery to Embellish the Idea

Ryken notes, "It is important for an audience that an explication [exposition or sermon] possess *a discernable strategy.* Jumping from one isolated detail to another, or from one part of a poem to another, is a sure path to an ineffective explication."[64] Each biblical

---

61 Matthew Arnold, *Literature and Dogma: An Essay towards a Better Apprehension of the Bible* (New York: MacMillan, 1914), xiii.

62 Ryken, *Words of Delight*, 210.

63 The first term was used by architect Ludwig Mies van der Rohe; the second by industrial designer Dieter Rams.

64 Ryken, *Words of Delight*, 207.

poem or unit within a poem has a unifying idea or theme, which every line, and perhaps every word, embellishes. My discernable strategy is (a) to find this idea, and (b) to explain how the imagery adorns it. Sadly, our sermons often simply identify, emphasize, and explain the idea,[65] while our commentaries often do the opposite: they give us plenty of information on the imagery but almost nothing on how such imagery fits into the idea. So put them together, and there you have it. Perfection.

For example, in my sermon on Song of Solomon 1:5–2:7,[66] I explained *the idea* of the beloved's transformation from negative self-perception to rapturous acceptance. And throughout the exposition I showed how each image enhanced the idea: she is ashamed of her looks because her skin has been blackened by the sun—"I am very dark . . . like the tents of Kedar" (1:5) / "Do not gaze at me because I am dark, because the sun has looked upon me" (1:6). She views herself as common, like a common countryside wildflower ("a lily of the valleys," 2:1). However, the beloved overturns her self-objections with his loving affirmation: "as a lily among brambles, so is my love among the young women" (2:2). Compared to all the women in the world, she is the best-looking and the only one worth eyeing.

In my above analysis I show, first, that the poet has "a game plan in mind based on the logic" of his images, and, second, "that exploring the logic of images is a very fruitful avenue to seeing how a

---

65 Sermons on a biblical a poem "should not flatten its poetry into prose," but should "seek to recreate the poem's sequence of images." For example, for Psalm 46, the preacher should "help listeners respond emotionally and imaginatively to the earthquake, river, battle, and especially fortress" (Langley, *How to Preach the Psalms*, 29).

66 See O'Donnell, *Song of Solomon: An Invitation to Intimacy*, 41–52. My ten sermons on the Song of Solomon can be found at https://www.youtube.com/channel/UCCe0I8FA_Nq0uS_ICuNBP1g.

passage of poetry gains its effects and communicates its meanings."[67] Images in the biblical poems do not merely awaken emotions; they communicate ideas. And for the poems of the Bible, as for any great poems, "we need to explore the connection between a given image and the subject of the poem or passage. A good question to ask in this regard is, Why this image for this poem or passage? What is the logic of it?"[68]

Paint the Picture

The other day, I asked my youngest daughter what she thought of my sermon on Sunday. She said, "I liked it." She paused and then completed her thought: "I liked it because it had lots of stories." After preaching for nearly three decades, I have learned that people—little girls, old men, and everyone in between—like stories. I have also learned that people like pictures. People think visually. People learn visually. When I was studying for my oral defense of my PhD dissertation, I watched dozens of videos from important scholars on key issues I might be asked about. Seeing someone talk, and seeing their lecture outlines on a screen, helped the facts I needed to know stick in my brain. The same is true of preaching poems. We should preach the imagery of biblical poetry with illustrative imagination!

For example, when I preached on Ecclesiastes 2:1–11, which is poetic verse retelling the story of Solomon's unfulfilling self-indulgence, I titled the sermon, "The Hollow House of Hedonism" and I used the picture of a house with four rooms to walk us through the text:

---

67 Ryken, *Sweeter Than Honey, Richer Than Gold*, 30.
68 Ryken, *Sweeter Than Honey, Richer Than Gold*, 30.

Here in the text . . . Pastor Solomon takes us to a place that we can name the *hollow house of hedonism*. Yes, the house is filled with wine and women, gardens and gold, songs and servants; but it is hollow when it comes to satisfying our deepest needs.

Within the hollow house of hedonism there are many rooms. Solomon will show us four of them in Ecclesiastes 2:1–11: the private pub, the garden, the treasury, and the bedroom. Take my hand now and I'll show you. Be careful, though, for seeing what Solomon saw might tempt you to want what he had. And that is not what we should truly *desire*.[69]

Preaching with pictures, however, is more than finding a visual (and thus, usually memorable) outline. It is also about explaining the details of the text so that people can see what God's Word is saying to them. Here is another example from Ecclesiastes. As I explained the imagery of the increase of bodily frailties before natural death, I sought to make visible the imagery of this awful reality:

Like a once-vibrant but now-unattended estate, our hands, legs, teeth, eyes, ears, vocal cords, and hair slowly deteriorate. Our hands, which once provided a living and protection, now shake ("in the day when the keepers of the house tremble"), our legs can't support the weight of our bodies for long ("and the strong men are bent"), our remaining molars can't chew food like they used to ("the grinders cease because they are few"), and our vision declines ("those who look through the windows are dimmed," Eccl. 12:3).

And if all that were not bad enough, other awful issues accompany old age. When we want our ears to work well, they

69 Douglas Sean O'Donnell, *Ecclesiastes: Enjoyment East of Eden*, Reformed Expository Commentary (Phillipsburg, NJ: P&R, 2014), 43.

don't (we can't even hear ourselves chew: "and the doors on the street are shut—when the sound of the grinding is low"), but when we would be fine with deafness, our ears work too well ("and one rises up at the sound of a bird," Eccl. 12:4). Moreover, we cannot sing like we used to. Our vocal cords "no longer have the elastic strength to make sweet music" or hit the high notes ("and all the daughters of song are brought low," v. 4b).

Finally, before we die (go to our "eternal home") and people grieve our passing ("and the mourners go about in the streets"), our hair turns gray or white ("the almond tree blossoms"), we lose our mobility and get around painfully ("the grasshopper drags itself along"), our motivation to work, our appetite for food, and our sex drive diminishes ("desire fails"), and a fear of falling and of other dangers increases ("they are afraid also of what is high, and terrors are in the way," Eccl. 12:5). And then the moment comes! What was once beautiful, precious, useful, and life-giving is destroyed ("the silver cord is snapped, or the golden bowl is broken, or the pitcher is shattered at the fountain, or the wheel broken at the cistern," v. 6). Light crashes to the ground and life spills out like water. "Life is broken beyond repair. Death is final and irreversible."[70]

Feel the Fire

The Song of Solomon is the perfect place to return to for this final point. If you preach the words, "Arise, my love, my beautiful one, and come away" (2:10), with the same intonation and affection as

70 O'Donnell, *Ecclesiastes: Enjoyment East of Eden*, 199–200. The first quote is from Philip Graham Ryken, *Ecclesiastes: Why Everything Matters*, Preaching the Word (Wheaton, IL: Crossway, 2010), 270; the second quote is from Sidney Greidanus, *Preaching Christ from Ecclesiastes: Foundations for Expository Sermons* (Grand Rapids, MI: Eerdmans, 2010), 293.

when you timidly turn to the passenger seat and ask your wife for driving directions, you've missed it. You must preach passion with passion, lament with lamentation, joy with joy, and so on. In other words, your heart should be so engaged that your tone is in tune with the lyrics. To preach, "As a deer pants for flowing streams, so pants my soul for you" (Ps. 42:1), without spiritual thirst in your voice is intolerable, and to preach, "My God, my God, why have you forsaken me?" (Ps. 22:1a), without anguish is unacceptable.

So while the question, "How did this passage make you feel?" is often a recipe for disaster in your average church Bible study, it is a very appropriate question for the preacher to ask himself, especially once all the details of the poetic structure and devices are in his head.[71] Feelings aren't everything, but they are something, something indispensable for the humble preacher of faithful sermons on the Bible's great poems. Thus, it is absolutely necessary for us to first understand and feel the power and play of words, what only poetry can do to the human heart and imagination. We should, in a sense (and with our senses), *smell* the frankincense, *touch* the polished ivory, *taste* the apples, *hear* the flowing streams, *see* the gazelles leaping over the mountains, feel (yes, feel!) the flashes of fire, the very flame of the LORD.[72]

---

71 Identifying a poem's tone or emotional mood is as crucial as, or even more crucial than, understanding its exegetical structure.

72 "Biblical poets express, model, commend and command deep feeling: joy, grief, gratitude, awe, reverence, contrition, fear, brokenness, elation, disappointment, loneliness, and even hatred are all evoked and expressed in relation to God. The psalmists do not merely report on their emotional experience; they invite us to make our own affective response to the reality of God, and they extend that invitation in richly emotive speech. Sermons on their psalms should attempt to do the same. We who preach psalms will try to help listeners join the psalmists in naming and learning from our shared affective experience. Together we'll explore what emotions can teach us about what's going on in our relationship to God and others. If this is going to happen, we will have to learn three skills or disciplines: (1) exegeting the emotion of texts, (2) sensing what the Spirit wants us to feel in appropriating these texts,

Every Word Counts; So, Lower Your Word Count

One final shortly stated suggestion. Compression is a trait of poetry. "Poetic language," as Langley well summarizes, "is compressed, densely packed."[73] Psalm 78, and other historical psalms (105; 106; 107; 114; 135; 136), cover years of salvation history in a very few lines. If these inspired poems can accomplish that important task in so few words, perhaps a sermon on such poems, and every other genre, can be compressed from 5,000 words to 3,000 words. Again, Langley's words on words are wise (and carefully crafted and concise): "What matters is not word count but that every word count."[74] By Thursday, I usually have a good draft of my sermon. What I do from Friday till the Sunday service is carefully edit. I change or explain difficult words. I shorten sentences. I diversify sentences—short and long, rhythmic and plain. I make sure each sentence is interesting to me. (If I'm not excited about preaching it, people likely won't be excited about hearing it.). I also delete lifeless words and replace them with something vivid and vital.

CONCLUSION

In his book *Sweeter Than Honey, Richer Than Gold: A Guided Study of Biblical Poetry*, Ryken lists four reasons people find it difficult to immerse themselves in the poetry of the Bible: it is too difficult to understand; optional in a person's life, not necessary for everyone; an unnatural form of discourse and therefore does not appeal to

---

and (3) helping listeners experience the emotional dimension of texts by how we shape and deliver sermons. More briefly, we have to know it, feel it, and then say it" (Langley, *How to Preach the Psalms*, 111–12). Our task as preachers is to "try to name what the [poet] felt as precisely as possible: is it anger? bitterness? weariness? defiance? bewilderment? gratitude? love? awe? relief? hope?" (116).

73 Langley, *How to Preach the Psalms*, 88.

74 Langley, *How to Preach the Psalms*, 88.

ordinary people; not worth the effort that it takes to master it.[75] Many preachers I know would express those same concerns. As Ryken, in that book, went on to answer those concerns, so I hope we have answered whatever concerns or hesitations you might have had. Put differently, I hope you know that learning how to read biblical poetry isn't as difficult as most think, that it is necessary to understand if one seeks to read through the Bible, that it is a natural, or at the least most fitting, way to talk about certain truths, and that it is definitely worth the effort of mastering it.

BUILD YOUR LIBRARY! HELPFUL RESOURCES

Alter, Robert. *The Art of Biblical Poetry*. New York: Basic Books, 1985.

Garrett, Duane A. "Preaching from the Psalms and Proverbs." In *Preaching the Old Testament*, edited by Scott M. Gibson, 101–14. Grand Rapids, MI: Baker, 2006.

Greidanus, Sidney. *Preaching Christ from Ecclesiastes: Foundations for Expository Sermons*. Grand Rapids, MI: Eerdmans, 2010.

Klein, George L. "Preaching Poetry." In *Reclaiming the Prophetic Mantle*, edited by George L. Klein, 59–77. Nashville: Broadman, 1992.

Langley, Kenneth J. *How to Preach the Psalms*, Preaching Biblical Literature. Dallas: Fontes, 2021.

Ryken, Leland. *Sweeter Than Honey, Richer Than Gold: A Guided Study of Biblical Poetry*. Reading the Bible as Literature. Bellingham, WA: Lexham, 2015.

Ryken, Leland, James C. Wilhoit, and Tremper Longman III, eds. *Dictionary of Biblical Imagery*. Downers Grove, IL: InterVarsity Academic, 1998.

---

75 Ryken, *Sweeter Than Honey, Richer Than Gold*, 12–13.

5

Words of Wisdom

Preaching Proverbs

EARLY LAST SPRING, I received this email from my youngest daughter's principal:

> I am wondering if you would be interested in being our graduation speaker? This is basically a charge to the graduates (especially spiritually and academically) for their years ahead but could also include some fond memories of Charlotte's class over the last few years. I am looking for 10-15 minutes. Would you have interest and availability? Thanks so much for considering!

After my agent who handles middle school speaking engagements negotiated terms ("money answers everything," Eccles. 10:19), I gladly replied, "Yes! I'm happy to speak." The next thing I did was pencil down on some scrap paper, "Go with three proverbial sayings." I jotted down tame the tongue, the race is not to the swift, and my grace is sufficient.

The Bible's proverbial maxims are perfect for such occasions. They are also great for personal daily devotions: a chapter of Proverbs a day keeps the fool in you at bay! They work well for small group studies, retreats, and one-on-one counseling. Speaking of one-on-one counseling, proverbs are best used for what they were designed for: "They are most effective," suggests Ryken, "when we can take them to a situation in life,"[1] and when we can fetch a proverb from the library of our memory and use it as a diagnosis and corrective for something in life. For example, when a friend is experiencing anxiety, we soothe him with the words, "Consider the lilies of the field" (Matt. 6:28); or, when we notice a brother is forming lazy habits, we prod him with, "All hard work brings a profit, but mere talk leads only to poverty" (Prov. 14:23 NIV); or when someone is struggling with envying the wealthy, we cite, "Godliness with contentment is great gain" (1 Tim. 6:6). Proverbs were designed to accurately observe human experience, help explain it, and offer God's proven wisdom into it.

But what about Sunday morning preaching? Should we preach proverbs? We *should*, especially if we want to preach through Proverbs, Ecclesiastes, Job, the Sermon on the Mount, and James. And we had *better* do so if we want to preach through just about any book of the Bible, as proverbs occur throughout God's Word. After listing eleven—e.g., sin will find you out (Num. 32:23); render to Caesar the things that are Caesar's, and to God the things that are God's (Mark 12:17); whatever a person sows, that he will also reap (Gal. 6:7)—Ryken states that "proverb is obviously a major

---

1 Leland Ryken, *Words of Delight: A Literary Introduction to the Bible* (Grand Rapids, MI: Baker, 1992), 316. "The best context for a proverb is the real-life situation where it applies" (Leland Ryken, Philip Ryken, and James Wilhoit, *Ryken's Bible Handbook: A Guide to Reading and Studying the Bible* [Carol Stream, IL: Tyndale, 2005], 256).

literary form of the Bible," and that "no form is more central to the teaching of the Bible than its proverbs."[2] The genre permeates the Bible from start to finish.[3] Did you know that? You know it now! Do you believe that now? We hope so. And if so, your next question, preacher, should be, "How do I preach proverbs?" In what follows, we offer answers. We also will showcase (a bonus for reading this far in the book!) how we can use what we find in proverbs to help our preaching of every genre.

HOW TO READ BIBLICAL PROVERBS

A proverb is a catchy, concise couplet that clearly captures a crucial concept. Said without alliteration, and thus more accurate but less memorable, a proverb is a saying that summarizes succinctly an important issue of life using specific concrete images, memorable words, and poetic structures that offer simple but profound practical wisdom. Or something like that. Ryken goes with, "A proverb is a concise, memorable statement of a general truth. . . . A proverb is an insight into the repeatable situations of life, and its aim is to make an insight permanent by expressing it in a short, memorable saying."[4] Someone named Cervantes texted me his offering: "A short sentence founded upon long experience, containing a truth." An anonymous author offered this

---

2 Ryken, *Words of Delight*, 313, 314. Cf. Robert C. Tannehill, "Proverb as a Literary Form," in *The New Testament in Literary Criticism*, ed. Leland Ryken, A Library of Literary Criticism (New York: Ungar, 1984).

3 Jeffrey D. Arthurs, *Preaching with Variety: How to Re-Create the Dynamics of Biblical Genres* (Grand Rapids, MI: Kregel, 2007), 130. Arthurs cites a prominent NT scholar who estimates that there are more than a hundred aphorisms in the four Gospels.

4 *Ryken's Bible Handbook*, 257. Elsewhere, Lee writes that a proverb is "a concise, memorable statement of truth—in the words of the English poet Alexander Pope, 'What oft was thought, but ne'er so well expressed'" (Leland Ryken, "Introduction," in *The Literary Study Bible, English Standard Version* [Wheaton, IL: Crossway, 2019], xxii).

okay effort: "A winged word, outliving the fleeting moment."[5] Whatever the best definition, the characteristics of the genre are evident. We offer eleven.

The Focus

Every culture around the world, and throughout world history, creates poems, stories, and proverbs. These are universal literary forms. Some world proverbs include,

It is the patient person who will milk a barren cow. (Ghanaian)

Talk does not cook rice. (Chinese)

Early to bed and early to rise, makes a man healthy, wealthy, and wise. (American)

Never argue with a fool; people might not know the difference. (Irish)

And here are some proverbs about proverbs:

As a boy should resemble his father, so should the proverb fit the conversation. (Ethiopian)

A proverb is the quintessentially active bit of language. (Turkish)

Honey is sweet to the mouth; proverb is music to the ear. (Tibetan)

5　These definitions are given in Arthurs, *Preaching with Variety*, 131.

What sets biblical proverbs apart from other proverbs is, obviously, that they are found in the Bible. Less obviously, but just as important, is that they focus on the God of the Bible. The opening prologue of Proverbs ends, "The fear of the LORD is the beginning of knowledge" (Prov. 1:7). The controlling principle for obtaining and amassing wisdom is not natural, acquired, or experienced intelligence that is unrelated to YHWH. It is the fear of God, which can be defined in Proverbs as "a continual (Prov. 23:17), humble, and faithful submission to Yahweh, which compels one to hate evil (8:13) and turn away from it (16:6) and brings with it rewards better than all earthly treasures (15:16)—the rewards of a love for and a knowledge of God (1:29; 2:5; 9:10; 15:33), and long life (10:27; 14:27a; 19:23a), confidence (14:26), satisfaction, and protection (19:23)."[6] The Bible's answer to the question "Where shall wisdom be found?" (Job 28:12) is "the fear of the Lord, that is wisdom" (Job 28:28; cf. Prov. 1:7; 9:10; Eccles. 12:13); it is a wisdom that comes from above and comes only "to those who take refuge in him" (Prov. 30:5). Tremper Longman summarizes the point we are attempting to make quite well, and adds an important Christ-centered dimension:

Proverbs is so much more than a collection of well-crafted insights into living. It is a thoroughly theological book, confronting us from the very beginning with the most fundamental of choices: What is or should be the driving force of my life? Will I enter a relationship with Wisdom or Folly? with God or

---

6   Douglas Sean O'Donnell, *The Beginning and End of Wisdom* (Wheaton, IL: Crossway, 2011), 37. In my commentary on Ecclesiastes, I summarize the concept in this way: "Those who, in the midst of all the hard truths and awful troubles of this fallen world, come before the Lord with *trembling trust* are given by him the gift of grateful obedience, steady contentment, and surprising joy" (Douglas Sean O'Donnell, *Ecclesiastes: Enjoyment East of Eden*, Reformed Expository Commentary [Phillipsburg, NJ: P&R, 2014], 9).

idols? A particular choice faces the Christian reader: In light of the New Testament's teaching on the nature of wisdom, is Jesus Christ, the epitome of God's wisdom, at the center of my life's decisions and actions?[7]

The Goal

The goal of Proverbs, as would be true of all the proverbs in the Bible, is "to lead readers to live a morally and spiritually ordered life by imparting wisdom (skill for living) that covers a wide range of human experience. Right thinking and right acting are the author's goals for his audience."[8] This is clearly expressed in Proverbs 1:2–6:

> To know wisdom and instruction,
>> to understand words of insight,
> to receive instruction in wise dealing,
>> in righteousness, justice, and equity;
> to give prudence to the simple,
>> knowledge and discretion to the youth—
> Let the wise hear and increase in learning,
>> and the one who understands obtain guidance,
> to understand a proverb and a saying,
>> the words of the wise and their riddles.

Here Solomon calls everyone who needs everyday wisdom—the young, the simple, and those already wise—to listen up. And he offers *practical* wisdom ("instruction in wise dealing" and "prudence . . . and knowledge and discretion," vv. 3–4); *intellectual*

---

7 Tremper Longman III, *How to Read Proverbs* (Downers Grove, IL: IVP Academic, 2002), 158.
8 *Ryken's Bible Handbook*, 251.

wisdom (insight into insightful words, vv. 2b, 4b); *moral* wisdom ("instruction . . . in righteousness, justice, and equity," v. 3b); and *mysterious* wisdom ("guidance" and the ability to understand or comprehend "the words of the wise and their riddles," vv. 5–6, difficult or complex concepts and sayings).[9] Our goal in preaching proverbs is to do the same.

Authoritative Tone

While all the books of the Bible assume a relationship between an authoritative leader (the author) and his subordinates (the audience), the book of Proverbs, and other biblical books wherein proverbs are found, assume more specifically a teacher-disciple relationship. David exhorts Solomon, King Lemuel's mother instructs her son, Lady Wisdom calls out to young men, and Jesus sits in authority on a mountain and teaches his disciples. This characteristic makes "proverbs sound authoritative."[10] They are wise words from wise people that were passed down from generation to generation, and thus in every present generation they are to be heeded.[11]

The Diverse Drumbeat

There is a certain monotony to a list of proverbs, most of which share a similar parallel structure. However, if you look and listen

---

9 See Duane A. Garrett, *Proverbs, Ecclesiastes, and Songs of Songs*, New American Commentary (Nashville: Broadman, 1993), 67–68.

10 Barbara Kirshenblatt-Gimblett, "Toward a Theory of Proverb Meaning," in *The Wisdom of Many*, ed. Wolfgang Meider and Alan Dundes (New York: Garland, 1981), 111.

11 "The wise men of ancient cultures possessed four chief traits: (1) they were careful observers of the human condition; (2) they were teachers; (3) they were masters of a particular kind of discourse (the proverb); (4) they were authority figures who asserted their wisdom without apology or reservation" (Ryken, "Introduction to Proverbs," 953).

carefully, there are a number of subgenres within this genre. For example, in the opening unit of Proverbs, we find an oration from Lady Wisdom (1:20–33); an encomium in praise of wisdom (3:13–20); and a father's dramatic monologue to his son, wherein he summons his son to listen, motivates and admonishes him how to act, and catalogs the consequences of disobedience (3:21–4:27). Proverbs 1–9 concludes with a temptation story (ch. 7), another oration from Lady Wisdom (ch. 8), and a narrative which leaves the reader with a choice between wisdom and folly (ch. 9).

Moments of Epiphany

Ryken labels proverbs "moments of epiphany" because they distill in a few lines a thousand stories of human experience.[12] Proverbs makes, he says, "an insight permanent" or memorable "by epigram-matizing an experience."[13] What emerges from the proverbs of the Bible, and preeminently from the books comprised wholly or mainly of proverbs, is a sense of life. Proverbs put us in touch with life as it is lived. As we immerse ourselves in the wisdom literature, virtually all of life passes before us, as captured by the French idiom *comédie humaine* ("the whole variety of life"). As such, this genre has the appeal of the authentic human voice, providing a good complement to theological preaching with its doctrinal abstractions. "I tell my classes," Lee says, "that the task of a literary author

---

12 Leland Ryken, *How to Read the Bible as Literature* (Grand Rapids, MI: Zondervan, 1984), 124. "Literature is the human race's testimony to its own experience, and proverbs do it as well as any other genre" (Leland Ryken, *Short Sentences Long Remembered: A Guided Story of Proverbs and Other Wisdom Literature*, Reading the Bible as Literature [Wooster, OH: Weaver, 2016], 56).

13 Leland Ryken, "Proverb as Literary Form," in *Dictionary of Biblical Imagery*, ed. Leland Ryken, James C. Wilhoit, and Tremper Longman III (Downers Grove, IL: IVP Academic, 1998), 679.

is threefold—to observe and record human experience, to interpret the experiences that are portrayed, and to entertain us with literary form and technique. The proverbs that make up wisdom literature perform exactly those three functions."[14]

John Bunyan was brilliant at developing characters in his *Pilgrim's Progress* that perfectly embody people we all meet in life and on our long and difficult journey to heaven. Like Bunyan, the authors of the biblical proverbs put perfectly into words and short poetic narratives people like the motormouth, the gossip, the shady merchant, the waffler, the boaster, the sloth, and so on. Similarly, we "intuitively *know*" that a proverb is true because it is truthful to our experience.[15] "The one incontrovertible proof of a proverb is a long, hard look at life around us."[16]

Chiseled Statements

A word fitly spoken is like apples of gold in a setting of silver. (Prov. 25:11)

All are from the dust, and to dust all return. (Eccles. 3:20)

Draw near to God, and he will draw near to you. (James 4:8)

These proverbs, and many others like them, captivate us with their insightfulness and succinctness, and they invite us to ponder and analyze them. Moreover, they serve as "examples of verbal beauty. They are chiseled statements, built out of carefully chosen words, artfully arranged and capturing a high point of human insight. This

14 Ryken, *Short Sentences Long Remembered*, 17.
15 Ryken, *Short Sentences Long Remembered*, 112.
16 Ryken, "Proverb as Literary Form," 679.

element of artistic beauty and skillful handling of style is an added avenue to enjoying proverbs. It also partly explains why proverbs are memorable."[17]

Types and Traits

Proverbs contain poetic images, figures of speech, and the usual structure is a parallelism. Types include one-sentence, one-line proverbs ("a threefold cord is not quickly broken," Eccles. 4:12); one-sentence, two-line proverbs ("For my yoke is easy, and my burden is light," Matt. 11:30); and various parallelisms.[18] Ryken offers these definitions and examples of the three most common types of parallelism:

> *Synonymous parallelism*, in which the second line restates the same truth as the first in a similar way: "A false witness will not go unpunished, / and he who breathes out lies will not escape." (Prov. 19:5)

> *Antithetic parallelism*, in which the second line states the truth of the first line in a contrasting way: "The way of a fool is right in his own eyes, / but a wise man listens to advice." (Prov. 12:15)

> *Synthetic* ("growing") *parallelism*, in which the second line adds to the first line or completes it: "The fear of the LORD is a fountain of life, / that one may turn away from the snares of death." (Prov. 14:27)

---

17 Ryken, *Short Sentences Long Remembered*, 34–35.

18 "The principle of organization that underlies parallelism is that of saying something twice in a similar grammatical form but in different words and images" (Ryken, *Short Sentences Long Remembered*, 33).

Robert Alter also includes *elaboration* and *answer* in his summary of the characteristic sentence structure of most of the two-part-sentence proverbs:

Elaboration. The second part intensifies the thought of the first or extends it in time. An example would be Proverbs 14:26:

> In the fear of the LORD one has strong confidence,
>   and his children will have a refuge.

Answer. The parts work together to create what seems to be the answer to a question which itself is not recorded. "To do righteousness and justice is more acceptable to the LORD than sacrifice" (21:3) is the answer to the implied question, "What is more acceptable to the Lord than sacrifice?"[19]

Table 5.1 highlights a few other types of proverbs.

Table 5.1: Various Type of Proverbs

Better Than	Two are better than one, because they have a good reward for their toil. (Eccles. 4:9)
Observation	House and wealth are inherited from fathers, but a prudent wife is from the LORD. (Prov. 19:14)
Command	Do not boast about tomorrow, for you do not know what a day may bring. (Prov. 27:1)

---

19 Robert Alter, *The Art of Biblical Poetry* (New York: Basic Books, 1985), 169, as explained and illustrated in Thomas G. Long, *Preaching and the Literary Forms of the Bible* (Philadelphia: Fortress, 1989), 60.

Table 5.1 (*continued*)

Incentive Formulas	My son, do not forget my teaching, but let your heart keep my commandments, for length of days and years of life and peace they will add to you. Let not steadfast love and faithfulness forsake you; bind them around your neck; write them on the tablet of your heart. So you will find favor and good success in the sight of God and man. (Prov. 3:1–4)
Rhetorical Questions	If salt has lost its taste, how shall its saltiness be restored? (Matt. 5:13)
Numerical Sequences	Three things are too wonderful for me; four I do not understand: the way of an eagle in the sky, the way of a serpent on a rock, the way of a ship on the high seas, and the way of a man with a virgin. (Prov. 30:18–19)
Positive Reinforcement	Humble yourselves before the Lord, and he will exalt you. (James 4:10)
Negative Reinforcement	Whoever troubles his own household will inherit the wind. (Prov. 11:29)
Straightforward declarative sayings	Trust in the LORD with all your heart. (Prov. 3:5)
Imperative exhortations	Hear, my son, your father's instruction. (Prov. 1:8)
Analogy	The fruit of the righteous is a tree of life. (Prov. 11:30)
Brief portrait	The drunkard (Prov. 23:29–35)
Riddle	Who has gathered the wind in his fists? (Prov. 30:4)

Under the final category (Riddle) we can speak of mysterious proverbs. For example, when we read, "The mercy of the wicked is cruel" (Prov. 12:10), we wonder, "How can mercy be cruel?";

and, when we read, "Cast your bread upon the waters, / for you will find it after many days" (Eccles. 11:1), we realize quickly that there is no time to "take a holiday of the mind."[20] To make sense of that tricky text, we need to carefully study the words, check out the context, and perhaps consult a commentary.

The defining traits that all of the above types of proverbs share are that they are (1) apt and memorable, (2) simple and complex (and profound!), (3) simultaneously specific and general or universal, (4) often use figurative language, and (5) express experiences and truths that are always up-to-date and are therefore continually confirmed in our own lives and observations.[21]

Understand the Imagery

As is hopefully noted by now (in all the examples above!), biblical proverbs are full of imagery. We need to observe those images, note their type, and see their traits. That's level one, as Ryken calls it. Level two is to interpret the imagery. Our good doctor offers three interpretative actions: First, we need to experience the literal properties of the image as fully as possible, making sure that we know what the proverb wishes us to picture. Second, we need to identify the connotations of the image, including the symbolism and emotion(s) the author intends us to feel. Third, we need to analyze the logic of the image: why did the writer choose this image for this particular subject?[22]

For example, let's take Proverbs 27:8: "Like a bird that strays from its nest / is a man who strays from his home." First, we must understand that this proverb gives us an analogy in the form of a

---

20 Ryken, *Short Sentences Long Remembered*, 42, 43.
21 *Ryken's Bible Handbook*, 257.
22 Ryken, *Short Sentences Long Remembered*, 37.

simile, leaving us to figure out how A (the first line) is like B (the second). What characterizes a bird that strays from its nest? Think about that for more than a second. Second, once we understand that "a bird that strays from its nest" represents a willful and stupidly self-sufficient creature, who, in the end, won't fare well in the world on its own, we then quickly figure out the symbolic connection with the young man who thinks he can live outside of his parent's authority and his family's protection. We also grasp that we are to feel sorrow over the situation, a tragic, unnecessary loss. Third, the logic of the image now comes into clear view: This is a warning! The author has used an everyday image of what looks like freedom to show the utter folly of following one's own way on one's own.[23]

General Truths, Not Certain Promises

Train up a child in the way he should go;
    even when he is old he will not depart from it. (Prov. 22:6)

Is this a promise? A guarantee? An immutable law? No. This is a principle that is generally true.[24] Personal experience and

---

23   Here is another example. On Proverbs 10:26 ("Like vinegar to the teeth and smoke to the eyes, so is the sluggard to those who send him"), Longman writes, "Have you ever gotten smoke in your eyes? Most readers have. Maybe fewer have taken a gulp of vinegar and swirled it around in their mouth. But this image is asking us to reflect on that experience and compare it to sending a sluggard on a mission, in essence giving the sluggard some responsibility to represent us. So how would you describe getting smoke in your eyes? I might use words like annoying, irritating, painful. Pure vinegar on the teeth? This is more difficult, if for no other reason than that we don't know how ancient vinegar tasted. Perhaps we would use the same words as for smoke, throwing in bitterness as well. These words add punch to the idea that a sluggard will let you down, and this will have repercussions for your own reputation. The effect of the proverb is both to warn the simpleminded against being sluggards, and to tell the wise not to hire them" (Longman, *How to Read Proverbs*, 44).

24   If someone took Proverbs 23:13–14 ("Do not withhold correction from a child, for if you beat him with a rod, he will not die. You shall beat him with a rod, and deliver his soul from hell," NKJV) as a law, it could lead to some dangerous applications, like "parents beating

observation of those around us tells us that good parenting and a consistent godly example at home usually leads to godly offspring. Likewise hard work usually results in the acquisition of wealth, and sowing seed results in a harvest. There are exceptions, of course. Think of Samuel's wicked sons, righteous Job's loss of possessions, and Elijah and Obadiah enduring a three-year famine. Biblical proverbs offer generalizations without qualifications about exceptions. "That is the nature of the genre," writes Jeffrey Arthurs:

> To be sure, they are inspired general observations, but they are not promises. God has arranged the world so that cause-effect and action-consequence are normal patterns, but as we all know, those patterns have plenty of exceptions. Proverbs summarizes the normal patterns, and the books of Ecclesiastes and Job handle the exceptions. They describe how the righteous think and behave when bad things happen to good people.[25]

Thus, to use the common analogy of forcing a round peg into a square hole, the preacher is to avoid unsuccessfully shoving "these round pegs of observation into the square holes of promise."[26]

---

their child [by a rod, not a mere spanking by hand] out of fear that otherwise the child would end up in the fire and brimstone of hell." Longman correctly comments, "But this is not a law. It is a general principle that encourages those who are reluctant to use a form of discipline by telling them that it is permissible and even helpful for delivering a child from behavior that may result in premature death. . . . one must know what kind of child one is dealing with. Some children won't respond at all to physical punishment; indeed, it may hasten their path to the grave. Others may not need physical punishment but simply a strong reprimand. The key is that parents must know their child and the situation as they apply any proverb" (Longman, *How to Read Proverbs*, 57).

25 Arthurs, *Preaching with Variety*, 141.

26 Arthurs, *Preaching with Variety*, 141.

Ryken gives examples (e.g., "The upright will inhabit the land . . . / but the wicked will be cut off from the land," Prov. 2:21–22; "No ill befalls the righteous, / but the wicked are filled with trouble," 12:21) and he offers this advice:

> We need to have a strategy for dealing with proverbs that seem to promise too much. The wrong path is to construct our whole attitude toward proverbs on the basis of this category. It is true that proverbs like these should not be viewed as absolutes or guaranteed promises, but they still obey the general rules of a proverb. All proverbs express general principles based on observation of life or on the nature of God's dealings with the human race. All proverbs express what is *typically* or *usually* true. The fact that there are exceptions does not mean that there is not a general rule. In fact, we have a proverb about "the exception that proves the rule." So the first requirement is that we not foreclose on the possibility that the difficult proverb states a truth. . . . We need to avoid turning descriptions of a general principle into a guarantee or promise. But instead of dismissing optimistic proverbs, we should operate on the premise that good interpretive alternatives to such dismissal exist.[27]

Proverbs are not to be applied "mechanically and absolutely."[28]

Investigative Questions

For each proverb, there is an observation level. That is the first floor. But often other, higher levels, are to be explored, such as the analytic, interpretative, and application levels. Ryken suggests three questions

27 Ryken, *Short Sentences Long Remembered*, 65.
28 Ryken, *Short Sentences Long Remembered*, 56.

to "probe the deeper meaning of any proverb,"[29] what he elsewhere labels "a foolproof way to extract the profundity of a proverb":[30]

1. What *value* is affirmed or praised? For example, in Proverbs 27:7, the value of moderation is applauded: "One who is full loathes honey, / but to one who is hungry everything bitter is sweet."

2. What *virtue* is celebrated or commended? For example, in Ecclesiastes 5:12, the work of the honest lower-class laborer is affirmed and admired: "Sweet is the sleep of a laborer, whether he eats little or much, but the full stomach of the [anxious] rich will not let him sleep."

3. What *vice* is denounced or prohibited? For example, in Ecclesiastes 7:9, anger is deplored: "Be not quick in your spirit to become angry, / for anger lodges in the heart of fools."

Some proverbs can embody all three: command or commend a *virtue*, explicitly or implicitly prohibit a *vice*, and affirm a *value*. As a specimen, consider Proverbs 27:1: "Do not boast about tomorrow, / for you do not know what a day may bring." To rescue that proverb from seeming to be a platitude, we can apply the proposed framework. First, what vice does this proverb prohibit? It prohibits presumption on God's providence and thinking that we are in control of our lives. Second, it implicitly commends the spiritual virtue of humility and submissiveness before God's providence. Third, it exalts the value of relating to God in a way that acknowledges his sovereignty over our lives. We do not need to remain at the surface level of a proverb. We can probe it for the virtue it prescribes, the vice it proscribes, and the value it commends.

---

29 *Ryken's Bible Handbook*, 257.
30 Ryken, *Short Sentences Long Remembered*, 60.

Comic Relief

Most of the biblical proverbs are quite serious. Yet, from time to time, and often unexpectedly, serious statements are interrupted with humor. Such humor brings respite to the reader. It also brings an I-know-what-you're-living-through sympathy. For example, the proverbs that describe the quarrelsome wife resonate with the loving husband who daily has to renew his covenant vows with his unlovely bride. Or when Jesus says, "leave the dead to bury their own dead" (Matt. 8:22), the point is serious—there should be no delay in following him—but the image, if we think of it, is not only impossible (dead people don't move, let alone bury other dead people), but humorous. It is laughable not to follow our Lord!

Here are three further examples of funny proverbial pictures from Proverbs:

> Like a gold ring in a pig's snout
>   is a beautiful woman without discretion. (11:22)

> The sluggard buries his hand in the dish
>   and will not even bring it back to his mouth. (19:24)

> It is better to live in a corner of the housetop
>   than in a house shared with a quarrelsome wife. (21:9)

HOW TO PREACH BIBLICAL PROVERBS

Having looked at how to read biblical proverbs we next, as we have always done thus far, turn to how to preach these catchy concise couplets that clearly capture crucial concepts. As we offered more than ten characteristics above, we offer nearly twenty suggestions below. How do we preach proverbs? Here's how!

Focus on the Fear

In his "Introduction to Proverbs" for the *ESV Literary Study Bible*, Ryken notes that one of the theological themes of Proverbs is "the view of God," namely, that various proverbs provide a "detailed outline of what God likes and dislikes, values and regards as worthless, and as we contemplate those things, we come to an understanding of God."[31] Put differently, and more specifically, the biblical proverbs as a whole have a Godward goal: the fear of the Lord. As preachers, our job is to focus on that fear.

If we focus on our proper response to God, it protects us from preaching moralistic sermons. Also, with this Godward goal in mind, it is difficult to preach the health-wealth gospel of the popular prosperity preachers. As Arthurs asserts, "Proverbs are not prescriptions for the American dream. They are prescriptions for how to live skillfully in a world created by the sovereign, generous, and fearsome Master."[32] If you are preaching that holy, awesome, powerful God whom you should revere with your face to the ground and sandals off (Eccles. 5:1–7), it is unlikely that you will in the next breath say something that makes you the center of the universe and your best life now the priority.

Observe Life

The art of observation is important in preaching.[33] The great preachers are excellent at observing both what is in the text and who is in their congregation. To be a great preacher of proverbs requires that

---

31 Leland Ryken, "Introduction to Proverbs," in *Literary Study Bible, English Standard Version*, 953.

32 Arthurs, *Preaching with Variety*, 142–43.

33 See Douglas Sean O'Donnell, "Spirit-Filled Sitzfleisch: The Prayerful Art of Sermonizing," in *Unashamed Workmen*, ed. Rhett Dodson (Fearn, Ross-shire, Scotland, UK: Christian Focus, 2014), 207–10.

you do what Solomon did in all his wisdom: "God gave Solomon wisdom and understanding beyond measure, and breadth of mind like the sand on the seashore," a "wisdom [that] surpassed the wisdom of all the people of the east and all the wisdom of Egypt" and "all other men" (1 Kings 4:29–31). And, due to this gift, "people of all nations came to hear the wisdom of Solomon" (v. 34).

What was the nature of Solomon's wisdom, as detailed in 1 Kings 4:32–33? "He also spoke 3,000 proverbs, and his songs were 1,005. He spoke of trees, from the cedar that is in Lebanon to the hyssop that grows out of the wall. He spoke also of beasts, and of birds, and of reptiles, and of fish." He learned to write carefully crafted sentences and lyrical poems. He learned to play music and sing songs. He learned to study creation. To speak of the cedars of Lebanon requires traveling from Jerusalem to Lebanon, and eying these magnificent trees, and perhaps writing down observations and comparing those trees with other trees. And to speak of birds and beasts, salmon and snakes, and likely many other creatures required time, travel, and thought.

Do you share Solomon's wisdom-growing lifestyle? When the sage says, "Go to the ant, . . . consider her ways, and be wise" (Prov. 6:6), he is directly addressing the sluggard, but some wisdom on hard work is to be gleaned by all who stop to see, and some nuggets of entomology regarding this insect and a thousand others can be used by the observant preacher for a number of illustrations and applications. Our Lord Jesus was a master of such. He used gnats, dogs, doves, moths, fish, sparrows, wolves, vipers, camels, and pigs to evidence or elucidate his points. What do you know of zoology? Biology? Botany? Do you observe life?

Maltbie Babcock (1858–1901) pastored First Presbyterian Church in Lockport, New York. He kept fit by running two miles from the church up the Niagara Escarpment that overlooks Lake Ontario and offers a panoramic view of upstate New York, two miles more to "a deep ravine where as many as forty different species of birds found a sanctuary," and then a few more miles back to his church office.[34] Babcock was also musical. He played the organ, piano, and violin, and penned (not surprisingly) the famous hymn, "This Is My Father's World." We don't have any of his sermons in print, but I would imagine something of the voice of creation that came to his "listening ears" ("all nature sings, and round me rings") made its presence known in his sermonic prose. And as he and his congregation sang of "rocks and trees, of skies and seas," singing birds ("birds their carols raise"), the sunrise ("the morning light"), flowers ("the lily white"), and "the rustling grass," they reminded each other of the truths of God's sovereignty over both creation and evil ("O let me ne'er forget / That though the wrong seems oft so strong, / God is the ruler yet"). You may not be an athlete and musician, but you can take a walk each day and consider the lilies, hear the bees buzz, watch birds swoop, and tell your congregation about your Creator from your observations of his creation.

Preach How to Live

A decade ago, I wrote a book on preaching Christ from Old Testament wisdom literature. I received a one-star review from a pastor who said, "I pity the congregation who sits under this man's preaching." Ouch! The reason for that review had to do that pastor's hermeneutics. He believed that books like Proverbs taught law, not gospel, and we are to preach them not as commands to keep but as commands that only Christ has kept. Well, I (still!) fundamentally

---

34 William J. Peterson and Randy Petersen, *The One Year Book of Hymns: 365 Devotions Based on Popular Hymns* (Carol Stream, IL: Tyndale, 2017), 137.

disagree with that theology as it relates to the wisdom literature of the Bible. The wisdom literature, found in both the Old Testament and New Testament, are not ethics to get into the kingdom but ethics for those already in. As Graeme Goldsworthy summarizes, "[The Wisdom Literature] complements the perspective of salvation history . . . [and offers] *a theology of the redeemed man living in the world under God's rule.*"[35]

I explained in the final chapter of my book, perhaps something my reviewer neglected to read, how the New Testament handles Old Testament wisdom literature. The first point I made, labeled "Gospel Ethics," was that the apostolic use of the wisdom literature merely reinforced Old Testament theology and ethics. I also claimed that this continuity and consistency between the Testaments was significant. And I clarified the nature of Christ-centered sermons on the books of Proverbs, Ecclesiastes, Job, and the like, in this way:

> Christ-centered sermons should call us to holiness in light of Christ's incarnation (2 Pet. 1:1–12, 17) and his second coming (3:11–12). Christ-centered sermons should promote the Great Commission's commission—"teaching them to observe all that I have commanded you" (Matt. 28:20a). Christ-centered sermons should make us wise in salvation through faith in Christ and train us in godliness (see 2 Tim. 3:16). Moreover, Christ-centered sermons should include Paul's confession of the work of the cross—"[Jesus] who gave himself for us to redeem us from

---

35 Graeme Goldsworthy, *Gospel and Kingdom: A Christian Interpretation of the Old Testament* (Exeter, England, UK: Paternoster, 1983), 142, emphasis mine. Cf. Duane A. Garrett, "Preaching Wisdom," in *Reclaiming the Prophetic Mantle: Preaching the Old Testament Faithfully,* ed. George L. Klein (Nashville: Broadman, 1992), 108–10.

all lawlessness and to purify for himself a people . . . zealous for good works" (Titus 2:14; cf. Acts 3:26); the author of Hebrews's firm exhortations toward endurance in light of Jesus's high priesthood (e.g., 4:14); and our Lord Jesus's final words of warning (not consolation) in the Sermon on the Mount (Matt. 7:21–27). Christ-centered sermons can and should have an ethical edge to them; our messages should carry a moral weight. As we walk under the cross from Proverbs to Philippians, Ecclesiastes to Ephesians, or Job to James, we must not dull this edge or lessen this weight. Our Christ-centered sermons on the Wisdom Literature must impress upon us, on the one hand, the greatness of God and, on the other hand, our response of obedient gratitude to grace, for as Paul says: the purpose of being "filled with . . . all spiritual wisdom" is so we might "walk in a manner worthy of the Lord" (Col. 1:9–10). This requires we keep in mind various broader issues that are closely related to the gospel in the New Testament—(1) faith: the proper response to the gospel, and (2) ethics: life under the gospel.[36]

What I have emphasized for a particular purpose (how we preach Christ from the wisdom literature), Ryken speaks on more broadly. In answer to the question, "What is wisdom?" he says,

Wisdom is *skill for living*. This implies that wisdom focuses on practical daily living and ties into the authors' task of observing life and human experience. . . . The book of Proverbs contains observations and advice on such far-flung topics as farming, lawsuits, table manners, money management, avoiding

---

36 O'Donnell, *Beginning and End of Wisdom*, 122–23.

bad companions, choosing a wife, and the delights of having grandchildren. This is not to minimize that other proverbs deal with the spiritual life—fearing God, worshiping properly, and enduring trial. Even here, though, the goal of the wise men is that people will navigate life well rather than poorly—with skill for living, in other words.[37]

Do you preach to your people skill for living? Do you give them God's wisdom? Do they understand that "there are standards by which we can differentiate between good conduct and bad conduct; actions invariably produce consequences; life requires us to make choices between good and bad options; the good life requires active choice and strenuous moral effort; all of life is momentous; the ultimate choice that people need to make is to choose to obey God's rules for living"?[38] Do you persuade your people to choose wisdom over folly in the daily decisions of life? Do you remind them of the rewards for righteous living, as Jesus does at the end of each Beatitude? Do you offer repeated warnings, as Proverbs and James do throughout, and as Jesus does at the end of the greatest sermon in history—the Sermon on the Mount? Do your sermons have any moral weight to them?

If you fail to preach to Christians the necessity of character formation, you fail to preach proverbs properly. "The real intent" of such literature, states Roland Murphy, "is to train a person, to form character, to show what life is really like and how best to cope with it."[39] God has not left us alone. He graciously gives us in his

---

37 Ryken, *Short Sentences Long Remembered*, 13.
38 Ryken, "Introduction to Proverbs," 952.
39 Roland E. Murphy, *The Tree of Life: An Exploration of Biblical Wisdom*, 3rd ed. (Grand Rapids, MI: Eerdmans, 2002), 15.

Word his pattern for the good life, offering lessons on discretion, purity, industry, hard work, justice, leadership, and controlling the tongue. To fail to preach Christian ethics is to fail to preach the whole counsel of God.

Follow the Formula

If you don't know where to start in heeding the above suggestion, just follow this God-inspired formula. Some proverbs, or strings of proverbs, offer all or a few of these four ingredients: (1) a summons to listen, (2) admonitions, (3) motivation for obeying, and (4) consequences of obedience. For example, Proverbs 4:1–9 combines all four, starting in verses 1–2 with a summons to listen ("Hear, O sons . . . be attentive"), a motivation ("for I give you good precepts"), admonition ("do not forsake my teaching"). It concludes with four more admonitions to "get wisdom" and the positive consequences for doing so: she will keep, guard, honor, and bestow a crown on you. In your preaching, follow that formula.

Adapt to the Audience

As I have argued elsewhere, the Song of Solomon is a book for girls: "The target audience is 'the daughters of Jerusalem,' who are the 'virgins' mentioned in 1:3 and 'the young women' in 2:2. These girls . . . are admonished to wait until marriage to enjoy sexual intimacy."[40] The book of Proverbs is a book for boys:

> Proverbs is primarily addressed to men, or more specifically, young men. In fact, the word son is used forty-four times.

---

40 Douglas Sean O'Donnell, "Song of Solomon," ESV Expository Commentary (Wheaton: IL, Crossway, forthcoming).

Compare that to the word daughter, which is never used, and you start to get this point. That's not to say that Proverbs has nothing to say to daughters, women, old men, or children, but it is to say that boys are the target audience here. That is why I call it, as others have called it, a book for boys. I think of it as a young man's devotional, for as there are thirty-one days in many months, so there are thirty-one chapters—a chapter a day to keep foolishness away. Stay away from the trap and snares of the adulterous woman (eight chapters focus to some extent on that topic). Stay away from the quarrelsome woman (there are five different references to her—you don't want her). But don't stay away from the wise woman, the excellent wife. Listen for her voice. Find her. Embrace her. Hold on to her like you would a rare and precious pearl. This emphasis on Proverbs being a book for boys is apparent throughout in the language and themes of the book but especially in this final chapter with its poem (31:10–31). In fact, the very structure of this skillfully crafted poem makes this point literally.[41]

Does that mean the Song of Solomon's wisdom admonition to young unmarried women has no relevance to men? No. Purity and patience should be a priority for both genders. Does that mean Proverbs 31 has nothing to teach old women? No. Older women need to model the excellencies of the excellent wife. Here, again, we reiterate the importance of (a) understanding a piece of literature's original audience and intention, and then (b) seeing how what was said to them there has application to your congregation now.

41 O'Donnell, *Beginning and End of Wisdom*, 48–49.

Structural Subtleties

It is possible, but not recommended, to organize sermons with the structural forms we find in some biblical proverbs. For example, I don't advise a twenty-two-point sermon on the acrostic poem in Proverbs 31:10–31, or a seven-point sermon based on its chiastic structure. Nor would I recommend dividing the five rhetorical questions (and their one answer!) into your five points. You could do a four-point sermon on the four things that are too wonderful and inexplicable—(1) the way of an eagle in the sky, (2) a serpent on a rock, (3) a ship on the high seas, and (4) a man with a virgin (Prov. 30:18–19)—but it would be a short sermon, I would imagine.

My point is this: where there is clearly structural order that fits a sermonic outline (e.g., the Beatitudes), use the inspired structure. However, a suggested way to preach most biblical proverbs, especially those in the book of Proverbs, is to group verses together thematically. Ryken elucidates: "Except in the first nine chapters and the encomium on the good wife at the end of the book, it would be futile to look for structural coherence and continuity as we read. . . . Although the proverbs in the book of Proverbs are not generally arranged in topical clusters, it is possible to peruse the book looking for proverbs on a topic and compose one's own proverb cluster."[42]

In "Appendix B: Book Summaries and Suggested Sermon Series,"[43] of my book on preaching wisdom literature, I write this on Proverbs:

---

42 Ryken, "Introduction to Proverbs," 953. Cf. Longman, *How to Read Proverbs*, 157.
43 O'Donnell, *Beginning and End of Wisdom*, 153–58. Cf. Raymond C. Ortlund Jr., *Proverbs: Wisdom That Works*, Preaching the Word (Wheaton, IL: Crossway, 2012), chs. 15–21.

There are places where we can take a purely linear approach (1:1–9:18) and other places where a thematic approach is more fitting (most of 10:1–22:21). However, there are editorial remarks within the inspired text itself that give us some structural guidance, headings such as "The proverbs of Solomon, son of David, king of Israel" (1:1), "The words of Agur son of Jakeh" (30:1), and so on. These headings, and other clues within the text, have led many scholars to view Proverbs as seven collections:

(1) 1:1–9:18
(2) 10:1–22:16
(3) 22:17–24:22
(4) 24:23–34
(5) 25:1–29:27
(6) 30:1–33
(7) 31:1–31

Doing seven sermons on each collection would prove valuable. Also, preaching Proverbs 1:1–9:18 in ten to fifteen sermons would make for a very helpful and practical sermon series. I have attached (brave man that I am) my attempt to plot out a sermon series for the whole book. Let us pray:

THE PROVERBS OF SOLOMON

1:1–7	The Beginning of Wisdom
1:8–19	Walk Not in the Way of Sinners
1:20–4:27	The Benefits of Embracing Wisdom
1:20–33	Wisdom Shouts in the Streets
2:1–22	Why Listen to Wisdom?
3:1–35	Trust in the Lord

4:1–27	Embrace Her (Wisdom)
5:1–23; 6:20–7:27; 9:13–18	Lady Folly
6:1–5	Go to Your Wronged Neighbor
6:6–11	Go to the Industrious Ant
6:12–19	Seven Abominations
8:1–9:6	Lady Wisdom
9:7–18	Correct a Scoffer

MORE PROVERBS OF SOLOMON

10:1–22:16	Contrasts ("but") and Consequences (do thematic sermons)

For 10:1–22:16, I suggest topical sermons on themes. I would start with an overview sermon explaining the motive for embracing wisdom: live wisely in attitude and actions toward God and others and (usually) you will prosper. Two titles I have come up with for this overview sermon are "The *What* and *Why* of Wisdom" and "The Rewards of Righteousness; the Outcome of Unrighteousness."

Below are my sermon titles for the topics to tackle: money, parenting, business ethics, the tongue, work ethic, politics, companionship, and godly attitudes and emotions. You should give at least one sermon on each.

Company Kept
The Power of the Tongue
Neither Poverty nor Riches
A Wise Son
Train Up a Child
O Sluggard

Tempering Our Tempers
Haughtiness and Humility
God's Guidance
Fear the Lord *and the King*
When the Earth Trembles: Injustices
Business as Usual?

THE PROVERBS OF SOLOMON VIA HEZEKIAH

THE PROVERBS OF AGUR

THE PROVERBS OF LEMUEL

Helen Sword notes how essayist Annie Dillard described writing as "an architectural endeavor, a continuous cycle of design, demolition, and rebuilding." Dillard compared sentences to bricks, paragraphs to walls and windows. A well-structured sermon, and

---

44 Often 22:17–24:22 is viewed as "thirty sayings of the wise," and 24:23–34 as "five more sayings." I join them together, for I see them connected by the key words "do not."

sermon series, "like a well-built house, requires careful thought and planning."[45]

Make Your Central Idea "Proverbial"

I borrow this suggestion, and the language for it (including the title above), from Arthurs. His words and my illustrations will suffice to summarize the suggestion:

> That central idea [of the sermon] will lodge in memory if you word it like a proverb, with brevity, balance, image, and sound values. By doing this, we preach not only as the sages spoke, but also as the listeners listen because in the age of secondary orality, the distilled, memorable phrase is as common as corn-flakes. Advertisers coin jingles to lodge in the memory ["I am stuck on Band-Aid brand, 'cause Band-Aid's stuck on me"], and politicians summarize their messages in sounds bites to make the evening news [or to create a movement—"Make America Great Again!"].[46]

Next, Arthurs offers four ways we can heed his advice. First, use the proverb itself and restate it throughout the sermon. If after every five minutes of exegesis, illustration, and application, you say, "Pride goes . . . before a fall" (Prov. 16:18), it is likely that each and every member of your congregation will walk away with the main point. Second, create your own proverbial saying. In his sermon on overcoming bitterness, John Piper coined this sermonic slogan: "If you hold a grudge, you slight the Judge." That's good! That will

---

45 Helen Sword, *Stylistic Academic Writing* (Cambridge, MA: Harvard University Press, 2016), 122.

46 Arthurs, *Preaching with Variety*, 140–45. The bracketed slogans are my examples.

preach. That will be remembered, and Lord willing, applied that week, if not for a lifetime. Third, rant a refrain. Okay, that's my alliteration, not Arthurs's, but it fits what he suggests. Tim Keller's ministry motto is the illustration Arthurs offers: "He [Jesus] lived the life I should have lived and died the death I should have died." Piper's refrain on Christian hedonism could fit here as well: "God is most glorified in you when you are most satisfied in him." Fourth, take a contemporary slogan ("seeing is believing") and give it a twist ("believing is seeing"). This slogan describes well the blind men in Matthew 20:30 who correctly perceive that Jesus is the powerful "Lord" and the merciful "Son of David."

A proverb is a concise, memorable statement of truth. Are your points that? And the biblical proverbs "express truth with a punch."[47] Do you? Do you not only express an insight, as God's proverbs do, but also compel your people to follow that insight, as proverbs also do?

The Traits in Teaching

As discussed earlier, the defining traits of biblical proverbs are fivefold: (1) apt and memorable, (2) simple and complex (and profound!), (3) simultaneously specific and general or universal, (4) often use figurative language, and (5) express experiences and truths that are always up-to-date and are therefore continually confirmed in our own lives and observations. All of these traits define a good sermon.

Make It Stick!

My wife works for *Administer Justice* (administerjustice.org), a ministry that provides legal assistance for low-income individuals.

---

47 Ryken, *Short Sentences Long Remembered*, 22.

She was tasked with writing a Bible study on the theme of justice. When she got to Proverbs, she said to me, "Proverbs are 'sticky sayings,' aren't they?" Precisely. The sages knew how to make it stick! As Ryken observes, "When we first hear or read a proverb, we obviously do not know whether we will remember it, but we sense that it has a striking effect on us, and we know that it is *worthy* of memory." He lists three examples,[48] including James 1:22 ("Be doers of the word, and not hearers only") and concludes, "Not all proverbs are that easy to remember, but the general tendency of proverbs is to stick in our minds."[49] Make an effort to make your points (and certain key sentences as well) memorable. For example, when I preached on the Beatitudes, my sermon online was,

A Broken Blessedness
A Future Blessedness
A Selfless Blessedness

As I preached through Ecclesiastes, I often followed Qoheleth's repeated refrain of "vanity," with this memorable phrase "depress you into dependence." Ecclesiastes was written to "depress you into dependence on our joyous God and his blessed will for your life."[50] Make it memorable!

Wordsmithing

What Sword says in her chapter "Smart Sentencing," in her book *Stylistic Academic Writing*, is apropos to preaching:

48 Some examples from Proverbs would include 3:5; 9:8; 10:2, 16, 25, 26; 13:12, 20; 15:17; 16:3, 9, 18, 25, 33; 17:22; 18:22; 22:4; 27:1, 6, 17; 31:30. Proverbs 24:33–34 is also lyrical (thus, memorable).

49 Ryken, *Short Sentences Long Remembered*, 22.

50 O'Donnell, *Ecclesiastes: Enjoyment East of Eden*, 221.

A carefully crafted sentence welcomes its reader like a comfortable rocking chair, bears its reader across chasms like a suspension bridge, and helps its reader navigate tricky terrain like a well-hewn walking stick. A poorly crafted or uncrafted sentence, on the other hand, functions more like a shapeless log tossed into a river: it might or might not help you to the other side, depending on how strong the current is and how hard you are willing to kick.[51]

She goes on to speak of stylish writers as those who are "sticklers for well-crafted prose," which includes sentences that "vary in length, subject matter, and style," and are governed by three key principles: "First, they employ plenty of concrete nouns and vivid verbs, especially when discussing abstract concepts. Second, they keep nouns and verbs close together, so that readers can easily identify 'who's kicking whom.' Third, they avoid weighing down their sentences with extraneous words and phrases, or 'clutter.' Far from eschewing theoretical intricacy or syntactical nuance, stylish academic writers deploy these three core principles in the service of eloquent expression and complex ideas."[52]

The wise men and women who spoke and wrote the wisdom proverbs of the Bible were keen observers of the human experience. They were also eloquent wordsmiths. The *Oxford English Dictionary* defines literary eloquence as "tasteful correctness, harmonious simplicity, in the choice and arrangement of words." An elegant writer, as Sword comments, is one who gives us the impression that "every word has been carefully chosen, like the words of a poem, for its weight, sound, and resonance."[53]

---

51 Sword, *Stylistic Academic Writing*, 48.
52 Sword, *Stylistic Academic Writing*, 49.
53 Sword, *Stylistic Academic Writing*, 167.

In Ecclesiastes 12:9–10, the Preacher, after "weighing and studying" words, arranged the proverbs he taught "with great care," and he "sought to find words of delight, and uprightly he wrote words of truth." The *Merriam-Webster Dictionary* offers this succinct definition of a wordsmith: "a person who works with words; especially a skillful writer." Preacher, you work with the Word. But do you work with your words on the Word? In the study, do you weigh words—one against another—until you find just the right one? Are you skillful in selecting the words for your Sunday's State of the Union—the union between Christ and his church? Do you use beautiful expressions to persuade your parishioners to think, feel, and act as God would want them to? Do you understand that "God created the human spirit with a capacity and longing for the true, the good, and the beautiful," that "something that is well phrased simply makes a greater impact"[54]? To the best of your ability and within the limits of your time, I encourage you to preach words fitly written and spoken. Yes, serve God's people apples of gold in a setting of silver (Prov. 25:11).

Talk Like Your People Talk

American poet laureate Billy Collins speaks of contemporary poetry as "using everyday language, with jazz added to it." The improvisational jazz solo was discussed above; the simple notes here.

There is a tone to the book of Proverbs, the Sermon on the Mount, and other great proverbial compilations in our sacred Scriptures. What is amazing is that both King Solomon and the Lord Jesus (who was far "greater than Solomon," Matt. 12:42) talked down-to-earth wisdom to everyone they encountered—from lowly

---

54 Ryken, *Short Sentences Long Remembered*, 103–4.

blind beggars to arrogant high priests. The metaphors, similes, and imagery in general employed in the biblical proverbs are ordinary and unpretentious; and the people, places, and things, along with the situations encountered are everyday: a sluggard in his bed; the constant arguments with a difficult spouse; the worldly temptations of sex, power, and money.

Do you talk like your people talk? Or, do you suffer from jargonitis? An easy way to do a self-assessment is to print out your last sermon and circle every word and phrase that the average teenager in your congregation would not find immediately understandable. If you have more than ten words circled, you need to learn that "clarity and complexity are bedfellows, not rivals."[55] And you need to start writing and preaching sermons that sound more like lines from the wisdom literature ("Light is sweet, and it is pleasant for the eyes to see the sun," Eccles. 11:7).

Tell and Show, or Show While You Tell

One day, the ten-year-old triplets in my church asked me questions about my sermons. To the question, "What was your favorite sermon to preach?" I replied, "The sermon on Ecclesiastes 2, the one I called 'The Hollow House of Hedonism.'" Each one of them nodded and said, "Oh, yeah, I remember that sermon." One of the children walked me through the whole sermon outline. No joke!

Why did I like it and why did they remember it, and like it too? Simple. It was perhaps the most visual sermon I ever preached. I don't always use PowerPoint or make use of screens, but I did that day, and as I walked through four rooms of Sol-

---

55 Sword, *Stylistic Academic Writing*, 156.

omon's House of Hedonism, an interesting and clear image accompanied each point. I have mixed feelings about screens in churches, but I have no qualms about saying, "Make your sermons as visual as possible!"[56]

Arthurs likewise admonishes that, as we preach proverbs, we should engage our imaginations by imagining images: "Try to see, hear, and feel the firebrands, pigs, jewels, trees, crowns, rods, scales, and fountains."[57] It is not a sin to fail to offer some visual commentary when you preach on the "forbidden woman" of Proverbs, but it is a shame. Offer visual commentary that corresponds to the visual nature of the text. With care and discretion, help your congregation *see* something of "the lips" that "drip honey," the "speech" that is "smoother than oil," and the awful consequences of submitting to the sin she offers: "in the end she is bitter as wormwood, sharp as a two-edged sword" (Prov. 5:3–4). Admonish the married men not to play with the fire of adulterous lust ("Can a man carry fire next to his chest and his clothes not be burned?" 6:27) and encourage them to enjoy the life-giving pleasure of their marriage bed ("Drink water from your own cistern, flowing water from your own well," 5:15). The imagery of the biblical proverbs is awesome (see the samplings above and below). Do justice to such imagery from the pulpit. Take care to image the ideas:

---

56 "As neuropsychologist Allan Paivio [*Mental Representations: A Dual Coding Approach* (Oxford: Oxford University Press, 1984)] and others have documented, words and images are processed by the brain along entirely separate pathways; unsurprisingly, readers understand new concepts more clearly and recall them more readily when they are presented both verbally and visually rather than just one way or the other. . . . Visual illustrations activate the eyes as well as the mind. . . . abstract concepts become more memorable and accessible the moment we ground them in the material world, the world that our readers can see and touch" (Sword, *Stylistic Academic Writing*, 108).

57 Arthurs, *Preaching with Variety*, 142.

They . . . drink the wine of violence. (4:17)

The path of the righteous is like the light of dawn, . . .
(4:18)

The teaching of the wise is a fountain of life, . . . (13:14)

The name of the LORD is a strong tower;
the righteous man runs into it and is safe. (18:10)

Bread gained by deceit is sweet to a man,
but afterward his mouth will be full of gravel. (20:17)

When your eyes light on it [wealth], it is gone,
for suddenly it sprouts wings,
flying like an eagle toward heaven. (23:5)

For a prostitute is a deep pit;
an adulteress is a narrow well. (23:27)

Wine . . . bites like a serpent . . . (23:31, 32)

Like clouds and wind without rain
is a man who boasts of a gift he does not give. (25:14)

Like a dog that returns to his vomit
is a fool who repeats his folly. (26:11)

As charcoal to hot embers and wood to fire,
so is a quarrelsome man for kindling strife. (26:21)

She is not afraid of snow for her household,
for all her household are clothed in scarlet. (31:21)

When you come upon a proverb in an epistle, discourse, or narrative, take the time to treat the proverb as a proverb. Unpack the proverb in its literary context. Clarify why it is there. Illustrate its importance. Apply it to the lives of your congregation. And, please, explain its imagery!

Relive the Story behind the Saying

Remembering that "a story, or a group of stories, lies behind each proverb," use "statistics, examples, current events, and stories" to "encourage and warn."[58] Here are three examples: When teaching on Proverbs 30:8 ("give me neither poverty nor riches"), offer statistics on spending habits. For example, Craig Blomberg begins his book *Neither Poverty nor Riches: A Biblical Theology of Material Possessions*, with a sampling of statistics: "At least one billion . . . people in our world today fall below any reasonable poverty line. . . . Americans spent annually twice as much on cut flowers as on overseas Protestant ministries . . . and a staggering 140 times as much on legalized gambling."[59] When instructing on "when the wicked rule" (29:2), illustrate with news clippings about the "cruel oppressor[s]" (28:16) of Myanmar or a dozen other countries. When preaching on the proverbs that warn young men to avoid keeping bad company (e.g., Prov. 1:10–19; 7:6–27), share the story of Augustine's youth, when he stole fruit solely due to the gang's collaborate misguided desire: "We took away an enormous

---

58 Arthurs, *Preaching with Variety*, 143.
59 Craig L. Blomberg, *Neither Poverty nor Riches: A Biblical Theology of Material Possessions*, New Studies in Biblical Theology (Grand Rapids, MI: Eerdmans, 1999), 17, 19.

quantity of pears, not to eat them ourselves, but simply to throw them to the pigs."[60]

Captive to Christ

What Paul writes in 2 Corinthians 10:5 can serve as an excellent motto for Christian preaching: "We destroy arguments and every lofty opinion raised against the knowledge of God, and take every thought captive to obey Christ." One way to do that when preaching biblical proverbs is to compare and contrast them with popular cultural slogans, what Alyce McKenzie labels "dueling proverbs."[61] Catchy political mantras and commercial jingles do more than clatter in your congregation's ears; they make their way into their memories, often offering an alternative, ungodly worldview. For example, due to social media platforms where people can say what they want when they want in a lightly filtered environment, it has become widespread for even Christians today to post their views of people and positions in highly uncharitable ways. The day before I wrote this page, a friend told me about an online post he wrote that got him fired. It was directly directed at an "untouchable" in the large organization. He said, "I took the post down. I know it was unloving. But I had to speak the truth." I thought to myself, "Hmm, how about speaking the truth in love?" He needed to know, believe, and apply Paul's proverb.

Another example was when billionaire Donald Trump ran for president in 2016. That year I read an article in *Politico* that talked about how "Trump made no effort to conceal his belief in the gospel of wealth." He regularly preached that a vote for

---

60 Saint Augustine, *Confessions*, trans. R. S. Pine-Coffin (New York: Penguin, 1961), 47.
61 Alyce M. McKenzie, *Preaching Proverbs: Wisdom from the Pulpit* (Louisville: Westminster/ John Knox, 1996), 127–28.

him equaled wealth for his voters: "You will all be rich. So rich," he promised. He also unabashedly announced, "We're going to make America wealthy again. You have to be wealthy in order to be great." Well, how does that philosophy fare with the teachings of Jesus on wealth and greatness? You know the answer. It doesn't fare well:

"If anyone would be first, he must be last of all and servant of all." (Mark 9:35)

"For what does it profit a man to gain the whole world and forfeit his soul?" (Mark 8:36)

When I used Trump's proverbial sayings as an illustration of a teaching not to heed, the backlash was felt. Some in my congregation were so attuned to hearing false proverbs that God's proverbs had become cause for concern. But that's just it. Your job as a preacher is to destroy all dueling proverbs. In love, of course.

There are many more examples you can use. For example, as it relates to sexual lust ("you can look as long as you don't touch" vs. "Can a man carry fire next to his chest and his clothes not be burned?" Prov. 6:27); modesty ("show a little leg" vs. "Like a gold ring in a pig's snout is a beautiful woman without discretion," Prov. 11:22); pride ("if it's going to be; it's up to me" vs. "the way of man is not in himself, . . . it is not in man who walks to direct his steps," Jer. 10:23); the tongue ("say the truth, no matter what," vs. "speak the truth in love," Eph. 4:15 NLT); and guidance ("trust your gut," vs. "Trust in the LORD with all your heart, and do not lean on your own understanding. In all your ways acknowledge him, and he will make straight your paths," Prov. 3:5–6).

With this suggestion in mind, here is how I preached, in part, on Jesus's Beatitudes:

What does it mean to be blessed by God? Does it mean good health—I hope that sneeze, by divine intervention, doesn't turn into something worse? Does it mean much wealth—I hope God prospers you and this country economically, bringing security and comfort? It can mean those things. Health and wealth can be great blessings from God. The Wisdom Literature of the Bible, especially Proverbs, speaks of such blessings. The Prophets also add their voices, as they predicted that when God's kingdom finally arrived there would be a reign of peace and plenty (see Isaiah 65:16–25; Haggai 2:6–9). Even as we look at the start of Jesus's earthly ministry, we get the impression that this "blessed" kingdom has arrived. What is Jesus doing in 4:17–25, right before the Sermon on the Mount? He is "proclaiming the gospel of the kingdom," *and* he is "healing every disease and every affliction among the people" (4:23). Jesus is teaching about God's kingdom and showing via healing that it was beginning to come.

If you lived back then, heard this message, and saw such healings (or were healed!), wouldn't you do what the crowd did in 4:25? You would crowd around Jesus, wondering, *What's he going to do next? What's he going to say next?* Well, what does he say? He talks about blessing. But he doesn't say what they likely thought he would say. Instead, he says what seems like one contradiction after another:

Blessed are the poor in spirit.
Blessed are those who mourn.
Blessed are the meek.

Blessed are those who hunger and thirst for righteousness.
Blessed are those who are persecuted.

According to Jesus, who is "blessed"? Is it the courageous, the
wise, the temperate, or the just? No. How about the agreeable,
the funny, the intelligent, the attractive, the sensitive, and the
fit? No. According to Jesus, the one who is poor, sad, lowly,
hungry and mistreated is blessed. . . . Welcome to the strange
world and wisdom of Jesus. Welcome to Jesus's narrow-gate
theology, teaching that separates the "crowds" who want health
and wealth in the here and now, and the "disciples," who are
willing to deny themselves, pick up their crosses, and follow Jesus
(cf. 5:1). Welcome not to "the few, the proud, the Marines," but
"the few, the humble, the followers of Jesus." Welcome to what
it means to be a "blessed" disciple of Jesus Christ.[62]

Biblical Illustrations

One of Tremper Longman's thirteen principles for reading the book
of Proverbs is particularly apropos to preaching: "Try to identify
biblical stories or characters who may illustrate the truthfulness
of the proverb(s) you are studying."[63] Allow me an illustration of
this suggestion.

When preaching on Proverbs 6:16–19, the narrative of the
beheading of John the Baptist can serve to perfectly illustrate the
vices listed. How would Herod, Herodias, and Salome fare when
assessed by Jesus's Sermon on the Mount? Lust? Check. Adultery?
Check. Breaking vows? Check. Hatred? Check. Revenge? Check.

---

62 Douglas Sean O'Donnell, *Matthew: All Authority in Heaven and on Earth*, Preaching the
Word (Wheaton, IL: Crossway, 2013), 109–10.

63 Longman, *How to Read Proverbs*, 157.

Murder? Check. And, what if we ran the data of their deeds through Proverbs 6:16–19: "There are six things that the LORD hates, seven that are an abomination to him: haughty eyes, a lying tongue, and hands that shed innocent blood, a heart that devices wicked plans, feet that make haste to run to evil, a false witness who breathes out lies, and one who sows discord among brothers." To steal his brother's wife surely sowed some discord. Abomination seven? Check. Herodias's quickly calculated plot to kill John is surely devising wicked plans. Abomination four? Check. Herod's exaggerated offer of his kingdom surely constitutes a lying tongue, and perhaps false testimony. Abomination two? Check. Abomination six? Check. Herod's proud oaths and offer, along with his saving face rather than John's head perfectly illustrates "haughty eyes." Abomination one? Check. They are all guilty of "shedding innocent blood." Abomination three? Check. Finally, the swiftness of the whole scene sure does remind me of that line—"feet that make haste to run to evil." Abomination five? Check. Seven out of seven. This trio is perfect in their imperfections.

Real-Life Examples

Earlier we spoke of the five defining traits of most biblical proverbs, the fifth being that they express experiences and truths that are always up-to-date and are therefore continually confirmed in our own lives and observations. Regarding this final trait, Ryken suggests that, accordingly, "we need to provide real-life examples . . . for a given proverb." When I recently preached in the UK on the theme of human transiency and the reality of the vanishing nature of our earthly accomplishment in Ecclesiastes ("There is no remembrance," 1:11), I opened with the illustration of my searching for my name online the night before. "Douglas Sean O'Donnell" was linked to a website, Irishdeaths.com. It listed various dead Irishmen. I was not among them but will be joining them soon enough. And my accomplishments, like yours, will be buried and soon forgotten. I shared that real-life example. Do the same.

Asides and Other Interruptive Instructions

Robert Alden writes, "Proverbs is truly a collection of sayings with no arrangement, outline, order, or progression. When you think about it, however, life is like that. We try to bring order to life, but opportunities, crises, and unexpected intrusions come. . . . Perhaps that is why Proverbs comes to us in the form it does."[64] Emulate that example.

One of the preachers who greatly shaped my preaching, Phillip Jensen, is a master of insightful and applicable asides. Listen to how he does it. You can listen to my poor imitations too. He has a website in his name; and the design team at Crossway has made one for me. Enjoy the examples. Or, think, "What vanity!"

Make 'Em Laugh

I married into a family that loves musicals. Pray for me! When I watched *West Side Story* and the two street gangs approached each other singing and dancing, I needed a break from *this* reality. Yet, when I was dragged to watch professional actors sing and dance to the production of *Singin' in the Rain*, I was impressed. I was especially impressed when I heard and saw the skit "Make 'Em Laugh." Brilliant!

The final tip is use humor, whether overt (a joke or cartoon clip) or minimalist (a witty one-liner). First, do so because Proverbs does

---

64 Robert Alden, *Proverbs: A Commentary on an Ancient Book of Timeless Advice* (Grand Rapids, MI: Baker, 1983), iv.

so. Here's another short-list of funny lines, or at least humorous images that make serious points:

Let a man meet a she-bear robbed of her cubs
    rather than a fool in his folly. (17:12)

As a door turns on its hinges,
    so does a sluggard on his bed.
The sluggard buries his hand in the dish;
    it wears him out to bring it back to his mouth. (26:14–15)

Second, do so because it works. A good joke or witty line, like a well-told story, engages, illustrates, and refocuses people.

Think of preachers whose sermons you admire. Do they convey passion and conviction? Do they engage you in a visceral way? Do you feel as if they are talking directly to you about the ancient text and the Ancient of Days? Are they personable, relatable, energetic, clear, honest, and persuasive? And do they offer concrete descriptions, engaging anecdotes, satirical riffs, clever turns of phrase, surprising insights, and wry asides? Do they make you laugh? And did you answer "yes" to the above questions? I'll bet you did. Copy the masters.

CONCLUSION

In his brilliant book *Short Sentences Long Remembered: A Guided Story of Proverbs and Other Wisdom Literature*, Ryken points out that the essential form of wisdom literature—the individual proverb—"appears on virtually every page of the Bible." He goes on to claim, "The Bible is the most aphoristic book of the Western world."[65]

---

65 Ryken, *Short Sentences Long Remembered*, 17.

Ryken also shares his journey from "undervaluing . . . proverbs as a form of literature" to having "a growing appreciation" for them.[66] He lists a number of obstacles that then stood in his way, and perhaps still stand in your way, the first three being: (1) a shift in cultural sensibility, (2) loss of memorizing, and (3) indifference to wisdom.

It is difficult to value biblical proverbs when our "modern age is not an oral age and is not oriented toward proverbial knowledge," and when the issue is not merely "not valuing proverbs," but also "lacking the mental equipment to cultivate them as a literary form."[67] We are immersed in a thousand shallow slogans, but not carefully crafted words of simple but profound truths that require sensibility of thought, deep meditation, and ready application. Moreover, we live in a print and digital culture where memory is undervalued and underused, and rarely do we use memorized proverbs to daily speak into each other's lives. It is hard to preach proverbs when we don't speak and hear proverbs! Finally, we live in the information age. Instead of walking outside, finding a flower patch, and taking the time to actually consider what a lily looks and smells like, we Google the info we need. As poet T. S. Eliot decried nearly a century ago, "Where is the knowledge we have lost in information?" we might ask today, "Can wisdom be found scrolling on our phones and watching five-minute video clips?" Biblical proverbs convey information, but so much more than mere data given at the touch of a screen. They bestow God's wisdom from the life experiences of God's people.

In this chapter, we have offered ways to surmount such obstacles, if surmounting is needed in your case. And in every preacher's

---

66 Ryken, *Short Sentences Long Remembered*, 19.
67 Ryken, *Short Sentences Long Remembered*, 20.

case, we hope, as Paul hoped for Timothy, "that all may see your progress" (1 Tim. 4:15). Paul speaks of progress in holy living ("train yourself for godliness," v. 7) but also in word-ministry ("be a good servant of Christ Jesus, being trained in the words of the faith," v. 6). Part of such training includes knowing how to rightly handle all of Scripture (2 Tim. 2:15), including proverbs. In the coming years, make it a priority to show your people your progress in understanding, explaining, illustrating, and applying proverbs.

BUILD YOUR LIBRARY! HELPFUL RESOURCES

Garrett, Duane A. "Preaching Wisdom," in *Reclaiming the Prophetic Mantle: Preaching the Old Testament Faithfully*. Edited by George L. Klein. Nashville: Broadman, 1992.

Longman, Tremper, III. *How to Read Proverbs*. Downers Grove, IL: IVP Academic, 2002.

McKenzie, Alyce M. *Preaching Proverbs: Wisdom from the Pulpit*. Louisville: Westminster/John Knox, 1996.

O'Donnell, Douglas Sean. *The Beginning and End of Wisdom: Preaching Christ from the First and Last Chapters of Proverbs, Ecclesiastes, and Job*. Wheaton, IL: Crossway, 2011.

Ryken, Leland. *Short Sentences Long Remembered: A Guided Story of Proverbs and Other Wisdom Literature*, Reading the Bible as Literature. Wooster, OH: Weaver, 2016.

6

And I Saw

Preaching Visionary Writings

EARLIER I TOLD OF Dr. Ryken recounting the time an older minister shared how he would often read a psalm to patients in a hospital
but would never consider preaching a psalm because he "didn't know
what to do with it." If that is true of poetry, how much more it must
be true of the visionary literature found throughout Scripture. I have
encountered many seasoned pastors who have avoided the second
half of Daniel, most of Revelation, the Olivet Discourse, and parts
of Paul and the prophets because they didn't know what to do with
the "visions and voices, symbols and signs, demons and dragons,"[1]
along with this sample of other bizarre and bewildering sights:

> "Four living creatures," each with "four wings" that featured
> "human hands" on the sides of the wings and "four faces"—the
> face of a human, lion, ox, and eagle . . . (see Ezek. 1:5, 6, 8, 10)

1   Jeffrey D. Arthurs, *Preaching with Variety: How to Re-Create the Dynamics of Biblical Genres*
(Grand Rapids, MI: Kregel, 2007), 179.

A floating goat ("behold, a male goat came . . . across the face of the whole earth without touching the ground") with "a conspicuous horn between his eyes" (see Dan. 8:5–6)

"Something like a great sheet descending" from heaven "upon the earth" filled with "all kinds of animals and reptiles and birds of the air" (see Acts 10:11–12)

"I saw a woman sitting on a scarlet beast . . . and it had seven heads and ten horns" (Rev. 17:3)

While it is unlikely that we would label the above images what George Bernard Shaw called the book of Revelation ("a curious record of the visions of a drug addict"[2]), what *do* we call them? More importantly, what do we do with them? What do they mean, and how do we preach sermons on such sights? In this final chapter, we offer help on the Bible's most perplexing genre.

HOW TO READ BIBLICAL VISIONARY WRITINGS

Let us begin by acknowledging that Presbyterians and non-Presbyterians alike, if they have read through good swaths of Scripture, agree with the Westminster Confession of Faith's statement that "all things in Scripture are not alike plain in themselves, nor alike clear unto all" (1.8) and that the Bible's visionary literature fits into the "not alike plain in themselves" category. And because that is the case, it is helpful to admit that we feel intimidated. The intimidation comes through ignorance

2   Shaw, quoted in Arthurs, *Preaching with Variety*, 178.

and inexperience.[3] Moreover, the abundance of obscure geo-graphical place names, elusive poetry and symbolism, topicality ("references to topics or situations that existed in the [author's] time and would have been understood by people living then but not by people [you!] living now"),[4] and confusion over time (has that happened, is it happening, or will it happen?) are all obstacles to our understanding. We start, then, in this first half of the chapter, with information that will, Lord willing, lessen the intimidation and give you the courage to take and preach what is not readily plain and clear and make it plain and clear to your congregation.

Wheels within Wheels

Let's start, as is only fitting, with a picture. I thought about starting with Ezekiel's gyroscopic image ("a wheel within a wheel," with "rims . . . full of eyes all around," Ezek. 1:16, 18). But in the end, I thought that an image of the glory of God was too grand to use for an illustration of the encyclopedic form of this genre. So, let's go with umbrellas!

Picture a bunch of little umbrellas under a large umbrella under a larger umbrella under a super-sized umbrella. The biggest um-brella is the genre of fantasy. Beneath that is visionary literature and then, below that, is apocalyptic literature. The Greek word *apokalypsis* "means 'unveiling or revelation,' and the apocalyp-tic literature chiefly unveils a world beyond and other than our

---

3 For example, in the whole of your ministry have you preached through Ezekiel, Zechariah, Revelation, and the second half of Daniel? This year, have you struggled in your devotional reading of Scripture to get through a book that is largely prophetic or apocalyptic?

4 Leland Ryken, *Symbols and Reality: A Guided Study of Prophecy, Apocalypse, and Visionary Literature* (Wooster, OH: Weaver, 2016), 14.

own."[5] Portions of apocalyptic literature can be called *prophetic apocalyptic* or *apocalyptic prophecy*. That genre is the dominant visionary genre in the Bible, and will thus be our focus. Within that genre (think of the books of Daniel and Revelation) other sub-genres are present, such as oracles, poems, songs, prayers, epistles, satire, and narrative fragments.[6] What Ryken says of Revelation fits portions of the prophetic apocalyptic throughout Scripture: "Two things primarily are unveiled," namely, "the nature of the unseen spiritual world and what will happen in the future."[7]

Sharp Two-Edged Sword

Why does the Bible reveal and record visionary writings, especially apocalyptic? First, the dreams and visions are often given to encourage the oppressed and bring hope to the hopeless. They are "designed to exhort and console oppressed believers by disclosing a transcendent vision of the future that God has prepared, which

---

5 Leland Ryken, *A Complete Handbook of Literary Forms in the Bible* (Wheaton, IL: Crossway, 2014), 25. "The word 'apocalypse' is derived from the Greek word meaning 'to reveal.' Accordingly, it has traditionally been used to describe writing which purports to be a revelation of phenomena which transcend the world of ordinary reality. Apocalyptic writing has usually denoted prophetic writing—writing which is predictive of future events. Within this broad framework there are two main types of apocalyptic writing. One is concerned with a transcendental state, outside of time, which will follow history; such writing is eschatologically oriented. The other views the apocalyptic state as attainable on earth, and describes a future state that will occur within the order of nature and within the ordinary temporal succession. Apocalypses of this type are frequently social in emphasis, with the reformed social order which is envisioned constituting a warning to contemporary society. Whether the future state is considered as falling within or beyond time, it is viewed as an ideal state—a type of golden age in which there is an ultimate triumph of good over evil" (Leland Ryken, *The Apocalyptic Vision in Paradise Lost* [Ithaca, NY: Cornell University Press, 1970], 2).

6 "Apocalyptic is a hybrid genre, partaking of narrative, poetry, and prophecy. As narrative, it has rudiments of plot, character, setting, and point of view. As poetry, it uses figurative language (especially symbolism) and heightened emotion" (Arthurs, *Preaching with Variety*, 180).

7 Leland Ryken, *Literary Introductions to the Books of the Bible* (Wheaton, IL: Crossway, 2015), 559–60.

will overturn present earthly circumstances."[8] Both the content and the form fit a specific audience and their specific historical circumstances. For example, in Babylon Daniel is given a vision of God's future vindication and everlasting reign to give him and those exiled with him a reminder of God's sovereignty; similarly, John, exiled on Patmos, sees the future final victory of God and his faithful people over the oppressive regime of the Roman Empire. For both saints, God's visions offer a reality counter to what they are experiencing; and, if they and their readers embrace those visions of God's supremacy, presence, and coming justice it will help them to endure suffering and continue in their faithful witness.

A second reason for this genre is to rebuke and discipline, and if necessary, judge unfaithful and worldly professing disciples. As Arthurs summarizes, "This genre consoles the persecuted faithful, but it also *chastises* the prosperous unfaithful."[9] The expressive language and evocative symbols of this literature hold its listeners' feet to the fire, or eyes to the Son of Man, whose "eyes were like a flame of fire" (Rev. 1:14). In this way, it functions like many of the biblical parables—it provides the necessary shock treatment. As Ryken writes,

> Visionary literature, with its arresting strangeness, breaks through our normal way of thinking and shocks us into seeing that things are not as they appear. Visionary writing attacks our ingrained patterns of deep-level thought in an effort to convince us of such things as that the world will not always continue as it now is, that there is something drastically wrong with the status quo, or that reality cannot be confined to the physical world that we

---

8 Arthurs, *Preaching with Variety*, 180.
9 Arthurs, *Preaching with Variety*, 182, emphasis mine.

perceive with our senses. Visionary literature is not cozy fireside reading. It gives us the shock treatment.[10]

What Ryken writes above obviously applies more broadly than just to those within the church who need to repent from sin and return to Christ. The expanded vision is to elicit the proper response and arouse godly affections in all.

A Third Edge

To my knowledge, there are no three-edged swords. (Although, I did find something called a Jagdkommando Tri-Dagger online!) So, let me state a third reason for this genre in a separate section, and thus for emphasis. Visionary writings present truths in unexpected and absorbing ways. Propositional statements are clear and helpful, but ideas embodied in imagery are more memorable, and offer perhaps an even clearer depiction of reality. For example, Ezekiel's expression of his vision of the divine chariot offers a sharper and unforgettable and fitting portrayal of our glorious God. As Ryken says, "An abstraction like 'God is glorious' does not pack the punch that Ezekiel's vision does."[11] D. A. Carson shares how this genre, "with its appeal to mixed metaphors and the like, has the unique ability to disclose things that are transcendent—right on the edge of ineffability. How do you talk about the throne room of God? How do you talk about the person of God? You can use a lot of abstract adjectives. Yet at the end of the day there is power in the multiplied, piled-up, sometimes formally mutually-contradictory images, which coalesce somehow

---

10 Leland Ryken, *How to Read the Bible as Literature* (Grand Rapids, MI: Zondervan, 1974), 169–70. Also quoted in Arthurs, *Preaching with Variety*, 183.
11 Ryken, *Symbols and Reality*, 79.

to make a powerful insight into realities for which we have no visual component in our brain."[12]

Ryken compares this genre to surrealistic art, the twentieth-century avant-garde technique of the seemingly irrational juxtaposition of images that are familiar with images that are unfamiliar, and normal with abnormal. Like those paintings, visionary literature can be said to follow common surrealistic techniques, including,

- [Using] the visible world around us as the starting point from which the author gathers material
- Bringing common objects into unrealistic combinations (making the ordinary suddenly seem extraordinary or strange)
- [Employing] distortion (sometimes called caricature) of the objects themselves, so that the parts, too, and not simply their juxtaposition, seem strange
- [Intermixing] fantasy elements (e.g., a dragon) to complement realistic objects.[13]

Ryken asks, "Why do prophetic and apocalyptic writers use surrealism?" His answer: "Surrealism has arresting strangeness and grabs our attention. The prophets and apocalyptic visionaries wish to overcome our numbness to truth brought on by sheer familiarity, and also to challenge our assumption that what we see around us is the only reality that exists. Related to that, one effect of surrealism is that it creates a sense of mystery, which is certainly appropriate when a writer portrays supernatural reality."[14]

---

12 D. A. Carson, "Apocalyptic Literature: Its Function and Usefulness." Available at simeon trust.org.
13 Ryken, *Symbols and Reality*, 118–19.
14 Ryken, *Symbols and Reality*, 120.

How true! Seeing the fearful image of a leopard-like "beast rising out of the sea, with ten horns and seven heads," whose "feet were like a bear's, and its mouth like a lion's mouth" (Rev. 13:1–2), and the grotesque image of a "woman, drunk with the blood of the saints" (Rev. 17:6) gets our attention. The images of people being "like thorns cut down, that are burned in the fire" (Isa. 33:12), locusts as big and strong as war horses with "tails . . . like scorpions" stinging people for five months (Rev. 9:7, 10), or one-hundred-pound hailstones falling "from heaven on people" (Rev. 16:21)—like scenes from a monster movie or a battle scene in *Lord of the Rings*—evoke terror as they open our ears (and eyes!) to God's revelation. With those pictures before us, it is hard to stay anesthetized to the truth of God's holiness and his coming judgments.

An Unfolding Pageant

Most visionary writings possess the rudiments of narrative. There is often a setting, with characters, and a semblance of a storyline. We say "semblance" because events are happening in some succession and to some end, but the story is not clearly structured with a beginning, middle, and end, with a rising tension, conflict, and resolution. "There is no unifying action, and there is no plot."[15] It doesn't follow a smooth narrative flow, but offers brief snapshots or vignettes that are "always shifting and never focus in for very long."[16] These "snapshots are often presented as dreams or visions, arranged as either a successive pageant or a kaleidoscope of constantly changing moments."[17]

15 Ryken, *Symbols and Reality*, 126.
16 Ryken, *How to Read the Bible as Literature*, 170.
17 Ryken, *Complete Handbook of Literary Forms in the Bible*, 26. "The overall genre is prophecy (22:19). Like biblical prophecy generally, the actual medium is visionary writing: the book [Revelation] unfolds as a pageant of visions, much a like a modern music video"

From Sensible Settings to Symbolic Strangeness

"The setting of a visionary realm is not *entirely* strange."[18] For example, in Isaiah's vision of God, it begins with a clear historical marker ("In the year that King Uzziah died"), and God is depicted as the ultimate king "sitting upon a throne" (Isa. 6:1). However, we then transition from the familiar to the strange. God's throne is "high and lifted up" (v. 1). Is it floating inches beneath the roof? The divine (and invisible!) sovereign is wearing a robe, and just the train of this garment fills the whole temple. The temple is about twenty stories high! That's a lot of space to cover. Can any creature breathe in the room with this giant robe? Obviously, both Isaiah and the six-winged angels can. For below God stands the prophet and above God are seraphim, who with two wings fly and with the other four cover their faces and feet. Ryken interprets the scene as follows:

> Even today we can picture a throne room, so we start with our feet on the ground. To say that God is "high and lifted up" introduces the first element of "otherness": *how* high and *how* lifted up? There is an element of mystery in the description. How can a robe fill an entire temple? And how did we move from a throne room to a temple? As for the seraphim, they defy all realistic images we have from the known world. The transcendent scene of Isaiah's call transports us to a strange world.[19]

(Leland Ryken, "Introduction to Revelation," in *The Literary Study Bible, English Standard Version* [Wheaton, IL: Crossway, 2019], 1945). Visionary writing "is not organized like a story" but "as a series of visions or dreams," with each vision unfolding like pictures in a slide show or frames in an action film (Ryken, *Literary Introductions to the Books of the Bible*, 558).

18 Ryken, *Symbols and Reality*, 72.

19 Ryken, *Symbols and Reality*, 72.

But we get ahead of ourselves. More on symbolism and its interpretation in a few pages. For now, let's stay with our feet on the ground and grounded in a real God who reveals realities to real people at real times and places in history.

Set in History

The throne room setting depicted above, like all of the dreams and visions in Scripture, is set in history. In fact, many of the visionary scenes start with a historical setting, like "In the year that King Uzziah died I saw" (Isa. 6:1) or "In the first year of Belshazzar king of Babylon, Daniel saw a dream and visions of his head as he lay in his bed" (Dan. 7:1). One sure way to misread visionary literature is to remove the interpretation of the details of the vision from its historical setting. For example, "Daniel and his fellow Jews about whom we read in the first six chapters had been carried into exile from Jerusalem in the first wave of captivity. In the stories about them in Daniel, we are given a clear picture of what it was like (and is like) to live as a displaced foreigner."[20] That setting sets the scene for the visions of chapters 7–12. After seventy years of exile, the return to Jerusalem is imminent, but the season of suffering is not over. Only after seventy sets of seven would God's final salvation arrive.

Symbolism

The most foundational characteristic of visionary literature is symbolism. "A symbol," according to Ryken's short and helpful definition, "is an image, character, setting, or event that exists in its own right (even if it is fantastic rather than real), but also points to or represents one or more things."[21] He notes, "Symbolism is

---

20 Ryken, *Literary Introductions to the Books of the Bible*, 277.
21 Ryken, *Symbols and Reality*, 87.

a common ingredient of visionary writing, in keeping with the fantasy element. Instead of portraying settings, characters, and events directly, the visionary writer portrays them by means of symbols. Thus, Christ becomes a lamb (Rev. 5:6) and churches are symbolically portrayed as lampstands (Rev. 1:20). In the prophecy of Daniel, four kings take the symbolic form of the four beasts (Dan. 7:15–27)."[22] Arthurs expands:

> This is not the world of the epistles with their flow of logic, or the worlds of narrative and parable with their feet planted in the soil of everyday life. It is closer to the world of poetry, but this is poetry amplified, at least in its use of symbols.
>
> The symbols can be animate beings such as a red dragon (Rev. 12:3–4), living creatures with "six wings . . . covered with eyes all around" (Rev. 4:8), a warrior on a red horse (Rev. 6:4), or two flying women with wings like those of a stork (Zech. 5:9). The symbols can also be inanimate objects such as candlesticks, bowls, trumpets, swords, and crowns. In the world of visions, these inanimate objects can themselves became actors, as when the earth helps the fleeing woman by swallowing a pursuing torrent (Rev. 12:13–16) and when the ram's horn grows to knock down stars (Dan. 8:9–10).[23]

Such symbolism is significant, for, "the symbols clarify the realities and make them vivid. The Christian worldview consists not only of *ideas* but also of *images or pictures* (a world picture in addition to a worldview)."[24]

---

22 Ryken, *Literary Forms*, 209–10.
23 Arthurs, *Preaching with Variety*, 185.
24 Ryken, *Literary Introductions to the Books of the Bible*, 565.

Color and Number Symbolism

This genre uses color and number symbolism. On color, Ryken writes, "In the Book of the Revelation, the color white is associated with Christ (1:4), the saints of God (3:18; 4:4; 7:9, 14; 19:18), the armies of heaven (19:14), and God's throne of judgment (20:11). Red, by contrast, usually appears in contexts of evil—warfare (6:4), the appearance of the satanic dragon (12:3), and the whore of Babylon and her beast (17:3–4)."[25] He adds, "The white garments of the saints (Rev. 3:18; 19:14) symbolize spiritual purity. A red horse (Rev. 6:4) symbolizes slaughter in warfare and a black horse (Rev. 6:5) death. The purple and scarlet cloth of the world empire 'Babylon' (actually Rome) in Revelation 18:12 represents affluence and mercantile prosperity."[26]

Regarding numerology, he summarizes, "The numbers 3, 7, 10, and 12 are good numbers that symbolize completeness, perfection, or victory. The number 6 is a sinister number similar to our bad-luck 13, approaching the perfection of 7 but falling short. Three and a half years (1,260 days) signal a short time, often in contexts of the temporary reign of evil. The number of the redeemed—144,000—symbolizes completeness (four-square symbolism of 12 times 12, and all 12 tribes represented) and magnitude (inasmuch as 1,000 symbolized a multitude in ancient times). The entire book of Revelation is based on patterns of 7 (letters to 7 churches, 7 seals, 7 trumpets, etc.); it is a fair inference that the number 7 symbolizes completeness."[27]

With both colors and numbers, we need the wisdom to understand the literary context, along with the type of genre of the

---

25 Leland Ryken, *Words of Life: A Literary Introduction to the New Testament* (Grand Rapids, MI: Baker, 1987), 139.

26 Ryken, *Symbols and Reality*, 99.

27 Ryken, *Symbols and Reality*, 99.

book or section of a book. For example, when the law in Numbers 19:2 speaks of "a red heifer without defect," the cow is literally the color red or orangish-red. However, the "red horse" of Zechariah's vision is an emblem of war and bloodshed. For example, within the historical narrative of Acts, when Luke writes, "we sailed away from Philippi after the days of Unleavened Bread, and in *five* days we came to them at Troas, where we stayed for *seven* days" (Acts 20:6), we are to understand the numbers literally. However, as Ryken states above, when John recalls his revelation, "Then I looked, and behold, on Mount Zion stood the Lamb, and with him 144,000 who had his name and his Father's name written on their foreheads" (Rev. 14:1), we are to understand the numbers symbolically, to represent the uncountable elect ("a great multitude that no one could number, from every nation, from all tribes and peoples and languages," 7:9).[28] The 144,000 are the ones who can stand in "the great day of . . . wrath" (6:17), the "sealed . . . servants of our God" (7:3), the "redeemed from the earth" (14:3).

Crazy Cast of Characters

A common feature of visionary writing is that the cast of characters includes *natural forces* such as the sun and moon, storms, wind, the sea, and rivers. In Jesus's Olivet Discourse, "the heavenly bodies are portrayed as actors in the final eschaton (climax of history): 'Immediately after the tribulation of those days the sun will be darkened, and the moon will not give its light, and the stars will fall from heaven, and the powers of the heavens will be shaken'

28 Following the pattern in Revelation 5, where John *hears* about a lion and then *sees* a lamb (with Jesus as the same referent of both animals), in chapter 7 John *hears* about 144,000 (7:1–8) but he *sees* the great multitude (v. 9).

(Matt. 24:29)."[29] The actors also might be *supernatural agents* such as angels, dragons, or fantastic creatures such as two women with wings like those of a stork. Or, sometimes there are combinations of natural forces and supernatural agents, such as a beast rising out of the sea, or an angel standing on the sun. In Ezekiel 10:9–14, the prophet sees "four cherubim who move through the air in co-ordinated formation accompanied by whirling wheels."[30] *Animals who behave like people* are a major category of visionary agents. The horses of John's vision that have serpentine tails and fire and smoke coming out of their mouths and that attack people as though they were warriors (Rev. 9:17–19) are one example. Another example is the killer locusts of Joel's prophecy:

> Their appearance is like the appearance of horses,
>   and like war horses they run.
> As with the rumbling of chariots,
>   they leap on the tops of the mountains,
> like the crackling of a flame of fire
>   devouring the stubble,
> like a powerful army
>   drawn up for battle. (Joel 2:4–5)

Transcends Earthly Experience

The visions portray supernatural occurrences or miraculous events, and often, these occurrences or events are set on a cosmic stage—the sea, the sky, the whole earth, or both in the heavens and on the earth. Moreover, the visions of altered earthly realities are intended to "carry us away in our imaginations to a supernatural realm that

29 Ryken, *Symbols and Reality*, 74.
30 Ryken, *Symbols and Reality*, 74.

transcends earthly experience."[31] This can be heaven. "The book of Revelation is an anthology of visions of heavenly reality."[32] Or, it can be some other place, like Isaiah's vision of God's glorious throne room. In those places we transcend our earthly experience and gain "a perspective 'from above.'" As David Helm writes, "By that I mean that they write from God's vantage point. Human history is orchestrated from God's heavenly throne room. Whether you are reading the great visions of Zechariah, Daniel, or even John, this divine perspective remains unchanged. Readers are given a behind-the-scenes look, or better yet, an elevated glance across heaven's threshold at the end of [or part of] human history."[33]

Worldmaking

The above traits all "create a strong sense of otherness and strangeness as we read," which "fits in well with the idea that apocalypse is an unveiling of a reality beyond the earthly."[34] Part of the strategic intention of this genre is to be subversive. Heaven entering earth, the future unveiled in the present, and the invisible merging with the visible disorients us for the purpose of reorienting us to a renewed vision of God, the future, and the present world we live in. Another intention is to create another world for its readers to enter. "Worldmaking," as Ryken puts it, "is an essential skill required of the composer of visionary literature. . . . Visionary literature

---

31 Ryken, *Complete Handbook of Literary Forms in the Bible*, 209–10.

32 Ryken, *Complete Handbook of Literary Forms in the Bible*, 209–10.

33 David Helm, "Apocalyptic Literature: Study Guide." Available at simeontrust.org.

34 Ryken, *Literary Forms*, 26. "The world of visionary writing is often 'strange' compared to the world in which we live (literary critics regularly use the formula 'strange-world motif'). This otherness might be temporal, as when the writer portrays a future state of affairs that differs from how matters stand at the time of the writing of the work. Another way of achieving this quality of strangeness is to portray settings, characters, and events that are fantastic, not belonging to life in this world" (209–10).

transports us to another, merely imagined world."[35] Elsewhere he adds, "Visionary literature does not give us a replica of the known world; instead, it whisks us away in our imaginations to an alternative world,"[36] where "horses can be red and a dragon can have seven heads and seven horns."[37]

Denunciation and Dualism

This genre "includes a strong element of denunciation and judgment of the present evil world system, along with a prediction of its end and pictures of an alternative world to the evil one that we know. The world that we enter in apocalyptic writing is dualistic, clearly divided between forces of good and evil, which are engaged in an ongoing conflict."[38]

A Time, Times, and Half a Time

How time relates to the Bible's visionary literature is not, strictly speaking, a literary phenomenon, but it is important for us to understand. First, there is a futuristic orientation (the vision "refers to many days from now," Dan. 8:26; "the things that must soon take place," Rev. 1:1); that is, most visions reveal future events.

Second, timelines usually work in three main stages—the immediate or near future ("Within a year . . . all the glory of Kedar will come to an end," Isa. 21:16); the intermediate future (e.g., the incarnation as a fulfillment of a variety of visions and prophecies); and the eschatological future (e.g., the return of Christ and final judgment).[39] On Zechariah 13:1 ("On that day there shall

---

35 Ryken, *Symbols and Reality*, 72.
36 Ryken, *Literary Forms*, 209.
37 Ryken, *Literary Introductions to the Books of the Bible*, 558.
38 Ryken, *Literary Forms*, 26.
39 See Ryken, *Symbols and Reality*, 27–29.

be a fountain opened for the house of David and the inhabitants of Jerusalem, to cleanse them from sin and uncleanness"), Ryken asks the following questions: "Is this a picture of the imminent future, namely, the return of a remnant from Babylonian captivity to resettle Jerusalem? Is the prophet Zechariah looking forward six hundred years to the incarnation of Jesus and the blessings that this brought permanently into the world? Is this an apocalyptic vision of the New Jerusalem of the millennium and eternity? Might all of these be simultaneously in view?"[40]

Third, the ordering of events is not always chronological. For example, the four beasts of Daniel 7:4–7 symbolize four kingdoms, in the order of their appearance or historical dominance: Babylon, Medo-Persia, Greece, and Rome. However, the start of Daniel 7 signals a break in the chronological sequence. We move from the reign of Nebuchadnezzar (1:1; 2:1) to Belshazzar, who followed Nebuchadnezzar (5:1), to Darius the Mede (6:1). Then, in 7:1, the vision takes us back in time to the first year of King Belshazzar.

Fourth, the symbols in these visions are "open-ended and capable of applying to many manifestations of something."[41] Put differently, what is depicted as past events (the letters to seven churches in first-century Asia Minor) and future events (the coming of the Christ and his judgments) can apply in the present. The visions are "sufficiently universal."[42] What happened *then* and will happen *later*, could happen, in some form or another (a temporary judgment or vindication), *now*.

This relates to the trait in visionary literature of recurring patterns. For example, the four beasts in Daniel's vision (Dan. 7:4–7),

---

40 Ryken, *Symbols and Reality*, 16.
41 Ryken, *Literary Introductions to the Books of the Bible*, 558.
42 Ryken, *Literary Introductions to the Books of the Bible*, 558.

who represent four successive kingdoms, become, in John's vision (Rev. 13:1–3), a single kingdom—the Roman Empire.[43] John was not reductionistic in his use of biblical imagery, and neither should we be. Just as Daniel's and John's communities needed to be comforted by God's promises about a coming King and his eternal kingdom and final vindication of the righteous, so our people need to take in the same message and take heart in the present as they long for the future. As Ryken states concerning Revelation, "Because of the literary form of the book, which portrays events symbolically, its relevance extends throughout the history of the world. Babylon, for example, may have been the Roman empire for John's first-century audience, but in Old Testament times it was literally Babylon, and it has taken many forms throughout history. The literary mode of symbolism means that the events portrayed in Revelation are perpetually relevant and will be ultimately relevant at the end of history."[44]

Cracking the Code

Earlier we stated that symbolism is the most foundational characteristic of visionary literature. We also offered this definition: "A symbol is an image, character, setting, or event that exists in its own right (even if it is fantastic rather than real), but also points to or represents one or more things."[45] It is helpful to have good definitions, but what about help in cracking the complex codes? In discovering the answer to the question, "To what reality does

---

43 The visions consistently collapse "one epoch in time upon another," something called *transtemporal*. Images—such as the four beasts in Daniel 7 and the composite of those creatures in Revelation 13—can be applied "to more than one period in history" (Helm, "Apocalyptic Literature: Study Guide").

44 Ryken, *Words of Life*, 144–45.

45 Ryken, *Symbols and Reality*, 87.

the unlifelike person, place, thing, or action point or symbolize?" we offer three possible steps.

The first step is to see if the symbol is interpreted for you. For example, in Revelation 1:12, "seven golden lampstands" are mentioned. Soon after, Jesus says that "the seven lampstands are the seven churches" (1:20). Easy enough! There are other examples from Revelation where the interpretation follows on the heel of the symbol, such as the "ancient serpent, who is called the devil and Satan" (12:9) and "it was granted her to clothe herself with fine linen . . . for the fine linen is the righteous deeds of the saints" (19:8). Likewise, in Daniel 2, the interpretation follows immediately after Daniel's retelling of the king's dream (e.g., Nebuchadnezzar is "the head of gold," v. 38).

However, as with parables, few of the symbolic details of visionary literature are quickly or ever interpreted for us. Thus, the second step will often be the first step we take: that is to review the book's literary context for clues, for often "the book itself will provide the interpretation."[46] Revelation 17:7–18 provides in interesting example. In verse 7, the angel tells John not to marvel about the revelation of "the woman, and of the beast with seven heads and ten horns that carries her" because he will "tell [reveal to him] . . . the mystery." In verses 9–10, John is told that "the seven heads are seven mountains on which the woman is seated" and "also seven kings," and in verse 12 he is told that the ten horns are "ten kings who have not yet received royal power." These kings "are of one mind" and "they hand their power and authority over to the beast" (v. 13), and as one army "they will make war on the Lamb, and the Lamb will conquer them, for

---

46 Ryken, *Words of Life*, 144.

he is Lord of lords and King of kings, and those with him are called and chosen and faithful" (v. 14). Later, John is told that "the woman that [he] saw is the great city that has dominion over the kings of the earth" (v. 18), and "the waters" where the woman is seated symbolize "peoples and multitudes and nations and languages" (v. 15).

At this point, the revelation is still quite cloudy. The kings and their power obviously represent earthly rulers and their armies, and the woman is an important city with a world dominion. The lamb and his army will defeat their enemies. But who is the beast? What city does the woman represent? Why is she called a prostitute? Who is the lamb? Why are his followers referred to as "called and chosen and faithful," and whom do they represent? How did they win the war? All of these questions are answered in Revelation. Our job is to find out where and how. Let's take the easiest one: who is the lamb, and how does he conquer? We are told in this text that he is "Lord of lords and King of kings" (v. 14).

As Christians, we are so familiar with the animal imagery and title as representative of Jesus. But the text itself makes only indirect connections. So, like a detective in a police investigation, the case can be solved only if we track down the clues and see where they lead us. If we turn from Revelation 17 to Revelation 19, the angel mentions Jesus's name, as it relates to those "who hold to the testimony of Jesus" and he says that that testimony "is the spirit of prophecy" (v. 10). The next scene is that of a rider on a white horse. Again, we know this is another image for Jesus, but the text itself doesn't make that direct claim. But what it does do is say that on this rider's robe is written, "King of kings and Lord of lords" (v. 16). Moreover, we read this description:

His eyes are like a flame of fire, and on his head are many diadems, and he has a name written that no one knows but himself. . . . *From his mouth comes a sharp sword* with which to strike down the nations, and he will rule them with a rod of iron. (vv. 12, 15)

Above we are given key clues, for we recall the description of Jesus at the start of the book, where "Jesus . . . the ruler of the kings on earth" (1:5) is described as having eyes "like a flame of fire" (v. 14) and a "sharp . . . sword" coming "from his mouth" (v. 16).[47] Mystery solved! Jesus is the lamb. And he conquers his enemies, as the context of the whole book makes clear, through his death and second coming.[48]

The identity of those enemies is made clear only through the final step: the context of the whole Bible. The important hermeneutical slogan of the Reformation—"Scripture interprets Scripture"— is crucial for cracking many of the codes of the Bible's visionary literature. What was said of John Bunyan (if you pricked his skin, he'd bleed Bible) could be said of the book of Revelation (if you dig beneath the surface, you'll strike the Hebrew Scriptures). In Revelation, the symbols Christ reveals to John come from "the storehouse of symbols" in the Old Testament.[49] There are nearly

---

47 "Nearly everything in the passage is a symbol. The seven golden lampstands are the seven churches of chapters 2–3. The son of man standing in the midst of them is Christ. The long robe and golden sash represent Christ as king and priest. The whiteness stands for spiritual purity and splendor. Fire, bronze, and the light of the sun in full strength are an example of enameled imagery, which combines a supernatural brilliance of light and hardness of texture to symbolize the glory and permanence of a transcendent place (heaven) and person (Christ). The seven stars are the angels of the seven churches. The sword is the word, power, and judgment of Christ" (Ryken, *Symbols and Reality*, 89–90).

48 See Rev. 5:6, 12; 13:8; 17:14.

49 Arthurs, *Preaching with Variety*, 186.

300 such allusions, according to Bruce Metzger.[50] For each section of visionary literature, we should acknowledge that the various symbols are likely rooted in other biblical texts. Thus, we should ask questions like, "Of what theological fact or event in salvation history does this passage seem to be a symbolic version?"[51] and "What familiar NT doctrine (such as God's judgment against evil) or event in salvation history (such as Christ's defeat of evil) or eschatological teaching (such as the degeneration of human history in its final phases) is pictured by the visionary details of the text?"[52] For, as Ryken notes, "The strange visions of Revelation keep referring to familiar doctrines and eschatological ideas taught elsewhere in the New Testament. . . . The book of Revelation fleshes out the blueprint that we can construct from elsewhere in the New Testament."[53]

For example, here is Ryken's brief interpretation of the symbols of Revelation 12: This text "begins with a vision of a woman (Israel) giving birth to a son (Christ), whom a red dragon (Satan) tries to destroy but who is miraculously protected and snatched up to heaven (the ascension of Jesus after incarnate life on earth)."[54] How does Ryken arrive at this conclusion? Here's how: "On the basis of the Old Testament symbols for the tribes of Israel (vv. 1–2), we can

---

50 Bruce M. Metzger, *Breaking the Code: Understanding the Book of Revelation* (Nashville: Abington, 1993), 13. "No other book of the NT is as permeated by the OT as is Revelation. . . . It is generally recognized that Revelation contains more OT references than does any other NT book, although past attempts to tally the total amount have varied [195, 226, 278, 394, 455, 493, 635, approximately 1000]" (G. K. Beale and Sean M. McDonough, "Revelation," in *Commentary on the New Testament Use of the Old Testament* [Grand Rapids, MI: Baker Academic, 2007], 1081, 1082). As Arthur Jackson put it, "All of the prophets rendezvous in Revelation" (quoted in Helm, "Apocalyptic Literature: Study Guide").

51 Ryken, *Words of Life*, 143.

52 Ryken, "Introduction to Revelation," *Literary Study Bible*, 1947.

53 Ryken, "Introduction to Revelation," *Literary Study Bible*, 1947.

54 Ryken, *Literary Introductions to the Books of the Bible*, 561.

identify the woman as Israel. The child who is to rule all the nations is obviously Christ. The dragon, we know, is Satan (12:9), who was unable to destroy Christ during his earthly life and redemptive history."[55] This provides an excellent summary of what should be our usual process of deduction. We need to have a keen eye for the obvious,[56] a firm grip on human experience in the world,[57] an understanding of the Bible's storyline, a knowledge of the history and cultural symbols of the original audiences, and the ability to connect one person or event in salvation history with another.

A Comment on Commentaries

What if taking the steps above gets us nowhere? If the symbol is not interpreted for you in the immediate context or elsewhere, the last step is to ask an expert. Consult with commentaries!

In the April 2011 issue of *Themelios*, Murray Harris reviewed J. Ramsey Michaels's commentary on the Gospel of John. In his review, as a brief aside on commentaries, Harris wrote, "what an embarrassment of riches we now have!" True. As such, for preachers, especially as we approach visionary texts, it is foolish to neglect reading a few good commentaries. Elsewhere, in detailing my regular weekly routine for sermon preparation, I wrote, "I use between five and thirty commentaries a week. Call me crazy? That's fine. I'd rather be called crazy than lazy. My logic is this: If I can gain insight from my intern on Monday, who is a Bible student at the local college [my usual practice at that point in my life], can't I also (and moreover!) gain insights from my commentator buddies on Tuesday, who are usually Bible professors at the most prestigious

55 Ryken, *Words of Life*, 141.
56 Ryken, *Words of Life*, 143.
57 Ryken, *Words of Life*, 144.

colleges, universities, and seminaries? Hanging out with commentators in the study or at Starbucks is the world's greatest Bible study. Don't neglect attending."[58] This bit of advice is especially true of the difficult genre of the visionary. After you do your own work—whether it is on Monday morning or Saturday night (God forbid!)—see what the experts have to say about the great goat who has a horn broken, burning sulfur falling from the sky, the birds eating the flesh of kings, and a thousand other tricky texts. See if their knowledge of Scripture and ancient history helps shed light on the mysteries you are seeking to solve.

HOW TO PREACH BIBLICAL VISIONARY WRITINGS

I must admit that I wrote this last chapter lastly not because it naturally fits—because it includes the book of Revelation—as the last chapter in a book on preaching the genres of the Bible, but because I lack experience in this genre and was thus intimidated. My experience is sparse. I taught a men's Bible study on Daniel, preached on the Olivet Discourse in Matthew and Mark, twice preached through Revelation 1–5, and one of my favorite go-to Christmas sermons comes from Revelation 12. But that is the extent of my teaching and preaching on the visionary literature in the Bible. So, needless to say, I learned a lot from reading Ryken's material on this topic, and other scholarly tomes as well (especially Arthurs), and reading and listening to pastors who are far more experienced. And, for this reason, I can't wait to share what I have learned; and, to someday, Lord willing, preach through all of the

---

58 Douglas Sean O'Donnell, "Spirit-Filled Sitzfleisch: The Prayerful Art of Sermonizing," in *Unashamed Workmen*, ed. Rhett Dodson (Fearn, Ross-shire, Scotland, UK: Christian Focus, 2014), 210–11.

visions in God's Word. Below I offer sixteen suggestions. (I know, it should be seven or twelve, but sixteen is the number I landed on.)

Earnest Prayer

On the Olivet Discourse, J. C. Ryle wrote, "All portions of Scripture like this ought to be approached with deep humility and earnest prayer for the teaching of the Spirit."[59] That is good advice for approaching all visionary literature. Get on your knees in the study before you stand in the pulpit.

A Pure Shade of Grey in an Ever-Growing and Ever-Increasingly Black and White World

The church is more polarized than ever, and many people in our congregations are demanding that we offer authoritative statements on everything from critical race theory to the identity of the antichrist. The advice here is simple, but surely controversial: Don't be afraid to give various interpretations and allow for some ambiguity.[60] If Daniel, who was given far greater wisdom and insider information than we will ever have or be given, can say that he "did not understand" a vision (Dan. 8:27), then we need to lower our soap boxes a few feet when it comes to this instinctively mysterious genre.

Don't Overemphasize Identification

Every symbol does symbolize someone, some place, or something, but sometimes identifying every person, place, and thing can be

---

59 J. C. Ryle, *Matthew: Expository Thoughts on the Gospels*, Crossway Classic Commentaries (1860; repr., Wheaton, IL: Crossway, 1993), 225.

60 For example, there may be a few exegetical options for Christ's consolation of "hidden manna" and "a white stone" (Rev. 2:17) to the church in Pergamum.

an unhealthy preoccupation, especially when Scripture itself offers no clues. So, please set aside your sermon on ten reasons why the ten horns in Revelation 13 represent the nations of the European Union. That is very likely not true. What is certainly true is that God will have the victory through his Son over every evil empire, those in present-day Europe and throughout the world. Avoid over-identification from the pulpit!

Play Not the Prophet (Thus Saith the Lord)

I began my sermon on Mark 13:24–37 with a long list of false predictions and the repetition of the phrase "Christ did not return." For example,

> A second and third century Roman clergyman calculated that Jesus would return in A.D. 500. His prediction was based on the dimensions of Noah's Ark. Christ did not return. On January 1, 1000, many Christians in Europe predicted the end of the world. Sadly, some reacted to that millennial mark in a military fashion. As the first of the year fast approached, Christian armies traveled to some of the pagan countries in Northern Europe in order to make converts, by force, if necessary, before Christ returned. Christ did not return. Also, in the Middle Ages, Pope Innocent III took the number 618 (the year Islam was founded) and added the number 666 (the number of the beast) to get 1284 as the year of Christ's final judgment. Christ did not return.[61]

I went on to include the predictions of Joseph Smith, Charles Taze Russell, Edgar Cayce, and Harold Camping. On six thousand

---

61 Douglas Sean O'Donnell, *Mark: Arise and Follow the Son*, forthcoming.

billboards across America, Camping decreed, "Judgment Day is coming/May 21 [2011]. The Bible guarantees it!" When the day came (and Christ did not), Camping merely offered another false prediction for the day of Christ's return.

When it comes to figuring out the details of the Olivet Discourse, or any of the apocalyptic prophecies, we must stay within the limits of what is revealed in Scripture.[62] If Jesus clearly states, "But concerning that day or that hour, no one knows, not even the angels in heaven, nor the Son, but only the Father" (Mark 13:32), it is sinful for us to pretend to know more than the incarnate Son.

We are not to play the prophet. And, if we have done so, we should repent, which is actually what Camping did a few months before he died. In a private interview, he stated what Jesus stated in Mark 13:32, that no human being can know the day the world will end.[63] Moreover, in a public letter to the listeners of his Family Radio network, he admitted that his predictions were "sinful," that he had not heeded what Jesus taught in the Olivet Discourse, and that he was now studying his Bible "even more fervently . . . not to find dates, but to be more faithful in [his] understanding [of it]."[64] Praise God. Do you need to repent of playing the prophet—of your fanciful prognostications and the fascination with prophecy charts and graphs and endless speculations that go with them?

Relive the Past; Present the Present

So many of the false predictions arise from failing to understand (or even seek out!) the author's intent for his original audience, as set

---

[62] "What will happen when" is not the right question; it misses "the intent of the apocalyptic message" ("Genre of Apocalypse," in *Dictionary of Biblical Imagery*, ed. Leland Ryken, James C. Wilhoit, and Tremper Longman III [Downers Grove, IL: IVP Academic,1998], 35).

[63] "Harold Camping Exclusive: Family Radio Founder Retires" (*Christian Post*, October 24, 2011).

[64] "Letter from Harold Camping to the 'Faith Radio Family'" (*Charisma News*, March 7, 2012).

within their cultural context. We identify the four living creatures in Ezekiel as political powers today without ever making sense of the significance of the book's detailed historic setting:

> In the thirtieth year, in the fourth month, on the fifth day of the month, as I was among the exiles by the Chebar canal, the heavens were opened, and I saw visions of God. On the fifth day of the month (it was the fifth year of the exile of King Jehoiachin), the word of the LORD came to Ezekiel the priest, the son of Buzi, in the land of the Chaldeans by the Chebar canal, and the hand of the LORD was upon him there. (Ezek. 1:1–3)

This book of apocalyptic prophecies starts with these fourteen historical details for a reason. If we overlook the details of *when* this vision happened and to *whom*, we cannot make sense of *what* the vision means, and certainly not its contemporary significance. As Helm cautions, "We get so caught up with where history is going that we neglect to consider what the history was, or where it went."[65] Arthurs gives an excellent example of reliving the text in its original historical context:

> Imagine that you are a devoted Christ-follower in the age of Domitian. You are harassed and marginalized, perhaps even imprisoned and tortured. Why? Because you love Jesus and have offered yourself to him as a living sacrifice. Imagine your feelings of vindication and relief when the curtain rises to show you God, called Faithful and True, who will soon strike down

---

65 Helm, "Apocalyptic Literature: Study Guide."

the nations (Rev. 19:11, 15). The tension of theodicy is resolved, and you determine to endure to the end.[66]

One reason to relive the past is to bridge the distance between the ancient audience and the contemporary church. As exiles on this earth, we can all relate to the themes found in exilic apocalyptic. In Daniel, for example, the stories of exile (chapters 1–6) along with the visions (chapters 7–12) both highlight "the contemporary issues facing Christians who live in a hostile culture."[67] Reliving the past also offers an opportunity to sympathize with and pray for the persecuted church today.

The week I wrote the draft of this chapter, I sat under the preaching of Pastor Jeff Frazier of Chapelstreet Church in Geneva, Illinois. In his sermon "Smyrna: The Persecuted Church, Revelation 2:8–11," he quoted the following statistics: "In just the last year there have been 340,000 Christians living in places where they experienced high levels of persecution and discrimination; 5,361 killed for their faith; 4,488 churches, schools, or other Christian buildings attacked or destroyed; 6,200 believers detained without trial, arrested, sentenced, and imprisoned." He paused, and then strongly exhorted us: "And we should be praying, praying on our knees for the persecuted church." Amen and amen.

Hold Out Hope

We might not be facing an unjust prison sentence, or threats to our lives or places of worship, but what Paul wrote to Timothy is true for all Christians throughout history: "all who desire to live a godly life in Christ Jesus will be persecuted" (2 Tim. 3:12). Moreover,

---

66 Arthurs, *Preaching with Variety*, 184–85.
67 Ryken, *Literary Introductions to the Books of the Bible*, 280.

we all live in a fallen world. We lose jobs, loved ones die, crises surface, and the wayward stay wayward. We experience all sorts of evils, and we have a heart that is prone toward evil. Thus, we all need to hear multiple messages on hope. Preaching from visionary literature will assure us that we have addressed that theme. What Ryken says about apocalypse and Revelation rings true of much of visionary literature: "Apocalypse is a genre of the happy ending. The book of Revelation ends with a hero on a white horse who kills a dragon, marries his bride, celebrates the wedding with a feast, and lives happily ever after in a palace glittering with jewels."[68] The Bible's inspired visions offer us a new vision. Through the violence, injustice, oppression, and natural catastrophes, we witness God's victory and vindication. We are taken to the mountaintop to "see through what is going on to what is really going on."[69] Our people need that! We need that! We all need hope. Hold out that hope.

Gospel Preachers

After his resurrection, Jesus made it clear that his sufferings play a central role in our understanding of the Old Testament (see Luke 24:25–27, 44–47). When preaching visionary literature, especially visions about future events, it is easy to forget the past and present, even the past event of Jesus's death and the present importance of it.

In his excellent study guide on apocalyptic literature, Helm illustrates the centrality of the cross in our preaching with King Nebuchadnezzar's vision in Daniel 2. It is clear, Helm instructs,

---

68 Ryken, *Symbols and Reality*, 98. "These previews of God's will being 'done on earth as it is in heaven' drew the attention of hearers away from the crises of everyday life. They caught glimpses of another time and another world where, devoid of the vice of the present global order, the virtue of God's universal order prevailed" ("Genre of Apocalypse," in *Dictionary of Biblical Imagery*, 35).

69 Fred B. Craddock, "Preaching the Book of Revelation" (*Interpretation* 40.3 [1986]: 278).

that the pagan king's divine revelation focuses on the future ("what shall be after this," Dan. 2:45) and that the great statue he sees "has something to do with the end of human history as we know it—complete with the setting up of an eternal kingdom."[70] Thus, typical sermons on this text focus solely on a future time when God's kingdom will reign supreme in the world. Fair enough. Preaching on God's present and future sovereignty is good. However, what is often overlooked is the detail that Jesus doesn't overlook, namely, the stone that "was cut out by no human hand" and that "struck the image on its feet of iron and clay, and broke them in pieces" (2:34). Yes, "it broke in pieces the iron, the bronze, the clay, the silver, and the gold" (v. 45).

In Luke 20:17–18, Jesus responds to the Jewish religious leaders' challenge, "Tell us by what authority you do these things" (v. 2), with the parable of the wicked tenants. This parable tells the story of Jesus's impending death, and it ends with the line on God's judgment of those who reject and kill his Son: "He will come and destroy those tenants and give the vineyard to others" (v. 16). The scribes and chief priests are aghast. "Surely not!" was their response. Jesus responded, then, with another judgment: "But he looked directly at them and said, 'What then is this that is written: "The stone that the builders rejected has become the cornerstone"? Everyone who falls on that stone will be broken to pieces, and when it falls on anyone, it will crush him'" (vv. 17–18).

Jesus quotes from Psalm 118 and Daniel 2. The first text is set in the context of the psalmist's hope of deliverance: "I shall not die, but I shall live . . . he has not given me over to death" (Ps. 118:17–18). The second is a clear allusion to Nebuchadnezzar's

---

70 Helm, "Apocalyptic Literature: Study Guide."

vision. Helm comments, "In alluding to Dan 2 Jesus connects his own death as the fulfillment of the apocalyptic dream of the stone that 'broke them in pieces.'"[71] In Jesus's exposition of Daniel 2 he found the "center of gravity" of the dream to be "his own death and resurrection."[72] Thus, Helm admonishes the preacher, "Our preaching of Dan 2 should highlight the cross of Christ as the time in human history when God broke in upon the world order and began his kingly reign. This commitment to grounding all of the Scriptures . . . in the cross of Christ makes us gospel preachers."[73]

Now-ness and Ought-ness

Helm also speaks of the relevance of the emphasis "on the 'now-ness' of apocalyptic literature for the Christian life."[74] Moreover, building on the work of Leon Morris, he speaks of "ought-ness."[75] He notes that the apocalyptic works of the Jewish and Greco-Roman world focus only on the otherness of the future, while "Biblical apocalypse is intimately concerned with ought-ness and the ethics of the here and now."[76] Visionary literature, across the various subgenres, offers some of the clearest calls to discipleship and examples of discipleship. As Helm states,

> When reading Amos, one is struck, not only with the impend-ing day of the Lord (a very apocalyptic idea), but also with the need for God's people to repent and begin living rightly again under God's Word. So too the book of Revelation. It is filled

---

71 Helm, "Apocalyptic Literature: Study Guide."
72 Helm, "Apocalyptic Literature: Study Guide."
73 Helm, "Apocalyptic Literature: Study Guide."
74 Helm, "Apocalyptic Literature: Study Guide."
75 See Leon Morris, *Apocalyptic* (Grand Rapids, MI: Eerdmans, 1983), 58–61.
76 Helm, "Apocalyptic Literature: Study Guide."

with prophetic-like ought-ness. It demands ethical change—it won't allow Christians through the ages to compromise their life commitments to appease a morally challenged age. In fact, John uses the word *keep* no fewer than 10 times—meaning for his readers to *heed* or to *obey*. Throughout, readers are exhorted to *remember*, to *do*, and to remain unstained from the world. He is bold in his intention to secure for God a people defined by the term "overcomers"—men and women who never compromise their Christian convictions in this hostile world.[77]

The same can be said of Daniel. As Ryken summarizes, "One of the most obvious applications of the book . . . is that it shows Christians how to live godly lives in an oppressive secular or non-Christian society."[78]

"Dare to be a Daniel" is no trite Vacation Bible School slogan. It should be the preacher's consistent plea with his people, in some form or another. Like Daniel, we should regularly pray, remain faithful, and courageously face persecution. We should also preach to ourselves and others what Daniel dared to preach to the most powerful king in the world: "break off your sins by practicing righteousness, and your iniquities by showing mercy to the oppressed, that there may perhaps be a lengthening of your prosperity" (Dan. 4:27). For we should not preach the prophetic visions without ethical exhortations; the Olivet Discourse without calls for watchfulness, faithful endurance, patient waiting, hard work, and loving service (see Matt. 24:13, 45–51; 25:14–30); and Revelation without calls to faith, endurance, obedience ("the endurance of the saints, those who keep the commandments of God and their faith

---

77 Helm, "Apocalyptic Literature: Study Guide."
78 Ryken, *Literary Introductions to the Books of the Bible*, 281.

in Jesus," Rev. 14:12; cf. 13:10), and holiness ("Come out of her, my people, lest you take part in her sins," 18:4).

Our preaching should follow the pattern of 2 Peter 3. After Peter writes of the sudden day of the Lord ("the heavens will pass away with a roar, and the heavenly bodies will be burned up and dissolved, and the earth and the works that are done on it will be exposed," v. 10), he offers this admonishment: "Since all these things are thus to be dissolved, what sort of people ought you to be in lives of holiness and godliness, . . . be diligent to be found by him without spot or blemish, and at peace" (vv. 11, 14). We wait for "the coming of the day of God" (v. 12), the promise of "new heavens and a new earth in which righteousness dwells" (v. 13), by acting ethically. "Peter wasn't concerned," Helm states, "with when Christ would return, he was contending for *what* Christians should live like until Christ returned."[79] We should share the same concern.

Feel the Tension

I thought about labeling this suggestion, "Preach the Whole Truth," or "Don't Tip-Toe around the Truth," or "Tackle the Tough Questions." We need to do what those three rejected titles state. However, I went with "Feel the Tension," because if you faithfully exegete these texts (preach the whole truth and nothing but the truth!), the tension will be tangible. Preaching truth causes tension.

My first sermon as a pastor was on September 16, 2001, five days after 9/11. My preselected passage was Revelation 19:11–21.[80] I preached a sermon on Jesus coming as savior and judge; and it was

---

79 Helm, "Apocalyptic Literature: Study Guide."
80 Ken Carr, the senior pastor, preached the week before on Philippians 2:1–11. He covered the incarnation. I was to focus on Christ's return.

precisely the message that God's people on that Sunday needed to hear. I prefaced the sermon, saying,

> The events of this week are indeed shocking, sickening, and sorrowful. That the rules of the kingdom of God have been violated is of little surprise, but that the soil of America has now been raped is revolutionary. We have witnessed this week acts of war against both God and man, episodes of evil that are too incredible to fully comprehend. But in God's great providence he has a word for us today. I am neither a prophet nor the son of a prophet but I must confess that it was months ago that I selected Revelation 19:11–21. At that time, I was obviously unaware of the future, and when I wrote most of it (before September 11) I was apprehensive about how well it would be received, due to the graphic nature of the text. Yet, in light of the events of this week I can think of no passage in the entire Bible more relevant, appropriate, and practical. I am convinced that it will do us well this morning to meditate on the great sovereignty of our God and the glorious return of his Son.

Then I read the text. We prayed. And I began the sermon like this:

> Vengeance has its place in the Christian faith. And it holds not an insignificant, unnecessary, or minor role in our salvation. It is as foundational and as crucial as the biblical concepts of grace, mercy, love, and forgiveness because at its center stands our Lord Jesus Christ. When most of us think of Jesus we rarely picture him, as the book of Revelation does, as a holy king, righteous judge, and victorious warrior. In our minds, we have little trouble imagining him as a baby wrapped in swaddling clothes, as a

child teaching in the temple, as a man miraculously walking on water, and as a dying savior. But we struggle to envision Jesus as a mighty conquering king—muscular, fierce, relentless, and vengeful. One reason we may have this difficulty is due either to our ignorance or to our misunderstandings concerning Christ and his second coming. On the one hand, we may simply be uninformed of the details of Christ's return; on the other hand, we may be able to recite some of the facts of the second coming, yet fail to comprehend its ultimate objective.

As I preached on the connection of salvation and judgment, namely, that Jesus will save his people through judging those who are not his people, it created tension. I could feel it. My congregation was exuding tension!

Faithful preaching of this genre will produce such tension. Resolution is good and needed, but don't be afraid of letting your congregation live in the tension created by the text. As they listen, let them ponder, "Am I for God or against him? Wearing a white robe or the mark of the beast? Is my name written in the Book of Life or the books of judgment?"[81] Help faithful witnesses rejoice over their perseverance, lukewarm believers lament over and repent of their capitulation, and unbelievers tremble before the coming judgment.

Turn Their Ears into Eyes

"On the one hand," writes Charlie Dates, "preaching has technical elements for exegesis, structure, theological and doctrinal proclamation. On the other hand, preaching, like jazz, can move within a structure, an invisible outline, a storytelling that makes

---

81 See Arthurs, *Preaching with Variety*, 184.

the point without necessarily announcing the point. It can invite hearers into the biblical narrative, turn their ears into eyes, and arrest their imaginations."[82] Earlier, I applied aspects of this quote to outlines for preaching narratives; let me apply it differently to preaching the genre of the visionary. There is both a science and an art to preaching. Sermons on the visionary literature require the blending of the two disciplines. Our sermons need clear structures and precise explanations. They also need to soar with raised song and elevated sights.

For example, in his sermon on Revelation 21, my friend Ed Copeland followed John's structure and emphasis, both of which are visual. Ed divided the text at the two natural points of division: "Then I saw a new heaven and a new earth . . ." (v. 1) and "Then . . . one of the seven angels . . . spoke to me, saying, 'Come, I will show you the Bride, the wife of the Lamb'" (v. 9). Notice the language: "I saw" and "I will show you." He settled on the title "Waiting for a Wedding" to fit the thematic emphasis of intimacy depicted in both halves of the chapters and each scene within it. In doing so, he offered this excellent advice to the preacher in his preface before the sermon: "Apocalyptic literature by its nature is evocative, visual, and visceral. Consequently, I focused on what the images were designed to convey and how they were intended to make the reader feel."[83] He succeeded. For with his five sermonic scenes—newness (of the recreated cosmos), bride, tabernacle, city, and nations—he brought the text's otherworldly imagery down to earth and to the real life of his congregation. His tour of what John

---

82 Charlie E. Dates, "Preface: The Treasure and Potential of African American Preaching," in *Say It! Celebrating Expository Preaching in the African American Tradition*, ed. Eric C. Redmond (Chicago: Moody, 2020), 18.

83 K. Edward Copeland, "Waiting for a Wedding: Expository Preaching from the Apocalypse," in *Say It! Celebrating Expository Preaching in the African American Tradition*, 202.

saw helped his people (and the reader!) to see that God has prepared a place of intimacy with us. He concluded, "We're resident aliens. That is not a cause for despair but a cause for rejoicing. One day, we will be at the wedding supper of the Lamb, without spot or wrinkle, and we will enjoy His unfiltered face in the place He has prepared for us forever and ever. Amen."[84]

There is too much left-side-of-the-brain preaching today. The left side, as Ryken summarizes, is "activated by abstract concepts, logical reasoning, and propositional thinking."[85] We need that in our sermons, but not to the neglect of the other hemisphere of the brain. The right side of our brain "deals with sensations, words that name concrete images, and figurative language."[86] When we process information with the right side, it is "by means of images and intuition."[87]

In his comments on Daniel 7:1–8, Helm notes how the genre shifts from narrative to apocalyptic, or, as he phrases it, "story-telling gives way to movie-watching." He also notes that, as difficult as some of the visions can be to understand, preachers need to remember that "many people prefer movies to books—something more overtly visual and vivid."[88] Question: Would your people categorize your sermons as visual and vivid?[89] Follow-up question: Would they say, "He helps me *see* what God's Word says"? Our people compre-

---

84 Copeland, "Waiting for a Wedding," 213.
85 Ryken, *Symbols and Reality*, 84.
86 Ryken, *Symbols and Reality*, 84.
87 Ryken, *Words of Life*, 144.
88 David Helm, *Daniel for You* (Epsom, England, UK: Good Book Company, 2017), 117.
89 "In order to communicate well, preachers should write and deliver their sermons in an oral style which the hearers can understand immediately." Sidney Greidanus lists sixteen suggestions, including offering "vivid, picture words—language that helps us to see the action" (*Preaching Christ from Daniel: Foundations for Expository Sermons* [Grand Rapids, MI: Eerdmans, 2012], 28).

hend the Word through both sides of the brain. Be balanced. Start preaching more to the right side! Turn their ears into eyes.

Encaustic Preaching

In his book *Small Preaching: 25 Little Things You Can Do Now to Become a Better Preacher*, Jonathan Pennington compares a season of preaching to a particular congregation to "encaustic" painting, an ancient technique that "uses hot wax colored with pigments and applied in layers" to create, over time, a final multidimensional and resplendent image. He comments, "It is a slow art, with each stratum and color cooling before the next is applied." As it relates to preaching, he advocates "taking a long-arc view of preaching, a layer-by-layer, slow approach to your life as a preacher," and he encourages preachers to "view each sermon they preach as but one layer of wax, one color for one bit of the overall picture," a picture that in time the Holy Spirit can use to create a masterpiece.[90] What excellent advice! This coming Sunday, pour out one of the diverse colors from God's creative palate. Let it sit. Repeat, with a new color, Sunday after Sunday till God calls you home, into a new church home or home to himself.

This excellent image and advice triggered in my mind a specific way to preach an individual sermon on visionary literature. You'll need fast-drying paint, or to stick the hot wax into a super cold freezer, but the idea is this: Take as many images as the text provides and offer a color for each one, a color for each part of an overall picture. Or, if you are preaching through Revelation, you can often use the colors provided. Here's an example of what I mean: Take Revelation 5. There are the obvious key images of (1) the scroll with

---

90 Jonathan T. Pennington, *Small Preaching: 25 Little Things You Can Do Now to Become a Better Preacher* (Bellingham, WA: Lexham, 2021), 33–34.

the seven seals, (2) the scroll-opening Lion of the tribe of Judah, who is also (3) the Lamb who was slain, and (4) the worship of the Lion-Lamb by the multitude of angelic and earthly creatures. Just an idea, but what if each of the four images above represented a color—blue (the tears because no one was found to open the scroll), purple (for the lion king), red (for the lamb's saving and conquering blood), and gold (for the golden bowls of incense, one of the images of worship)—and each color combined created a throne, with the point of the passage (or part of the point) being that the Lion/Lamb is seated next to "him who was . . . on the throne" (5:1), whom God described in Revelation 4. Just an idea. Maybe a bad one. Or, maybe one that stirs your homiletical imagination as Pennington's idea did mine.

Jigsaw Puzzle

Another idea I've borrowed and modified from Pennington relates to the idea of "conceiving and crafting a sermon" as one would "a jigsaw puzzle." The philosophical foundation here is that learning can happen "in a systematic and linear manner," but more often for most people learning happens in a "more associative way—encountering and connecting bits of data and thoughts that we experience somewhat randomly." There are some systematic ways we might put together a puzzle (such as starting with the edge pieces), but "for the most part it is a very non-linear process of discovery." Pennington explains the analogy as it relates to preaching:

> Sometimes a text speaks to a complicated issue that has several points and perspectives that must be considered carefully, such as issues of economics, race, gender, or sexuality. Instead of trying to make a simple, linear argument, a jigsaw puzzle approach could free the preacher to recognize and explore this complexity

en route to painting a helpful and clear picture. Several different ideas can be held up and examined before putting them together. In this type of sermon, it will likely be best to make three moves: framing the issue (putting the edge pieces together); exploring several distinct issues (examining pieces that may not appear to be connected); and completing the picture (showing how all the pieces fit together).[91]

Here then is my modification, as it relates to preaching visionary literature: Sometimes with an image-laden text, it is best to follow these three moves: (1) make clear the section of Scripture (e.g., Revelation 5), (2) briefly walk through the key aspects of each image (Jesus is the lion, then the lamb), and (3) put the pieces together and provide a picture of the pictures (Jesus rules through his sacrificial death).

A Three-Staged Rhythm

Okay, one more borrowed and modified idea. Pennington suggests that Alfred North Whitehead's observation about education can provide a helpful framework for structuring and crafting the moves of our messages. Whitehead observed "growth in knowledge . . . as a process or *rhythm* that generally goes through three stages." The first stage is romance, wherein people are intrigued by an idea and want to learn more about it; the second stage is precision, wherein "curiosity leads to comprehension" (connections are made and questions find answers); the third stage is generalization, wherein "people move to considering how this precise topic connects with the rest of life."[92] Applied to preaching, Pennington writes,

91 Pennington, *Small Preaching*, 52–53.
92 Pennington, *Small Preaching*, 50–51, summarizing Whitehead.

The preacher starts with the Romance stage, inviting hearers indirectly to become intrigued in an idea, helping the topic of the text catch their eye, maybe for the first time. This can often be effectively done with well-honed questions that stimulate interest. The second move . . . is the Precision stage. This is the center of the sermon, in which the preacher works hard to move from the initial interest into increasing appreciation and knowledge of the complexity and importance of the text's idea. Finally, the Generalization stage is analogous to the crucial turn toward application that sermons typically make, though with an emphasis more on how the idea of the sermon connects with other concepts and truths and with life generally.[93]

I highly commend this movement when preaching visionary literature. For example, in a sermon on the vision of Jesus in Revelation 1, start with a question like, "Who is Jesus?" Offer ideas ranging from popular perceptions and to various world religions' misconceptions. Then, dive into the details. Answer the questions the curious should ask, after your interesting, engaging, and enticing introduction; ask, "Why is Jesus depicted with white hair, a sword coming out of his mouth, etc.?" Once the code is cracked, get practical. Answer the "So what?" question.

The Non-Verbal

Visionary literature covers the big themes of the Bible. We should "preach [these] big themes in big ways."[94] Arthurs offers three ways to accomplish this.[95] First, use befitting illustrations. Sec-

93 Pennington, *Small Preaching*, 51–52.
94 Arthurs, *Preaching with Variety*, 193.
95 Arthurs, *Preaching with Variety*, 194.

ond, use "a slightly elevated style." Third, use "the nonverbal channel."

One of the most moving displays I have seen in a Christian service was when someone at a school chapel was reading from Scripture about the creation of the universe as three artists drew on three separate canvases what appeared to be three totally different paintings. Yet, when the Scripture reading ended, and the sound of subtle music with it, and the three canvases were placed together, they formed a unified picture with the phrase (if I remember correctly) "In the beginning, God." As Arthurs exhorts, "If you have gifted artists in your congregation, why not unleash them when preaching from apocalyptic? Discover the joy that comes from working with a team, and discover the power of proclaiming visionary literature with symbol and song."[96]

Liturgy: Scripture, Songs, and Supplications

Let the pageant or parade-like organization of visionary litera-ture, along the mix of subgenres within it (songs, confessions, and prayers), help you to create new liturgies based on these ancient texts. On Revelation, Fred Craddock counsels,

Let the whole liturgy bring Revelation to the congregation. The sermon is not alone the bearer of the Word of God. Anthems drawn either in spirit or in text from Revelation, hymns inspired by the Apocalypse, and healthy portions of Revelation well read but without comment do not simply serve as context for a ser-mon but, on their own, can say and do what the prophet John sought to say and do. In fact, given the highly liturgical nature

---

96 Arthurs, *Preaching with Variety*, 198.

of Revelation, this final suggestion to the preacher is weightier than an option; the book itself demands it.[97]

Arthurs offers an excellent example of an arrangement of Revelation 7:9–12 for readers and a choir.[98] Here I offer my own special service of Scripture, Sermon, and Song on Revelation 5:

Welcome and Opening Prayer

Responsive Reading Revelation 4:2, 6, 8b, 9–11

At once I was in the Spirit, and behold, a throne stood in heaven, with one seated on the throne. . . . And around the throne, on each side of the throne, are four living creatures, full of eyes in front and behind. . . . and day and night they never cease to say,

"Holy, holy, holy, is the Lord God Almighty,
who was and is and is to come!"

And whenever the living creatures give glory and honor and thanks to him who is seated on the throne, who lives forever and ever, the twenty-four elders fall down before him who is seated on the throne and worship him who lives forever and ever. They cast their crowns before the throne, saying,

"Worthy are you, our Lord and God,
to receive glory and honor and power,

---

97 Craddock, "Preaching the Book of Revelation," 282; quoted in Arthurs, *Preaching with Variety*, 193.
98 See Arthurs, *Preaching with Variety*, 194–95.

for you created all things,
  and by your will they existed and were created."

Song	Holy, Holy, Holy (Reginald Heber)
Scripture	Revelation 5:1–5
Choral Anthem	Is He Worthy? (Andrew Peterson)
Scripture	Revelation 5:6–10
Sermon	Worthy is the Lamb
Song	Worthy Art Thou, O Christ (Douglas Sean O'Donnell)[99]

Responsive Reading Revelation 5:11–14

Then I looked, and I heard around the throne and the living creatures and the elders the voice of many angels, numbering myriads of myriads and thousands of thousands, saying with a loud voice,

  "Worthy is the Lamb who was slain,
  to receive power and wealth and wisdom and might
  and honor and glory and blessing!"

And I heard every creature in heaven and on earth and under the earth and in the sea, and all that is in them, saying,

  "To him who sits on the throne and to the Lamb
  be blessing and honor and glory and might forever and
    ever!"

---

[99] See Douglas Sean O'Donnell, *God's Lyrics: Rediscovering Worship through Old Testament Songs* (Phillipsburg, NJ: P&R, 2010), 187.

And the four living creatures said,

"Amen!"

and the elders fell down and worshiped.

Go Big or Go Home

Our next suggestion follows well the Jesus depicted in Revelation 5 and throughout the book.[100] When preaching on the Son of God described at the start of Revelation and throughout, or the Lord God Almighty of Ezekiel 1 or the Ancient of Days in Daniel 7, go big or go home. I use that somewhat trite sales or sports slogan to "go all-out" or "give it all your effort," to make an extremely serious point: We need to stop preaching (go home, or stay home) if we do not preach a big God.

In an article in *Preaching Today*, Dr. Duane Litfin shares this story:

I remember a student preaching a sermon on the Gospel of Mark, where Jesus is casting out demons. The student preached a sermon

---

100 "In Revelation we finally see Jesus unveiled: 'the ruler of the kings of the earth' (1:5), the 'Alpha and the Omega' (1:8), 'with a voice like the sound of rushing waters' and his face 'like the sun shining in all its brilliance' (1:15–16). He stands on Mount Zion and sits on clouds (14:1, 14). He wears a crown of gold (14:14) and rides a white horse (19:11). He wields a sharp sword and rules with an iron scepter (19:15). The Jesus we meet in Revelation, with his robe dipped in blood (19:13), has come a long way from the Jesus we met in the Gospels, where his glory occasionally flashed from behind the curtain. To be sure, he is still the Lamb of God, but now the Lamb is also 'the Lion of the tribe of Judah, the Root of David, [and he] has triumphed' (5:5). 'Thousands upon thousands, and ten thousand times ten thousand' angels sing in a loud voice, 'Worthy is the Lamb, who was slain, to receive power and wealth and wisdom and strength and honor and glory and praise!' (5:12). He wipes away the tears of the faithful, spreads his tent over them, and leads them to springs of living water (7:17), but for the wicked, the hour of his wrath arrives as the kingdom of this world becomes the kingdom of Christ (11:18, 15). Ask God to help you catch this vision, and ask him to help you convey it to the listeners" (Arthurs, *Preaching with Variety*, 192).

basically on how to cast out demons. When he was through, we began probing what he had done with the text. I asked him, "Do you think Mark was trying to tell us here how to cast out demons?"

He said, "Mmm, no, probably not."

"What do you think Mark was doing?"

"Well, Mark was teaching us about Jesus."

"What was he teaching us about Jesus?"

"That he had power over the occult, the forces of evil, and the universe."

I said to him, "Why didn't you preach it that way?"

He said, "I couldn't think how to apply it."

And I said to him, "How about if we apply it this way: 'Let's all get down on our knees and worship Jesus?'"

And he said, "I didn't think of that."[101]

What Litfin applies to a miracle story, we can apply to the way the Bible's visions and dreams depict God. And in the study, as in the pulpit, we should make it a habit to humbly worship our awesome Lord ("Worship God," Rev. 19:10; 22:9), tremble before him (see Dan. 10:10, 11), know that "there is a God in heaven who reveals mysteries" (Dan. 2:28), seek to understand such mysteries ("I sought to understand" the vision, Dan. 8:15), confess our sin ("I am a man of unclean lips," Isa. 6:5), acknowledge his rule ("know that Heaven rules," Dan. 4:26), and praise his name: "Blessed be the name of God forever and ever, to whom belong wisdom and might" (Dan. 2:20).

Eschatological Exaltation

In his insightful and eye-opening article "Sermonic Eschatonics in Preaching," Robert Smith Jr. argues that there is "an inextricable

101 http://www.preachingtoday.com/skills/themes/redeeminghowtopreaching/200304.18.html.

relationship between preaching and eschatology," and he illustrates this through the African American preaching tradition, wherein the goal of an "eschatological presence in preaching"—or what he labels "sermon eschatonics"—is "to paint the future of believers on the canvas of the biblical text in spite of their present crisis."[102] He writes,

> There is a proclivity and a proneness for preachers of the 21st century to become nearsighted in their preaching and to *gaze* at the now and not *catch* a glimpse of the glory of the One who makes all things new. There is a tendency for the contemporary preacher to look at the biblical text microscopically and see its implications for the already without looking through the biblical text telescopically and discerning its truths in light of eternity. Both the penultimate and ultimate observation of the biblical text determine whether the preacher is looking at holy writ bifocally or with one eye closed![103]

Playing off of Bryan Chapell's FCF (Fallen Condition Focus), wherein the preacher connects the biblical text to an aspect of our fallen condition, Smith speaks of our need to have an FCF (Future Condition Focus) that "highlights the consummation of redeemed humanity which entails celebration—what God designed for us in eternity past even prior to the fall of humanity through sin," an "eschatological celebration [that] begins in this life and reaches its fulfillment in eternity future."[104]

---

102 Robert Smith Jr., "Sermonic Eschatonics in Preaching," *Preaching* (Fall 2020): 18.
103 Smith, "Sermonic Eschatonics in Preaching," 19.
104 Smith, "Sermonic Eschatonics in Preaching," 20. "God declared the *Christus Victor* in the book of Revelation (11:15) before He announced the protoevangelium in Genesis 3:15" (20).

Smith recalls most of the sermons he heard as a youth ending with such celebration, and how this tradition was rooted in the worship of the slave community. He describes it in this way: "After a week of the slaves being torn, being told that they were 3/5 humans who had tails but no soul, the slaves would put on their Sunday-go-to-meeting clothes because they were going to meet the Lord at church. There was freedom to express themselves; freedom to cry; freedom to feel the Spirit; freedom to preach, sing, and shout. They had been waiting all week long to exhale on Sunday morning."[105] Our congregations too need to exhale! Let them. Encourage them. Show them how. Set before them—as some face discrimination and marginalization, others relationship rifts and financial losses, and some death itself—their glorious Savior and their brilliant future.

CONCLUSION

John Barton wrote, "We instinctively know that a sentence that begins: 'the stars will fall from heaven, the sun will cease from its shining and the moon will drip blood' will not end 'and the rest of the country will be partly cloudy with scattered showers.'"[106] True enough. But what is not instinctive, especially for those growing up in the evangelical church in the last century, is that the above imagery should be taken *literarily*, not literally. Hopefully, you have learned that foundational truth in this chapter. And hopefully, you have gained greater confidence on how to read and preach this difficult genre. More than that, we pray that you are so open "to the wonder, mystery, and otherness" and the "imaginative energy and brilliance" of "the strange worlds of the visionary

---

105 Smith, "Sermonic Eschatonics in Preaching," 21.
106 John Barton, *Reading the Old Testament: Method in Biblical Study* (Philadelphia: Westminster, 1984), 17.

imagination"[107] and so "receptive to the imaginative power of the images and symbols"[108] that you allow your imagination to soar. Try to fly beyond the stars![109]

BUILD YOUR LIBRARY! HELPFUL RESOURCES

Arthurs, Jeffrey D. *Preaching with Variety: How to Re-Create the Dynamics of Biblical Genres.* Grand Rapids, MI: Kregel, 2007.

Copeland, K. Edward. "Waiting for a Wedding: Expository Preaching from the Apocalypse," in *Say It! Celebrating Expository Preaching in the African American Tradition.* Chicago: Moody, 2020.

Greidanus, Sidney. *Preaching Christ from Daniel: Foundations for Expository Sermons.* Grand Rapids, MI: Eerdmans, 2012.

Ryken, Leland. *Symbols and Reality: A Guided Study of Prophecy, Apocalypse, and Visionary Literature.* Wooster, OH: Weaver, 2016.

Ryken, Leland, James C. Wilhoit, and Tremper Longman III, eds. "Genre of Apocalypse," in *Dictionary of Biblical Imagery.* Downers Grove, IL: IVP Academic, 1998.

Smith, Robert, Jr. "Sermonic Eschatonics in Preaching," *Preaching* (Fall 2020): 18–23.

---

107 Ryken, *Symbols and Reality*, 77, 93.

108 Ryken, notes on Daniel, in *Literary Study Bible, English Standard Version*, 1368.

109 Francis Schaeffer wrote that Christians "do not need to be threatened by fantasy and imagination. . . . The Christian is the one whose imagination should fly beyond the stars" (Francis A. Schaeffer, *Art and the Bible* [Downers Grove: InterVarsity Press, 1973], 61).

Conclusion

A Final Word on Your Work in the Word

IT WAS SUNDAY MORNING. I was at the church office about to head over to the sanctuary for the first service. I noticed a message on my phone. It was from Kent Hughes. He was inviting me to write a volume for Preaching the Word, the commentary series he edits. He said, "I'd love to have you contribute. Think about what book of the Bible you'd like to do." The Gospel of Matthew quickly came to mind. But I had never published anything at that point and I thought it would be presumptuous to call him back and say, "I'll do it! And, oh yes, sign me up for the big book of Matthew." I determined to ask for John's little letters, and I would do so after the service. When I returned to my office, there was another message from Kent: "I'd like you to do Matthew, if you'd be up for it." By God's strength, I was up for it!

Kent's editor's preface for each book in the Preach the Word series is titled "A Word to Those Who Preach the Word."[1] In that preface, he answers the question, "How do we account for the sense of God's

---

1   Kent Hughes, in Douglas Sean O'Donnell, *Matthew: All Authority in Heaven and on Earth*, Preaching the Word (Wheaton, IL: Crossway, 2013), 13–14.

pleasure in our preaching?" through the Aristotelian categories of logos, ethos, and pathos. Aristotle used these categories to speak of persuasion: "Now the proofs furnished by the speech are of three kinds. The first depends upon the moral character [the ethos of the speaker], the second depends upon putting the hearer into a certain frame of mind [pathos], the third upon the speech itself [logos]."[2] As it relates to preaching, and the question Kent sought to answer, he writes, "The pleasure of God is a matter of *logos* (the Word), *ethos* (what you are), and *pathos* (your passion)." Obviously, a manual on preaching the literary genres of the Bible likely won't change or improve your character. But Lee and I hope we have offered some help with pathos (e.g., we hope you feel the emotions of the biblical text before and as you preach it), and much help with logos. We hope you know more how to faithfully proclaim the stories, parables, epistles, poems, proverbs, and visions found in God's holy Word. We hope we encouraged you to do Word-work.

Moreover, we hope this book has given you an awareness and appreciation of the artistry of the inspired Word, has helped you to understand that a literary analysis of the Bible is invaluable to faithful preaching, and has offered you an arsenal of analytic tools to explore and exposit the entire canon. Finally, we hope, as Paul did for Timothy, that your people "may see your progress" (1 Tim. 4:15). Progress, not perfection, is the preacher's goal! May your congregation notice in this coming year, and in the many years to

---

2   Aristotle, *Art of Rhetoric* 17 (1.2.1356a). Abraham Kuruvilla offers this interesting observation: "Several centuries later [after the fourth century BCE], Paul seemed to echo those same ideas: 'Our gospel did not come to you in word only [i.e., *logos*], but also in power and in the Holy Spirit and with great and complete confidence [i.e., *pathos*], just as you know the kind of men we were among you for your sake [i.e., *ēthos*].' 1 Thess. 1:5" (Kuruvilla, *A Manual for Preaching: The Journey from Text to Sermon* [Grand Rapids, MI: Baker Academic, 2019], 257).

come, that your sermons on the Psalms sound different than your sermons on Philippians, and that your sermons on Philippians don't share the same shape, style, mode, and tone as your sermons on Proverbs. And may they come to grow, as your progress in your genre-sensitive preaching grows, in their love for our good God and his good book.

General Index

Scripture Index

Also Available from Leland Ryken

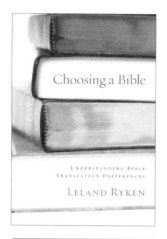

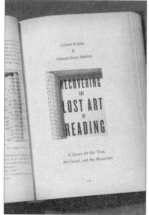

For more information, visit **crossway.org**.